Embattled Freedom

Chronicle of a Fugitive-Slave Haven in the Wary North

Jim Remsen

Mechanicsburg, PA USA

Published by Sunbury Press, Inc.
Mechanicsburg, Pennsylvania

SUNBURY
P R E S S
www.sunburypress.com

For information about special discounts for bulk purchases, please contact Sunbury Press Orders Dept. at (855) 338-8359 or orders@ sunburypress.com.

To request one of our authors for speaking engagements or book signings, please contact Sunbury Press Publicity Dept. at publicity@ sunburypress.com.

ISBN: 978-1-62006-811-3 (Trade paperback)

Library of Congress Control Number: 2017932022

FIRST SUNBURY PRESS EDITION: February 2017

Product of the United States of America
0 1 1 2 3 5 8 13 21 34 55

Set in Bookman Old Style
Designed by Crystal Devine
Cover by Lawrence Knorr
Edited by Erika Hodges

Continue the Enlightenment!

Contents

Author's Note

———◆·●·◆———

My old hometown, Waverly, is a proud and pictur-
esque village in the hills of Lackawanna County in
northeastern Pennsylvania. By the 1850s it numbered
three hundred souls, most of them original Yankee
settlers who exuded industriousness and Protestant
rectitude. The Waverly of the time included a distinc-
tive other group as well: runaway slaves—indomitable
freedom-seekers from the South.

As a boy a century later, I knew vaguely about this.
I knew our village had been a stop on the Underground
Railroad, that mysterious network of sympathizers who
aided the fugitives' flight northward in the decades prior
to the Civil War. We baby boomer kids heard stories
about hidden rooms and passages. We'd bicycle past the
row of snug homes on the edge of town that once housed
two or three generations of black families who had made
Waverly their home. The fugitive-slave settlement had
passed into memory by then, the village reverting to
lily-white decades before my time. I ended up departing
Waverly, too, moving away as a young adult—yet that
dimly understood aspect of the town's past stuck in the
back of my mind. Why had the whites taken in the fugitives? Why had the freedom-seekers felt safe enough to
stay? It seemed an exceptional chapter of local history.
Frustrated that more wasn't known and written about
it, I decided a few years ago to dig in. Being a retired

journalist from the *Philadelphia Inquirer* and a history buff with time on my hands, I relished the opportunity. A three-year-long research adventure followed. Local, county, and state histories, church records, census schedules, military paperwork, land deeds, scholarly papers, family genealogies, period newspapers, local chronicles, conversations with specialists, and walking tours of key sites enabled me to piece together a fairly rich picture of that distant, complex era.

As discovery led to discovery, I decided to expand the scope of the book beyond the particulars of Waverly and its immediate environs. The narrative that follows describes the white yeomen of the area who defied law and custom by aiding fugitive slaves, but also the outside pressures they would have felt, both for and against their activism. You will meet a number of the individual black residents—I have compiled a three-generation database of nearly three hundred people of color, including fifty-six probable runaways—and you'll read how they constructed an unlikely new future on the edge of Waverly. But equally important is taking a step back to look at crucial context about the wider world they had to navigate and the attitudes they had to tolerate. In time, you will head into battle with Waverly's black Civil War soldiers, thirteen gallant men and teenagers who are a central focus of the book. I document not only their bravery but also the scorn that rained down on them. You'll learn about the challenges they and their people faced afterwards from the larger society. In this way, the book aims to go beyond a micro-history of Waverly to a broader social history of race relations in the vicinity, the county, and beyond into northeastern Pennsylvania. The period under review is roughly 1820 to 1920, which traces the life spans of the thirteen individual soldiers, from the birth of the first to the death of the last.

The picture is not altogether complete. Waverly had no newspaper and was covered only sporadically by the ones based in the county seat. Unfortunately, it seems none of Waverly's black inhabitants left behind diaries or journals—the original fugitives were illiterate due to Southern slave rules, after all. The origin stories of only four Waverly fugitives have survived, and only in scant detail. I came upon old references to diaries by a few of the local white allies, which might have shed light on their secretive work, but alas, I couldn't locate any of those writings. The descriptions that remain of the part of town called Colored Hill are, for the most part, spotty recollections from a few white old-timers. Their vignettes are sometimes fond and sometimes condescending, but the chroniclers never interviewed the black subjects themselves so their voices are regrettably absent. I wish I could take you right to the kitchen tables, rocking chairs, and church pews of Colored Hill to hear that perspective, but the best I can accurately provide is a view from the treetops. There they are below, silhouettes moving faintly through the years, the focus on them sharpened now and then thanks to outside insights from historians, or the writings of black contemporaries. I have injected those extra viewpoints, and sometimes added informed conjecture of my own, to provide immediacy to what otherwise might seem like a misty world beyond our grasp. One memorable fact that old-timers noted over and over was how deeply, *exuberantly* faithful Waverly's people of color were. It's said their heartfelt prayers and singing could be heard from a block away when they were at worship. I hope that spirit rises from the pages to you.

The project brought many personal delights. Through a professional genealogist I tracked down three living descendants of two important figures in this story: white abolitionist Leonard Batchelor and black fugitive Lot

Norris. The descendants all live far from Waverly now and knew nothing of their ancestors' accomplishments, so my information surprised and thrilled them. On a more personal note, I discovered that my boyhood home had been part of a white abolitionist hive at Waverly's southern entryway. Two anti-slavery activists once lived right across the street. The house next to mine had been the residence of the fugitives' white medical doctor and, at one point, of the ringleader, Batchelor. Best of all, my own house had belonged to one of the area's earliest white abolitionists, Rodman Sisson. The opening chapter of the book presents Sisson's exploits in harboring George Keys, the first black runaway to settle in the village. Plus, I learned that Keys had joined the very church I attended as a boy, Waverly Methodist, and he lies buried today in the old Methodist churchyard. I discovered that the fields behind my house where I would "play guns" as a boy, fittingly with a Civil War theme, had been tilled and tended by the men of Colored Hill. On top of that, I saw how the black soldiers' headstones at Hickory Grove Cemetery overlook my parents' graves like sentries standing guard. I like to think that would have pleased my father, who was a Civil War aficionado. These realizations combined to make me feel a certain *kismet*, fate, was at work in the project.

Special satisfaction came from delving into George Keys and the others who enlisted in the US Colored Troops and went off to war. Old accounts mention them in passing, without detail. How exemplary, I thought, that those thirteen men and teens left their safe havens to head south voluntarily, to return into the lion's mouth, freedom-seekers turned freedom fighters. They had gone from the humblest of existences to being champions in a grand endeavor. What, exactly, did they experience during the war? Research trips to the National Archives in Washington brought much of that to light. Further reading, and a road trip to battlefields where they fought, added to the picture. As you'll learn in Chapters 8 and 9, they had brushes with famous figures—Abraham Lincoln, Frederick Douglass, John Wilkes Booth, Ulysses S. Grant—and braved gunfire, shelling, and disease. Some of their units went behind enemy lines to liberate slaves directly from Southern plantations. Three Waverly men were in an early black force that performed so ably in the siege of Charleston that the federal government was persuaded to expand black recruitment. Six other Waverly recruits spearheaded a heroic charge into battle at Petersburg that helped to transform white attitudes about black soldiers. Their regiment's Petersburg triumph became so heralded, in fact, that a painting of it hangs today at West Point. Most of the thirteen returned to Colored Hill and died unsung. I'm honored to provide them with some overdue tribute, especially on the heels of the nation's one hundred and fiftieth anniversary of the Civil War. They are both the book's narrative arc and its beating heart.

Other findings weren't as positive. I'd hoped, even expected, to see my old stomping ground emerge as an inspiring community of conscience. It was and it wasn't, the documentary evidence revealed. Waverly certainly had a cadre of humanitarians who aided the fugitives and saw to their well-being over the long haul. They provided religious fellowship, education, housing, employment, and, after the war, a variety of assistance to the black war veterans. There was clearly a synergy between the village and its Colored Hill. On the other hand, it is a perplexing fact that Waverly, or at least its all-male electorate, was long dominated by political reactionaries. From the 1830s onward, the county and most of the region were solidly in the camp of Jacksonian Democrats who trumpeted a "white republic" credo and warned against race-mixing. They celebrated white rule as though it were a divine patrimony. Abolitionism and black people's aspirations were lumped together and condemned as mortal threats to domestic harmony. It was painful to realize that this was being peddled not by fringe crackpots, but by community leaders, public officials, and jurists—the ruling establishment—and that most voters went along with it. All through the Civil War, local reactionaries fomented grassroots dissent against the war and President Lincoln's "abolition rule." They knew that slave labor was the driver of the Northern and US economy, and they extolled that fact. The rhetoric went beyond simple economic self-interest to a full-throated demonizing of black people and their white allies. For years afterward, Democrats in northeastern Pennsylvania kept playing the white race card as a sure way to stay in power. If, as Martin Luther King Jr. stated, "the arc of the moral universe bends towards justice," the Democrats of old were pressing hard against it.

As I say, Waverly did not stand apart. Chapter 2 chronicles how a mixed-race farmer's attempt to vote in adjacent Greenfield Township in 1835 led to the removal of voting rights for *all* people of color in Pennsylvania, and how one of Waverly's white patricians was a central player in that historic travesty. Over time, the vicinity became what we would call politically purple: majority-Democratic here, majority-Republican there. Many young men of the village did rally round the flag and Lincoln during the Civil War—but, paradoxically, election returns show that up until 1885, most Waverly voters continued to throw their support to the retrograde Democrats. Those villagers had had black people as neighbors and employees for decades by that point. Had they never come to see them as worthy or equal? Was their apparent tolerance really just a grudging toleration? How did they ever coexist with the abolitionists who'd incubated Colored Hill? And how did Waverly's black residents cope with the fraught situation? Those puzzles are explored at length, especially in Chapter 4. As a journalist, I'm wary of presentations that cheerily "celebrate our heritage," yet I *had* assumed the Waverly of yore would be a bit more true-blue. Well, the evidence is the evidence, however disconcerting. It's a whipsawing story in the end, and all I can do is invite you to enter it, consider its people, and ponder where you might have positioned yourself had it been your world.

THREE STYLE NOTES: First, be aware that the chapters are presented chronologically rather than according to themes or subjects. All the relevant developments in a certain time period, whether with the fugitives or in the white society, on the battlefield or in politics, unfold together in that period's chapter. Thus each chapter heading displays its particular time period in jumbo type to help fix those years in your mind.

Second, many of the region's place names and jurisdictional lines have changed over time. Abington Township was established in 1806 as the mother township of the vicinity and spread from present-day La Plume over to Scott, up to Nicholson, and down to Chinchilla. Waverly today is in Lackawanna County—but there was no such county until 1878. The entire Abington area was originally within sprawling Luzerne County, with Wilkes-Barre as its county seat. That is why Luzerne County and its politics and culture are such a dominant part of the book. The Abington vicinity was originally known as Northern Luzerne and its communities were known as "the outer townships." When Lackawanna County was carved out of Luzerne in 1878, the Abington-Waverly area became part of the new county, with Scranton as its new county seat. Another geographic quirk is that when Abington Centre split away from Abington Township in 1854 to become Waverly borough, the Colored Hill settlement was left straddling that boundary line. This has left me at times resorting to fuzzy descriptions like "greater Abington" or "Waverly and environs," but in all cases, Waverly is at the focal core. I hope any geographic confusion is minimal.

Last, there's the matter of racial terminology. Unfortunately, the bigots of the day reveled in the N-word in both print and speech. You'll find the slur muted in the book as "N**," but understand that it was spewed to the local public in raw form. In that regard, the Waverly settlement was called not only Colored Hill but also Sable Hill, Darkie Town, and even N** Hill. I've decided to use Colored Hill throughout, *colored* being a ubiquitous term that evokes the norms of the era.

SO MANY TO THANK. This project draws heavily from the research of academic and folk historians, whose work is attributed in the endnotes of each chapter. Of particular importance was the late William Lewis, who conducted primary research and interviewed a number of old-timers when he was a Waverly schoolboy in the mid-1900s.

Meanwhile, my utmost thanks go to the Willary Foundation, whose generous financial support enabled me to complete all aspects of the project. Because of Willary, I was able to create the educational website embattledfreedom.org as a free, corollary resource for both public and classroom use. Special thanks go to Joe Scranton for championing the project and to Richard Maloney and Laird Sapir for partnering with me on the website. The early backing and encouragement of Will Chamberlin and Kathryn Lesoine and of Peter and Sally Bohlin also were priceless to me.

Sherman and Cindy Wooden of Montrose stepped forward as invaluable resources over the last few years. I hope that *Embattled Freedom*, as a project of their Center for Anti-Slavery Studies, builds on the center's seminal 2009 resource book *The Place I Call Home: How Abolition and the Underground Railroad Shaped the Communities of Northeastern Pennsylvania*. Sunbury Press and editor Erika Hodges helped to develop the professional product you're holding today.

Archivists and local history staffers toil far too thanklessly, and I must extend gratitude to those who extended themselves in extra measure for me, from Montrose to Maryland to Virginia: Betty Smith, Mary Ann Moran-Savakinus, Sarah Piccini, Joe Long, John Fielding, Michael Gilmartin, Cara Sutherland, Paula Radwanski, Aslaku Berhanu, Jim Mundy, Theresa Altieri, Krystal Appiah, Maya Davis, Mary Mannix, Annique Dunning, Robert Kelly, Rick Smith, Milton Loyer, and Anna Kephart. Special thanks also go to Marie Wilson and Gia Reviello of the Waverly Community House.

This work would never have been possible without the stellar crew of hosts, advisors, guides, readers, confidantes, and friends who eased my way. Bouquets go to Ellie Hyde, Beth Perry, Barry Singer, Reginald Pitts, Randy Watkins, Tim Coyne, Michael Haight, Aaron B. Miller, William Gershey, David Key, Emilie Amt, Steve Saunders, Amy Broadbent, Curt Bogart, Anne Lewis, Drew Bednar, Bernard Humbles, Richard Frey, Carol Malkin, Ben Remsen, and Phil and Marj Lohman. And all power to my wife, the wise and patient Harriet Katz. Let's keep making history together, dear.

Finally, I wish to dedicate *Embattled Freedom* to the memory of a beloved boyhood playmate from Waverly, USMC Sgt. Robert B. "Herm" Banks (1952-1994). *Semper fi*, comrade.

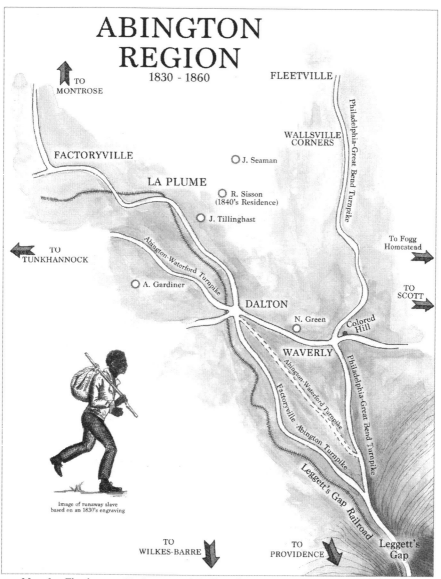

ABINGTON REGION
1830 - 1860

TO MONTROSE

FLEETVILLE

Philadelphia-Great Bend Turnpike

WALLSVILLE CORNERS

FACTORYVILLE

○ J. Seaman

LA PLUME

○ R. Sisson
(1840's Residence)

○ J. Tillinghast

TO TUNKHANNOCK

Abington-Waterford Turnpike

To Fogg Homestead

TO SCOTT

○ A. Gardiner

DALTON

N. Green ○

Colored Hill

WAVERLY

Abington-Waterford Turnpike

Factoryville-Abington Turnpike

Philadelphia-Great Bend Turnpike

Image of runaway slave based on an 1830's engraving

Leggett's Gap Railroad

TO WILKES-BARRE

TO PROVIDENCE

Leggett's Gap

Map 1 – The known Underground Railroad routes, as described in Chapter 3.

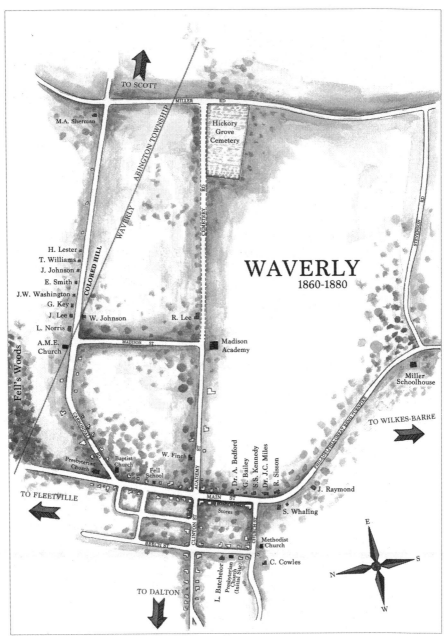

Map 2 – Showing Colored Hill and environs at their peak.

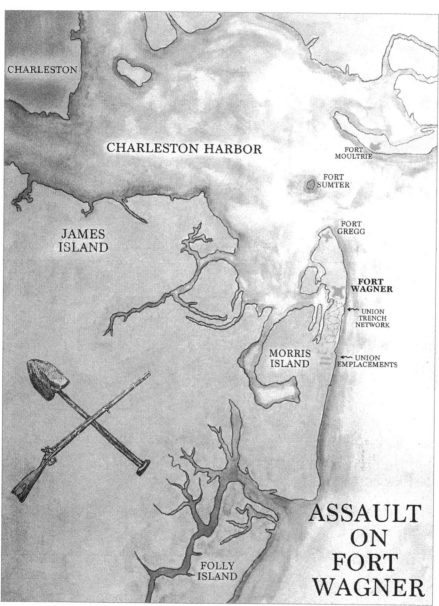

CHARLESTON

CHARLESTON HARBOR

FORT
MOULTRIE

FORT
SUMTER

JAMES
ISLAND

FORT
GREGG

**FORT
WAGNER**

← UNION
TRENCH
NETWORK

MORRIS
ISLAND

← UNION
EMPLACEMENTS

FOLLY
ISLAND

ASSAULT
ON
FORT
WAGNER

Map 3 – The 3rd Regiment's mission, as recounted in Chapter 8.

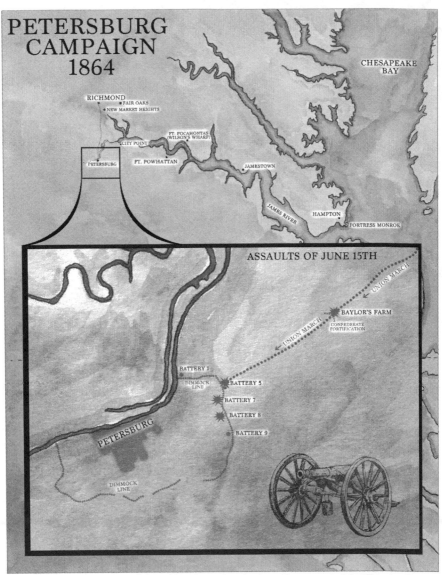

Map 4 – Showing the 22nd Regiment's mission, as recounted in Chapter 8.

CHAPTER ONE

1843

Crossing the Threshold

-------◄•►-------

THE YOUNG MAN had come to the right place, led by God's hand, sheer luck, or perhaps an inside tip. He was in dire straits: a runaway slave from Maryland adrift in northeastern Pennsylvania, still hundreds of miles from the promised land of Canada. Slave-catchers had caught wind of his whereabouts and were closing in. In all probability it was dusk, the best time to start moving, but he hadn't been able to shake his armed pursuers. The lone farmhouse, prominent on a bare hilltop, must have beckoned like a lighthouse.

As the story goes, the white farmer was at home and answered the knock on his door. Rodman Sisson was one of the area's many Rhode Island transplants, an upright Baptist and devoted abolitionist. He belonged to a movement that fought human slavery by both word and deed, even if it meant breaking the law by harboring a fugitive from bondage. Perhaps Sisson took his time scrutinizing the stranger standing there in the gloom, a light-skinned black man in his early twenties, dressed in sweaty garb, panting his plea with a Southern drawl. More likely, he immediately yanked the fellow inside, keenly aware of the danger facing them both.

Many years later, Sisson would chuckle when he told a friend what happened next. It went like this: he hurried the fugitive to an upstairs bedroom and directed him to its open, unlit fireplace. With seconds to spare, the stranger clambered up into the chimney. There he hid like a spider, precarious and grimy, but out of sight.

More sounds were heard at the front door—loud pounding this time. Sisson opened it to a blast of hostility and threats. Yes, he knew harboring a runaway was against the law, yet he insisted no runaway had come his way. He let the slave-catchers check the first floor while, with a flourish of bluff and bluster, he managed to keep them from the bedroom. The posse eventually stalked off, empty-handed.

Hours later, once the coast was clear, the runaway was whisked to an outbuilding for safekeeping. From there he was moved overland to a nearby village, where Sisson's newlywed daughter would see to his well-being.

That fateful showdown occurred in the early 1840s (most likely summer of 1843) at La Plume Corners, in what was then North Abington Township. The nearby village was Waverly, known at the time as Abington Centre. A handful of villagers had already helped other runaway slaves journeying through toward Canada, but the young farmhouse fugitive was different. He lingered around Waverly, took its measure, and decided to stay—thus launching an extraordinary chapter in the annals of northeastern Pennsylvania. By putting down roots there, he became the founding father of Colored Hill, the long-lived fugitive colony that soon sprang up from nothing on the edge of otherwise all-white Waverly. In time, it would become the largest black enclave for thirty miles around.

The young man would be known to the locals as George Keys. That may not have been his birth name. As with most runaways from bondage, facts about his origins are sketchy and inconsistent. On occasion, Keys claimed that he came from the uplands of western Maryland, birthplace of many of Waverly's ex-slaves. His son said Keys actually had fled a tobacco plantation in tidewater southern Maryland—from an area that was to erupt in slave resistance in 1845.

Before his auspicious arrival in Waverly, Keys seemed to have tarried thirty miles to the south, in the county seat of Wilkes-Barre, where freeborn blacks and a few white allies were known to safeguard fugitive slaves. Unfortunately, Wilkes-Barre also was home to a number of white roughnecks and bounty-hunters, and a group of them might have set their sights on Keys. While one version has Keys being chased to Sisson's door by his slave master's son, it's more likely he was dogged by local hired guns. Chances are, some sympathizers had given Keys directions to Sisson's safe house. They might have seen it as distant enough to elude the would-be captors while still close enough to Wilkes-Barre—home of a freeborn black woman whom Keys had begun courting and would, in time, bring to Waverly as his bride.

THE TALE OF RODMAN SISSON'S farmhouse standoff was recounted by one of his friends many years afterward. The friend told the dramatic story to a Scranton newspaper;[1] unfortunately, he gave no insight into Sisson's motivation to defy the law. Sisson ran for county office on the abolitionist Liberty Party ticket in 1847[2] and kept up his secret Underground Railroad work for many years, even after moving from La Plume to Waverly in 1857. But what drove him to civil disobedience is unknown. Like other pious Christians, Sisson may have felt commanded by scripture to welcome all strangers. Perhaps he was inspired by Congressman Galusha Grow, a lifelong family friend who declaimed against slavery on the national stage.[3] Whatever his reasons, they are lost to history. Sisson could read and write, unlike George Keys, yet he left behind no journal or other records about his covert activities.

One thing is clear. Through those activities, Sisson and his compatriots carved out a durable zone of safety that was rare for its time and place. Keys must have spread the word to other freedom-seekers down the line that if they delivered themselves unto Waverly, they, too, might find lasting sanctuary.

As it happened, George Keys was not the first person of color to live in greater Abington. William Fogg of Connecticut had quietly settled five miles away, on the eastern edge of the township, with his blended family back in 1811.[4] Whereas Keys began thriving in Waverly's climate, Fogg ran headlong into the state's bigoted white power structure. Fogg fought back—but, as shall be seen, his legal fight produced a pair of landmark setbacks that would stymie all black Pennsylvanians for decades to come.

---

1. Twining, Alfred. "Waverly an Important Station on the 'Underground Railroad,'" *Scranton Times*, (Scranton, PA), Oct. 3, 1916, p. 37.
2. *Wilkes-Barre Advocate* (Wilkes-Barre, PA), Sept. 29, 1847, p. 2.
3. *Historical Record: The Early History of Wyoming Valley and Contiguous Territory* (Wilkes-Barre, PA: Press of the Wilkes-Barre Record, 1893) p. 99.
4. *Weekly Notes of Cases Argued and Determined in the Supreme Court of Pennsylvania, the County Courts of Philadelphia, and the United States District and Circuit Courts for the Eastern District of Pennsylvania, Vol. 2*. (Kay & Brother, 1876, online as Google eBook) p. 709.

CHAPTER TWO

1835–1838

A Giant Step Backward

————◆•◆————

SOMETIME IN 1811, a decade before George Keys was born, 18-year-old William Fogg left New London, Connecticut, to test his fortunes in the stony soil of Abington Township. He and his mother, Elizabeth Fogg Allen, and stepfather, Pardon "Paddy" Allen, came with the early waves of white settlers from eastern Connecticut and western Rhode Island who were drawn to northeastern Pennsylvania for its newly opened land and fresh opportunities. Yet there was one profound difference: The Fogg-Allen family was of mixed race, and evidence suggests they were escaping particular hardships and social stigma.

Elizabeth Fogg Allen, an illiterate mulatto woman, had spent her girlhood in enforced servitude to a prosperous couple in New London.[1] Though freeborn, she had been "bound out" to the couple in 1780 by the city's selectmen, a practice under which children of indigent, idle, or "immoral" parents could be sent away for apprenticeships in what were deemed honest callings. Then, in August 1793, Elizabeth gave birth out of wedlock to her son, William. The unnamed father died a few months later. In 1803, after a decade of struggle for her and her fatherless boy, Elizabeth married Paddy Allen, a freeborn black man, in the New London First Church.[2]

The new family must have longed for a fresh start elsewhere. Life for Connecticut's six thousand free-blacks was circumscribed. "They could testify in court and own property, but their place was still at the bottom of society," historian David L. Parsons writes. "They could not vote; they were not welcome as social equals in the educational and social institutions of the state."[3]

In July 1808, Paddy Allen took a gamble. Exercising his right to hold property, he purchased one hundred wild acres listed as "lying on the waters of the Tunkhannock creek in the county of Luzerne" in faraway Pennsylvania. He was acting sight-unseen. Luzerne County's old deed books record that the sale occurred in New London and that the property was in arrears. Allen secured the title for $100, which covered the original grantee's back taxes.

Three years later, the family was able to move west to claim the acreage (on rolling land in present-day Scott Township, a stone's throw from Interstate 81).[4] Once there, they set up camp and leaned into the backbreaking work of clearing land, sinking a well, building a cabin, and making the rocky fields arable. Their presence was duly recorded. The 1820 Abington census includes the three among the township's one thousand white residents.[5]

In late 1821, William Fogg trekked back to Connecticut to marry a black woman he'd wooed. Abigail Hazard had been the "faithful handmaiden" of a wealthy widow from Colchester who'd died earlier that year and willed her $50.[6] The newlyweds returned to Pennsylvania to start their own family. County deed records notate that Paddy and Elizabeth Allen transferred forty of their hundred acres to Fogg for $1.

Busy years followed. William and "Nabby" developed their new farmstead and had three baby boys. William's mother and stepfather worked the adjacent farm and had three children of their own. Sometime prior to 1830, however, Paddy Allen abandoned them and vanished for reasons unknown, burdening William with extra responsibilities.

By then, the vicinity had become part of the new Greenfield Township, which was carved out of Abington as the population grew. The 1830 census shows 1,310 people living in Greenfield. Though the area's inhabitants had diversified beyond the original Yankee stock, the five Foggs and four Allens stood apart as Greenfield's only people of color.

William Fogg, then nearing 40, was a landowner and taxpayer, and must have seen himself as a respectable man. Whether he was close to his white neighbors, (many of them landless tenants) or kept his distance is not known. There is no record of his joining a church, of being involved in civic affairs beyond paying his county property taxes, or before 1835, of attempting to vote.

On election day of 1835, Fogg stepped into the public arena, and into history. At the Greenfield polling place, he tried to cast his vote for governor and was turned away solely because of his racial status.

FREE-BLACK MEN IN PENNSYLVANIA had managed to vote here or there for decades because the state's 1790 constitution did not expressly prohibit it; the suffrage clause said nothing about race. In practice, the matter was often left to the whim of local officials. By the 1830s, that whim was turning into hostility as efforts to deprive black men of the voting franchise were becoming widespread.

Whether he knew it or not, Fogg was being caught up in a powerful resurgence of "white republic" ideology. The prior, paternalistic approach of granting some rights to Pennsylvania free-blacks was being swept aside by xenophobic whites who espoused that the nation was founded by and for white people. Even though the labor of enslaved blacks had literally built much of

ENFORCING WHITE SUPREMACY

Up until the 1850s, Northern white attitudes about black people generally ranged from indifference to wariness to visceral repugnance. In Pennsylvania, the loudest voices—often those of elected officials—peddled open contempt. "Blacks were seen as slothful, idle, vagrant, and inherently inferior. Consequently, they were unwelcome,"[7] writes Pace University political scientist Christopher Malone. This mindset, called "racial ascriptivism," took hold strongly in Pennsylvania during the early decades of the nineteenth century, according to Malone.

Some firebrands in Luzerne County and elsewhere proclaimed Southern slavery to be a moral and economic good, and argued that black people were enslaved by divine sanction. The hard-liners, labeled "doughfaces" by their critics, freely supported slaveholder rights and in many ways were mouthpieces of the Southern slave system.

Less fanatical, more civil Northern whites held mixed feelings. They, too, saw black people as lesser—they'd been bred to assume white superiority, after all—but they weren't vehement about it. They might be uneasy with the doughfaces' desire to expel or ostracize free-blacks in their states. Unlike the fanatics, they regarded human slavery as a moral evil, one that the British overlords had regrettably imposed on the "infant" colonies long ago, and they might even hold a vague sympathy for the misery of the Southern slave.

Where the fanatical white chauvinists and the less vehement ones were in full agreement was on the imperative of keeping the nation intact—holding the Union together. If suppressing black rights both North and South would help mollify the slaveholding states, so be it. Anything that jeopardized the delicate national peace, especially the emerging abolition movement, was branded "disunionist." By the mid-1830s, the civil racists assented as doughfaces began attacking black rights as a mortal threat to the Union.

Both fear and partisan politics figured into the crackdown. The Nat Turner slave revolt of 1831, in which sixty white people were killed in Virginia, had sent a chill through the white populace of the

the nation North and South, the xenophobes branded black people as unworthy and unwelcome aliens. (See box, "Enforcing White Supremacy," above.)

The rural counties of north-central and northeastern Pennsylvania were bulwarks of Jacksonian Democracy, their leaders "the most inflexible and rigid partisans"[8] of white supremacy. In years past, the predecessor Democrat-Republicans had actually courted and received the black vote in some parts of the state.[9] By 1835, however, the Democrats saw their new rivals, the Whigs, gaining

North and South. In the slave states, the slayings unleashed the vicious "Great Reaction," a campaign of mass whippings, executions, black codes, and slaveholder militias. In Pennsylvania, doughfaces circulated rumors that free-blacks in their midst were plotting to take up arms, and that uppity, unruly mulatta women were causing trouble in Philadelphia and beyond. The "negrophobia" bore fruit. Across the state, people of color found themselves shut out of public schools and openly harassed. In Harrisburg, gangs of white youths invaded black churches to toss hot peppers into the sanctuary stoves, the fumes hitting the churchgoers like pepper spray. In Columbia, Pennsylvania, white laborers assaulted residents and burned homes in the prosperous free-black community. Copycat attacks followed, along with extralegal orders to expel blacks.[10] Some of the state's black leaders suggested forming a network of independent agricultural enclaves so as to avoid the fury of malicious white nationalists.[11]

Jacksonian Democrats—who controlled Pennsylvania politics and the statehouse itself—took pains to appease their party's Southern wing and encourage the enforcement of white supremacy. The populist party of Andrew Jackson was known for advocating for "the common man" and against the moneyed aristocrats with their banks and market controls. At the same time, however, "appealing to the worst strains in white racism . . . had long been the stock in trade of one Jacksonian politician after another," in the words of University of Massachusetts historian Leonard L. Brooks.[12]

Predictably, abolitionists in the North found themselves targeted as menaces to public order. Democrats were a driving force in this effort. James Buchanan, a Pennsylvania doughface who went on to be US president, put it this way: "In my own State, we inscribe upon our party banners hostility to abolition. It is one of the cardinal principles of the Democratic Party; and many a hard battle have we fought to sustain this principle."[13] As one abolitionist wrote in an 1833 letter to the editor from Luzerne County, "I am astonished to find the people of this part of this state so generally in favor of slavery AS IT IS."[14]

support, and they worried that black voters were leaning to the Whigs. In response, Democratic operatives stepped up their policing of the polls.[15]

On Election Day, October 13, 1835, Fogg was turned away at the Greenfield polling place by Hiram Hobbs, a white farmer who doubled as township election inspector. Hobbs' words during the confrontation are not known, but his courtroom stance would be that "a free negro or mulatto is not a citizen, within the meaning of the law of the constitution and the laws of the United

States and the state of Pennsylvania, and therefore is not entitled to the right of suffrage."

Pride and gumption aroused, Fogg hired a pair of lawyers and filed a civil damage claim. The suit accused Hobbs and local election judges Uriah A. Gritman,[16] Levi Baldwin, and John Miller of "contriving, and fraudulently and maliciously intending to injure and damnify him."

In building their case, Fogg's advocates cited empowering language in the Federal Articles of Confederation: "the free inhabitants of each of these states, paupers, vagabonds, and fugitives from justice excepted, shall be entitled to all privileges and immunities of free citizens in the several states." That clause, they argued, meant free-blacks of good standing were entitled to vote by federal privilege in state elections.[17]

The lawsuit came before David Scott, president judge of the state's Eleventh Judicial District—and the namesake of present-day Scott Township. The Eleventh District covered Luzerne County and was based in Wilkes-Barre, where the judge lived. A judicial colleague later remembered Scott as "the autocrat of the bench, the determined and courageous man with a will of iron, who decided questions with most decided decision."[18]

Fortunately for Fogg, Judge Scott's decisiveness favored him. After hearing all the arguments, Scott instructed the jury to bring a verdict for the plaintiff. Once it did, he held the election board liable for damages, writing: "We know of no such expression in the constitution or laws of the United States, nor in the constitution or laws of the state of Pennsylvania, which can legally be construed to prohibit free negroes and mulattoes, who are otherwise qualified, from exercising the rights of an elector. The preamble to the act for the gradual abolition of slavery, passed on the 1st of March 1780, breathes a spirit of piety and patriotism, and fully

William Fogg's barn site, in present-day Scott Township northeast of Waverly. (Courtesy Jim Remsen.)

Chief Justice John Bannister Gibson (left) and Judge David Scott are both enshrined in mosaic in the Luzerne County Courthouse rotunda. (Courtesy Luzerne County Convention and Visitors Bureau, John Maloney.)

US Supreme Court Chief Justice Roger Taney said the Fogg decision influenced his Dred Scott ruling. (Courtesy Library of Congress.)

indicates an intention in the legislature to make the man of color a *freeman*."[19]

(While Scott may have been driven by noble principles, an examination of local records reveals that he had a startling connection to Fogg's two attorneys, Ebenezer Greenough and Luther Kidder. He was their immediate in-law! Scott's daughter Martha was married to Kidder,[20] and Scott's son William was married to Greenough's daughter Susan.[21] Such a familial bond, whether or not it caused the judge to favor Fogg unduly, would be considered a clear conflict of interest today.)

HOBBS, THE LEAD DEFENDANT, immediately appealed Scott's unfavorable ruling to the Pennsylvania Supreme Court. The high court was headed by Chief Justice John Bannister Gibson of Luzerne County, a former Democratic legislator who had once practiced law in Hagerstown, Maryland, and would have moved in its slaveholder circles. "Judge Gibson was a large and handsome man, six feet four inches tall, and a profound scholar and lawyer," said one memoirist.[22] Indeed, by 1835, he'd already had a town named after him: Gibson, in present Susquehanna County, Pennsylvania.

The five justices of the Supreme Court met in Sunbury in the summer of 1837 to consider the Fogg case. Gibson himself penned the unanimous decision—although precisely when is not known. The ruling is officially dated July 1837 but was not announced for seven months. Legal historians and others suggest Gibson may have withheld it for strategic reasons. A state constitutional convention, then in session, was considering revoking black suffrage. Only in late February 1838, once the convention delegates made their majority opposition to black voting official, was the *Fogg v. Hobbs* opinion made public. It came down like a hammer.

"[N]o coloured race was party to our social compact," Gibson declared, ". . . our ancestors settled the province as a community of white men; and the blacks were introduced into it as a race of slaves—whence an unconquerable prejudice of caste which has come down to our day, inasmuch that a suspicion of taint still has the unjust effect of sinking the subject of it below the common level. Consistent with this prejudice, is it to be credited that parity of rank would be allowed to such a race? Let the question be answered by the statute of 1726 which denominated it an idle and slouthful [sic] people. . . . In interpreting the [US] constitution in the spirit of our own institutions, we are bound to pronounce that men of colour are destitute of title to the elective franchise."

Gibson maintained that Article 4 of the US Constitution "presents an obstacle to the political freedom of the negro" by specifying that a class of people held in bondage in one part of the confederacy should not be treated as citizens in another. In addition, he cited what he said was a prior rejection of black suffrage by Pennsylvania's High Court of Errors and Appeals in the mid-1790s. Gibson relied on his father's "perfect" recollection of that supposed case, even though no written record of it could ever be found.

By that point in time, the chief justice knew his decision dovetailed with the position of the state constitutional convention. For the better part of a year, convention delegates had taken up a host of issues—chartering of banks and corporations, executive power, patronage, judicial tenure, and black suffrage—and developed a package of amendments to put before the electorate in October 1838.

During their 1837 deliberations in Philadelphia, several delegates had actually proposed a continuation of race-neutral suffrage language. But on May 16, a member of the Luzerne County delegation struck back at that notion. He introduced a counter-resolution to flatly restrict the vote to "every white male citizen" who met the age and residency requirements.

That delegate was Andrew Bedford of Waverly.

When Bedford's resolution and a similar one were debated later that month, like-minded delegates rose to defend the preferential treatment of whites as sacrosanct. Some framed their position as patriotic, claiming that disenfranchising people of color would improve North-South harmony and thereby strengthen the nation's bonds. Others appealed to raw prejudice. They said the black vote was bound to produce black officeholders, a situation they were certain would be abhorrent to whites. They warned that political equality would draw swarms of poor Southern blacks along with their ills including, in time, "racial amalgamation."[23]

Two of Luzerne County's other delegates, Democrats Ebenezer Warren Sturdevant and George Washington Woodward, joined in. Sturdevant dismissed the existing colorblind suffrage clause as an oversight, saying its framers "unquestionably regarded [black people] as a degraded race, and therefore took no notice of them. Esteeming them neither citizens nor freemen, they left them where they had found them, in the enjoyment of no political rights . . . I call upon delegates on this floor to pause before they yield a right to the Negro, which by an attempt to elevate him will degrade us."[24]

Woodward, in turn, argued that "our citizens would be outraged by a decision that Negroes are to vote, and this will be decided if you reject the [whites-only] amendment. At no stage of our history have our people been willing to give them this right, and now let us not offend against nature, and do violence to the general feeling, by saying in all time to come they shall possess it. Let us not reduce the inestimable right of suffrage to this degradation, lest the people spurn it from them as unworthy any longer of their affection, but let us preserve and bequeath it as we have inherited it, and then posterity will have no reproaches against our memory."[25]

Woodward was instructing black men, as the author of *Families of the Wyoming Valley* wrote approvingly years later, that "his race was a *caste*, and that for their benefit, as well as the benefit of the white population, his position of political and social inferiority must be recognized."[26]

Delegates from elsewhere in the state rose to defend free-blacks as upstanding, and to note that voting requirements were meanwhile being loosened for poor whites. Their arguments were cast aside. Pressure had risen over the months from the US Congress, where Southerners were calling on their Northern allies to suppress abolitionism. James Buchanan, then a US senator, was sending dispatches about it to the delegates, more of whom "began connecting the local question of black suffrage to the national controversy over slavery and abolition," writes historian Nicholas Wood.[27] On January 20, 1838, the delegates voted, 77-45, to formally endorse the whites-only voting amendment. By 73-36, they rebuffed a compromise bid by the minority faction to let people of color vote only "after the year 1860." Woodward, Sturdevant, and Bedford voted with the majority—which included not only doughface zealots but also political moderates whose foremost goal was "harmonious perpetuation" of North-South ties.[28] (Similarly, a proposal to grant jury trials to accused fugitive slaves went nowhere. Most delegates dismissed it as "offensive to southern countrymen," writes Towson University historian Andrew Diemer. "Black citizenship rights needed to be sacrificed on the altar of slavery.")[29]

Gibson's *Fogg v. Hobbs* court ruling followed, making "the creation of the white republic of Pennsylvania more complete by stamping the seal of the Pennsylvania Supreme Court upon it."[30] Scott, the trial judge, "came down pell-mell" against the decision, telling people the high court reversed him only because Gibson had waited until the convention delegates provided him political reinforcement.[31]

THE ONE-TWO PUNCH of the ruling and the constitutional amendment shocked the state's black community and its white allies. Gibson's ruling "has been received by one universal expression of astonishment by the people of Pennsylvania," reported the *Pennsylvania Freeman* newspaper.[32] In Montrose, the *Spectator* and *Freeman's Journal* denounced the amendment as

EMERGENCE OF THE 'ONE-DROP RULE'

In November 1837, as the constitutional convention was debating the black-suffrage clause, a warning was raised by an unlikely voice. Democrat Amzi Wilson of Carbondale was a lawyer and owner-editor of the *Northern Pennsylvanian*, a strongly Democratic weekly. "We are no abolitionist," Wilson editorialized. "Still, we are of the opinion that little should be said in Pennsylvania in relation to color—if our inhabitants own property—pay taxes—and otherwise bear the burdens of government, and are every way good citizens, we cannot see the equality of disenfranchising any portion of them—if the negroes are disfranchised, the mulattoes ought also to be deprived of the privilege of voting—and then, doubts will arise whether those of a still lighter complexion ought not to be excluded, which will ever create contention, at our elections."[33]

Wilson was wise to anticipate unintended consequences. The state may try to draw a line between white and black, but where, precisely, was that line? What admixture of "black blood" counted, and how was it proven? What if one was simply swarthy in complexion? In time white supremacists, especially in the South, would enshrine a so-called "one-drop rule," which held that any scintilla of black ancestry was enough to relegate a person to the lower social station.

According to historian Frank W. Sweet, the one-drop concept was birthed in the North—in the Fogg case. "[U]ntil William Fogg admitted under oath in court that he descended from Negroes, the court records made no mention of the fact," Sweet writes in *Legal History of the Color Line*. "The record does not state that the man looked more European than African, but one cannot help reaching this conclusion, given that he was compelled to admit African ancestry only under oath. Hence, *Hobbs v. Fogg*, 1837 Pennsylvania, may be the earliest documentary evidence of a decision in favor of something like a one-drop rule in a U.S. court of law."[34]

bearing "not a vestige of civilization, republicanism or Christianity."[35]

A petition of dissent entitled "Appeal of Forty Thousand Citizens Threatened with Disfranchisement, to the People of Pennsylvania" was immediately drafted by African American leaders in Philadelphia, including James Forten, Robert Purvis, and Bishop Morris Brown. "Reject, fellow citizens, the partial, disenfranchising Constitution offered you by the Reform Convention, and we shall confidently expect that the Supreme Court will do us the justice itself and honor to retract its decision," the petition stated. "Should it not, our appeal will still be open to the conscience and common sense of the people."[36]

Bedford and his four fellow delegates from the region issued a caustic response. In a statement that ran in two leading newspapers, they called on citizens in Luzerne, Monroe, Wayne, and Pike Counties to ratify the whites-only amendment because "the Government was made by white men, and it must be preserved by white men." Black people "are a *caste*, and to confer suffrage on them would be political amalgamation," the five declared. "Against amalgamation in all its monstrous and hideous aspects the instincts of nature rebel. Whether it be social or political, it [amalgamation] is alike opposed to all the indications of the Divine will and all the sensibilities of human nature."[37] The *Republican Farmer and Democratic Journal*, a Kingston weekly, tried to shape public opinion in a similar vein. Blacks are uniformed and their votes easily bought with whisky, the paper claimed in a ruthless editorial: "The colored population of the free states as a mass are notoriously a degraded, worthless, and half-savage race, with all the vices of the whites, and without one of their virtues."[38]

Those sentiments prevailed over the "Forty Thousand Citizens" plea. In October 1838, Pennsylvania voters ratified the full package of constitutional amendments including whites-only suffrage. Black leaders mounted appeals to the state legislature and to the US Congress, but their efforts were "met with indifference."[39] Pennsylvania's people of color would be barred from voting for the next thirty-three years.

The Fogg ruling reverberated and on both sides of the Mason-Dixon Line. In 1845, in Charles County, Maryland—the very county that George Keys had recently fled—white slaveholders cited the opinion to help justify their clampdown following a local slave uprising. A "select committee" called for evicting free-blacks from Charles County, its report declaring them nuisances who had "no part in the social compact." Nor are they entitled to vote, the report said: "This is settled by a decision of the Supreme Court of Pennsylvania, and although it is not absolute authority in this State [Maryland], yet coming from a judicial tribunal distinguished for its legal learning, it ought to be conclusive, and more particularly when that judicial tribunal is located in a region with every disposition to favor the negro. It is the case of Hobbs and others vs. Fogg."[40] The complete text of Gibson's ruling accompanied the article in the Charles County newspaper.

As time went on, Gibson's opinion of exclusive white entitlement became a guidepost for jurists and policymakers. By the mid-1850s, writes University of Maryland law professor Mark A. Graber, "nearly every state court that ruled on black citizenship concluded that free persons of color were neither state nor American citizens. Four attorneys general of the United States rejected black citizenship. Their view was endorsed by the leading Northern treatise on jurisprudence, James Kent's *Commentaries on American Law*, and by Chief Justice John Marshall."[41]

Most significantly, the Fogg opinion served as a precedent for the US Supreme Court's notorious Dred

Scott decision of 1857. In that opinion, which lurched the nation closer to civil war, the slaveholding US Chief Justice Roger Taney wrote that the Constitution's framers intended that people of African ancestry, slave or free, "had no rights which the white man was bound to respect; and that the negro might justly and lawfully be reduced to slavery for his benefit." In comments afterwards, Taney said Gibson's ruling was an important marker due to "the just weight and authority of the court by which the opinion was given" and because "it maintains precisely the same principles" that his own ruling advanced.[42]

While Taney offered his reflections on the *Fogg v. Hobbs* opinion, Gibson himself did not, at least not in writing. His memoirs express neither satisfaction nor regret. The ruling seemed to be a non-issue in Gibson's social and civic circles, and it hardly harmed his standing over time. Nor did the area's other agents of black disenfranchisement face recriminations.

Luzerne County's Hendrick Bradley Wright and John N. Conyngham, the trial lawyers who had opposed Fogg in court, went on to distinguished careers. Voters elected Wright to the state House of Representatives in 1841, and after he authored a bill to ban interracial marriage (which passed the House but not the Senate), they re-elected him. He was floated as a possible Democratic presidential candidate in 1844, served four terms in the US Congress, and was in the running to be the Greenback Party's 1880 nominee for president. Conyngham, meanwhile, became Luzerne County president judge in 1839 and served 31 years, being regarded as "one of the most eminent judges of his time."[43]

The county's three anti-black delegates to the constitutional convention also found their stars rising. The first, Ebenezer Sturdevant, was Wilkes-Barre's city council president from 1841 to 1846, then became county district attorney. The second, George W. Woodward, served as president judge of the state's fourth judicial district from 1841 to 1851, then became a Pennsylvania Supreme Court justice. In October 1860, Woodward was a featured speaker at a Democratic rally at Independence Square in Philadelphia, where he railed against the "vain and mad attempt at Negro freedom. This is the poor, the abortive, the absurd, the wicked purpose for which we are expected to sacrifice our sacred inheritance.—God forbid it!"[44] Three years later, the implacable white supremacist became his party's nominee for governor of Pennsylvania and was nearly elected in a tight race. Following that, Woodward was the state supreme court's chief justice from 1863 to 1867 and, finally, was a US congressman for four years.

BACK IN GREATER ABINGTON, the third county delegate, Andrew Bedford, received accolades that summer of 1838. He was chosen to preside over the July Fourth celebration in Waverly and was formally toasted for "his worthy efforts in amending the constitution."[45] (Another Waverly patrician, Horatio Nicholson, added a holiday toast against abolitionism: "may it expire with religious intolerance; [otherwise] both would *rise* together.") In coming years, Bedford served as town doctor, burgess, postmaster, and church leader, as well as county prothonotary, county court clerk, and successful businessman. He also would ascend to the presidency of the powerful Luzerne County Democrats and oversee its continued attacks on abolitionism. After his death, an official profile characterized Bedford as "venerable and much esteemed."[46]

In Greenfield Township, election inspector Hiram Hobbs slipped from public life, but election judge Uriah Gritman did not. Gritman represented Greenfield at the

Luzerne County Democratic convention of 1841. He also became one of Luzerne County's three elected commissioners in 1863—the same year, as shall be seen, that he added his name to a wartime manifesto denouncing the federal government's "negro fanaticism" and "Abraham Lincoln's bloody Abolition rule."

And what of William Fogg? After stirring the hornet's nest, he fell back into obscurity. There is no indication he ever took part in black-rights or abolition activities during the remaining four decades of his life. Fogg would have become aware of the unusual fugitive-slave settlement over the hill in Waverly, but there's no trace of his having mingled there, sought support, given counsel, joined its church, or had words with Andrew Bedford. However radicalized his court experience had made him, Fogg chose to stick to his farm and mind his own business. Still, trouble found him. His wife, Nabby, died in 1841.[47] By 1850, his three young sons were gone from the census, so death may have claimed them as well. Fogg remarried and had a son by his new wife, Ellen, a black woman from New York. Money was tight and deed records show the couple selling off parcels of land. In 1877, what was left of the homestead, including house, barn, outbuildings, and apple orchards, was sold at a sheriff's sale for $1,550, in part to cover unpaid debt. The 1880 census records Fogg as no longer a farmer but a "farm laborer." His earthly toil ended in August 1888, when he died and was laid to rest in the nearby Carpenter Cemetery.

Whatever his personal setbacks, the man did attain ultimate political vindication. In 1870, the Fifteenth Amendment to the US Constitution was adopted, guaranteeing citizens the right to vote regardless of "race, color, or previous condition of servitude." In 1873, the Pennsylvania Constitution was changed to eliminate *white* as a voting requirement. Celebrations were held across the black community. It's not known if William Fogg ever partook of the franchise again, but he had lived to see the precious right to vote restored for his people.

1. Brown, Barbara W., and Rose, James M. *Black Roots in Southeastern Connecticut, 1650-1900* (New London, Conn.: New London County Historical Society, 2001) p. 127.
2. ibid. p. 4.
3. Parsons, David L. *Slavery in Connecticut 1640-1848* (New Haven, Conn.: Yale-New Haven Teachers Institute) online curricular unit.
4. Based on a 1864 county map, Fogg's property was on what is now Joe Lick Road, an unpaved lane in Scott Township.
5. The 1820 Abington census applies the free-black designation to only one 1820 Abington household, that of a Thomas Colard. Nothing further is known about the Colard family, which vanished from the local record thereafter.
6. Marshall, Benjamin T., editor. *A Modern History of New London County, Connecticut, Volume 2* (New London: Lewis Historical Publishing Co., 1922) p. 562.
7. Malone, Christopher. "Rethinking the End of Black Voting Rights in Antebellum Pennsylvania: Racial Ascriptivism, Partisanship and Political Development in the Keystone State," article in *Pennsylvania History*, Vol. 72, No. 4, 2005, p. 480.
8. Blackman, Emily C. *The History of Susquehanna County* (Baltimore: Regional Publishing Co., 1873, reprinted 1970) p. 524.
9. "Negro Suffrage," article in the *Jeffersonian* (Stroudsburg, PA), June 15, 1865, p. 2.
10. *Lancaster Journal*, Aug. 15 and 19, 1834.
11. Lapsansky, Emma. *Black Presence in Pennsylvania: Making It Home* (University Park, PA: Historical Association, Pennsylvania History Studies, No. 21, 2001) pp. 16-17.
12. Brooks, Leonard L. *Who Freed the Slaves? The Fight Over the Thirteenth Amendment* (Chicago: University of Chicago Press, 2015) pp. 158-9.
13. Wood, Nicholas. "A Sacrifice on the Altar of Slavery: Doughface Politics and Black Disenfranchisement in Pennsylvania, 1837-1838," article in *Journal of the Early Republic* (Philadelphia: University of Pennsylvania Press, Spring 2011), p. 83.
14. *Liberator*, Boston, Mass., Nov.9 1833, p.1.
15. Malone, op. cit., pp. 470-71.
16. Note that court records sometimes refer to Gritman incorrectly as 'Gritner.'
17. Moss, Emerson I. *African-Americans in the Wyoming Valley, 1778-1990* (Wilkes-Barre: Wyoming County Historical and Geological Society, 1992) p. 32.
18. Johnson, Frederick C. *The Historical Record of Wyoming Valley: A Compilation of Matters of Local History from the Columns of the Wilkes-Barre Record* (Wilkes-Barre: Press of the Wilkes-Barre Record, 1902), p.32.
19. Malone, op. cit., p. 484.
20. Kulp, George B. *Families of the Wyoming Valley: Biographical, Genealogical and Historical* (Wilkes-Barre: E.B. Yordy, 1885) p. 392.
21. Kulp, George B. *Luzerne Legal Register, Vol. 13, 1884* (Wilkes-Barre: E.B. Yordy, 1884) p. 456.
22. Johnson, op. cit., p. 33.

23. Price, Edward. "The Black Voting Rights Issue in Pennsylvania, 1780-1900," article in the *Pennsylvania Magazine of History and Biography*, Vol. 100, No. 3, July, 1976, pp. 356-373.
24. *Wyoming Republican* (Wilkes-Barre, PA), January 31, 1836, p. 2.
25. *Lackawanna Register*, Aug 27, 1863, p. 2.
26. Kulp, op. cit., *Families of the Wyoming Valley*, pp. 1152-3.
27. Wood, op. cit., p. 87.
28. Wood, op. cit., p. 81.
29. Diemer, Andrew. "Pennsylvania, Black Citizenship Rights, and Slavery in the 19th Century," article in the *Historical Society of Pennsylvania Legacies* magazine, Fall 2016, p.16.
30. Malone, op. cit., p. 499.
31. Kulp, op. cit. *Families of the Wyoming Valley*, p. 395-6.
32. *Spectator and Freeman's Journal* (Montrose, PA), March 29, 1838, p. 2.
33. "Negro Franchise," *Northern Pennsylvanian* (Carbondale, PA), Nov. 18, 1837, p. 3.
34. Sweet, Frank W. *Legal History of the Color Line: The Rise and Triumph of the One-Drop Rule* (Palm Coast, Fla.: Backintyme, 2005), p. 334.
35. *Pennsylvania Freeman* (Philadelphia), March 12, 1838, p. 3.
36. "African Americans in Pennsylvania: The Quest for Civil Rights," online publication of the Pennsylvania Historical and Museum Commission, p. 244.
37. "The New Constitution," *Wyoming Republican and Farmer's Herald* (Kingston, PA), June 6, 1838, p. 2; The *Advocate* (Wilkes-Barre, PA), June 6, 1838, p. 1.
38. *Republican Farmer and Democratic Journal* (Wilkes-Barre, PA), March 21, 1838, p. 3.
39. Price, op. cit., p. 364.
40. *Port Tobacco Times and Charles County Advertiser*, Feb. 26, 1846, p. 1.
41. Graber, Mark A. *Dred Scott and the Problem of Constitutional Evil* (Cambridge, England: Cambridge University Press, 2008) p. 28.
42. ibid, p. 28.
43. *Encyclopaedia of Contemporary Biography of Pennsylvania* (New York: Atlantic Publishing & Engraving Co., 1890), p. 244.
44. *Lackawanna Register* (Scranton, PA), Aug. 20, 1863, p 1.
45. *Republican Farmer and Democratic Journal* (Wilkes-Barre, PA), July 18, 1838, p. 2
46. Johnson, F.C., editor. *Historical Record, Vol. I*, Sept. 1886-Aug. 1887 (Wilkes-Barre, PA: Press of the Wilkes-Barre Record), p. 83.
47. Lewis, William. "Underground Railroad in Abington, Pa.," unpublished manuscript, 1944, p. 4.

CHAPTER THREE

1838–1843

To Help or Hinder

————◆•◆————

AS THE CIVIL WAR raged around him in early 1863, Pvt. Willard J. Whitney received some bad news from home. He was encamped with his 57th Pennsylvania Infantry in Virginia when word arrived that his uncle, Alvinza Gardner, had passed away back in West Abington. The rugged farmer had raised Whitney from boyhood after his parents died, so the news hit hard. The young soldier took time to pen a passionate tribute and mail it off to the *Wyoming Republican* newspaper in Tunkhannock[1].

The community, Whitney wrote, had just lost its best citizen, a faithful Baptist and a temperance pioneer, "the first to raise a barn without liquor in his neighborhood." But it was his uncle's abolitionist work from the late 1830s onward that drew the utmost praise: "He was also the first to establish a 'depot' on the 'underground R.R.,' where the poor, down trodden black fleeing from oppression could always find an open purse, a good meal, clothes if needed, and a helping hand to bid him God speed on his way to the land of freedom, which he failed to find under the stripes of our *free* (for whites) country. His conscientiousness was very large and his hatred of wrong doing, intense."

Uncle Alvinza, the private proclaimed, was a shining example of the "positively good" man, "one who devotes his whole energies to elevate the moral, physical and

24

Pennsylvania Hall in Philadelphia, a meeting place for abolitionists, was burned to the ground by a mob in 1838. (Courtesy Library of Congress.)

religious states of the community in which he lives." The "negatively good" man, by contrast, "is a quiet inoffensive sort of person who lacks force of character enough to make an enemy. One who never crosses the path of evil doers, by bringing them to 'grief,' one whom everybody calls a 'good old soul,' who is hardly known outside of his own immediate circle of friends, and whom no others miss when he dies."

If being a "positively good" person meant following Alvinza Gardner's example, then every white inhabitant of greater Abington had a choice to make. Would he or she, like Gardner, become a friend of the fugitive slave, or merely be a "negatively good" person who demurs from fighting wrong?

In the late 1830s and early 1840s, when circumstances were forcing that choice on people, one could find abundant reason to demur. The disenfranchisement events of 1837-38 made clear that abolitionism and black advocacy were hostile acts in the eyes of Pennsylvania authorities and most of the state's electorate.

Underground Railroad work ran afoul of the Fugitive Slave Act of 1793, still on the books with a steep $500 fine for aiding runaways. It could even risk physical harm. Anti-abolitionist riots had swept across New York City in July 1834. A racist mob in Philadelphia had torched Pennsylvania Hall, an abolition site, in May 1838. The financial Panic of 1837 fed into the malice toward black people by causing many working-class whites to fear that blacks would steal jobs and depress wages. An informed citizen of Abington would have known all that. Closer to home, he probably would have heard how hooligans violently prevented Wilkes-Barre abolitionist William Gildersleeve from hosting anti-slavery lecturers in 1837 and again in 1839—tossing a pail of black dye on Gildersleeve in one incident—and were never punished. A person might recall what had happened up in Montrose in 1835, when the call to form an anti-slavery society drew 86 signatories, but also 143 foes who publicly denounced "the dangerous principles and projects of the Abolitionists." In Carbondale, a meeting in 1837 to form an anti-slavery society was taken over by foes claiming to represent "nine-tenths" of the town, and who declared abolitionists to be "enemies of the Union of the states."[2] A few anti-slavery branches did form up in neighboring Susquehanna County, as well as in Bradford County, but the do-gooders predictably ran into angry opposition.

In those early days, a would-be abolitionist from greater Abington knew she might risk being a renegade in her own church. While agitation against slavery was increasing in churches elsewhere in the North, the large Abington Baptist Association took no official position until the mid-1850s. The area's Methodist hierarchy also was sidestepping the issue. Presbyterian leaders in the area were actually on record *against* abolitionism. In 1837, the Presbytery of Susquehanna, which encompassed greater Abington, called on its congregations to "avoid all unnecessary excitement on the subject of slavery and abolitionism."[3] The resolution, unanimously adopted at a meeting in the town of Kingston, advanced a commonly held position. While not wanting to "justify or extenuate the Evils of slavery," it declared that "the present system of agitation, adopted and acted on, in non slave holding states, by the zealous advocates of abolitionism, is unnecessary, unscriptural, and pernicious." (Unnecessary, the presbytery argued, because slavery had been abolished in Pennsylvania; unscriptural, because Jesus never crusaded against the Roman slavery of his day; pernicious, because "it tends directly to the division of the church, and ultimately to the destruction of the Federal Union.")

On top of that, in 1842, a group of civic and business leaders in the county seat of Wilkes-Barre, organized as the Friends of the Union, issued a public denunciation of abolitionism as a movement based on "a total misapprehension of the great purposes of God's providence."[4] Open scorn emanated from Waverly itself. As early as 1838, ceremonial toasts were being raised against abolitionism at the village's July Fourth celebration. In November 1840, the *Weekly Standard* of Raleigh, North Carolina, published a letter datelined Abington Centre, PA (Waverly), and signed simply "A Jeffersonian Democrat." The anonymous writer warned Southerners that abolitionists "would prefer the annihilation of this republic, to the continuance of the institutions of the South. Such is the infatuation that exists among them. Wake up, then, and do your duty—defend your rights at the ballot boxes, People of the South, or our exertions to support your constitutional rights may fail."[5]

In 1844, extremists in the abolitionist movement provoked further antagonisms when they declared that the free states should actually form a separate union in order to avoid the taint of Southern slavery.[6] While most opponents of slavery were not that radical, the purists' talk of seceding only fed the suspicions that abolitionists were, at heart, unpatriotic "disunionists." Judge George Washington Woodward, the fiery Luzerne Democrat, would later express the depth of doughface contempt in a letter to a fellow jurist. Woodward termed abolitionists "Boston infidels whom unitarianism had thrown up to the surface. . . . Their weapons were sometimes gross blasphemies—sometimes literary platitudes—sometimes humanitarian philosophies—but whichever they were, they were directed against slavery not because they cared for blacks or whites, but because slavery was an Institution of civilized and Christianized society. They saw the plain evidence that the principle of human bondage had received Divine sanction. This intensified their hate of it. They knew that we as a people were not responsible for the institution, but that we had dealt wisely with it and had turned it to good account, making it the instrument of blessings to both ourselves & the slaves. This maddened their rage. Here was a chance to war against God, Native Country, political & social institutions, and the vultures whetted their beaks for an unusual feast."[7]

DESPITE THE WIDESPREAD ANTIPATHY, a number of Abington-area whites did begin to stand up as pioneering friends of the fugitive slave. At first it was just a few, but steadily, to one degree or another, others joined the radical vanguard. This was underway by 1840, though the exact timing is unknown. Nor is it known how many runaways these pioneers eventually assisted, and when the assistance took the shape of the fabled Underground Railroad with agents, conductors, and relay stations. At first, their assistance would have been ad hoc and localized. Their individual reasons for getting involved varied, and in most cases, are lost to time. Still, evidence from the era does point to four likely factors.

As in other places in the North, the happenstance of geography was a major factor. The early wave in West Abington that included Rodman Sisson and Alvinza Gardner had farms situated near the Abington-Waterford Turnpike, one of the area's principal roads northward, thus making it a corridor on the freedom trail to Canada. On occasion, probably at dusk or dawn, they would have noticed fugitives slipping past Bailey Hollow (Dalton) and La Plume on their way north to Montrose, Tunkhannock, Sugar Run, Towanda, Elmira, and beyond.[8] Two miles to the east, a second trunk road, the Philadelphia-Great Bend Turnpike, ran right through the village of Waverly and would have been another route that the runaways followed northward. [*See Map 1 "Abington Region (1830-1860)" on page xv.*]

By offering the passing fugitives a bite to eat and an open manner, the Abington area pioneers could hear about life in the South. These might be vague snippets—or be graphic descriptions of the realities of bondage. Such testimonies, sometimes with physical scars for evidence, powerfully refuted the reassurances that Northerners often got about slaveholder benevolence. Physical abuse was the most common cause runaways listed for their escaping, according to Underground Railroad historian Eric Foner: "their words of complaint included 'great

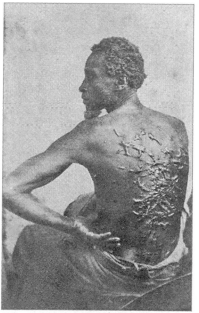

This freed slave, known as Gordon, bore the stripes of servitude.

violence,' 'badly treated,' 'ruff times,' 'hard master,' 'very severe,' 'a very cruel man,' and 'much fault to find with their treatment.'"[9] Direct slave testimonies about gruesome treatment prompted many Northerners to action, and they must have galvanized the Abington vanguard as well.

Their Christian hearts, in fact, would have been quickened. Sisson and Gardner were among the original settlers who had brought Yankee piety with them from New England, a piety that upheld conscientious living and collective uplift in the here and now. They would have heard those values reinforced by revivalists traveling the land in those days. Much of the country was in the midst of the Christian mass revival known as the Second Great Awakening. The message was urgent: Jesus was coming so people needed to repent of their sins—and also reform worldly affairs by purifying society of the sins of alcohol, idleness, and human bondage. At least one large revival was held in greater Abington, in 1837.[10] "The revival fires burned most brightly where transplanted New Englanders had achieved a critical level of stability and maintained a rural perspective," historian Carol M. Hunter writes. "The two key words for the revivals as experienced in the white communities are perfection and control. The enemy was personal sin and societal chaos. The remedy was personal pietism and attempts to usher in the realm of God via reform and social control, creating a more nearly perfect society."[11]

The Abington pioneers who were Presbyterians like Waverly's Leonard Batchelor could also take inspiration from the insurgent New School Presbyterians. In 1837, the New Schoolers broke away from the Old School establishment, which they felt was too tolerant of the South. New School Presbyterians were "Immediatists" who believed that enslaved people should be emancipated without delay and that the church must purge itself of "the scourges of slavery."[12] The New Schoolers were a strong force in the Montrose-based Presbytery to the north, and Batchelor would help align his Waverly congregation with Montrose, spurning the Presbytery of Susquehanna's ruling Old Schoolers.

An early declaration of defiance came in January 1839, when six Abington area radicals—Alvinza Gardner, John Raymond, Rodman Sisson, Isaac Tillinghast, Lyman Green, and Benjamin F. Bailey—joined 136 others activists from four adjacent counties in calling for a region-wide anti-slavery convention. Their declaration, published in the *Montrose Volunteer* newspaper, said the signatories "are in favor of the immediate abolition of slavery in our country, and are desirous of more energetic action in this cause."[13] The convention took place at Montrose Presbyterian Church in February 1839, with more than four hundred people attending for guidance and fellowship. The movement was debating a number of topics in those days such as Immediatism; the American Colonization Society, whose goal was to buy slaves' freedom but then deport them to Africa for resettlement; and the Free Produce movement, which advocated boycotting the products of slave labor. Attendees heard cautions from the movement's conservatives that direct aid to fugitives was "injurious" to the greater cause of ending slavery because it might inflame Southerners whose consciences they were trying to reform in order that they might voluntarily free their slaves.[14] In the end, people were urged to speak out in their communities and to stick to peaceful, moral suasion such as public lectures.

The Abington vanguard renounced the cautious stance and launched "more energetic action." As more fugitive slaves came through their vicinity, the pioneers began systematically offering meals, clothing, safe places to rest and sleep, and a vigilant eye. If it was planting

Masthead of the Liberator, *William Lloyd Garrison's influential abolitionist newspaper.*

The Slave's Friend *was a children's magazine that promoted abolitionism. (Courtesy American Antiquarian Society.)*

William Gildersleeve, leading Wilkes-Barre abolitionist. (Detail from an image in the collection of the Luzerne County Historical Society, Wilkes-Barre, PA.)

or harvest time, they might provide fieldwork for pay to ease the fugitives' journeys.[15] By such hands-on support and protection, the vanguard was rejecting the arms-length stance of the colonizationists. They were flouting the accommodationist theologies of the day. And they often were agitating their own pastors who, while perhaps opposing slavery, worried about schism in the pews. If challenged, the radicals needed only to remind people of the words of the revivalists. They could also cite the biblical call to hospitality, the Golden Rule, and the Declaration of Independence. The clincher for many activists was Deuteronomy 23:15-16: *"Thou shalt not deliver unto his master the servant which hath escaped unto thee; he shall dwell with thee, even among you, in that place which he shall choose in one of thy gates where it liketh him best; thou shalt not oppress him."*

MEMBERS OF THE ABINGTON CELL—who would begin calling themselves "the sons of freedom"[16]—managed to draw others to their side. Sisson and Gardner were in a network of family and intermarried neighbors that spread from present-day Glenburn up through La Plume, and eastward to Benton, Waverly, and South Abington. As kinfolk and neighbors heard reports from the activists, or perhaps dropped by to see and hear for themselves, they, too, got involved. Among them were Charles Bailey, Eunice Chase, Archa Mumford, William Mason, and John Seamans. In Waverly, pioneers Batchelor and Esther Sisson Stone could enlist the likes of John G. Fell, Wanton Sherman, William Finch, and Samuel Whaling. Those folks, in turn, might carefully recruit others. For instance, Seamans, "a deep sympathizer with the slaves of the South," was a shoemaker who traveled the area to cobble boots,[17] and could discreetly peddle abolitionism in the process. John Raymond would travel about with his pharmaceutical wares and high ideals. Networking in that way was a common factor in the spread of abolitionism, even if some recruits were initially joining out of loyalty to friends as much as personal conviction.[18]

The vanguard also might have tried to prick people's consciences by sharing abolitionist literature. Anti-slavery writings, which foes were trying hard to ban from the mails, included William Lloyd Garrison's newspaper the *Liberator* and the autobiographies of ex-slaves Frederick

Douglass, Charles Ball, and Josiah Henson. There was even a magazine for children, the *Slave's Friend*, which aimed to raise up a new generation of abolitionists. An 1839 volume entitled *American Slavery As It Is, Testimony of a Thousand Witnesses* might have been especially influential since it included the witness of a local abolitionist, Wilkes-Barre's William Gildersleeve, who had seen slavery up close during his boyhood in Georgia. As Gildersleeve wrote, "Acts of cruelty, without number, fell under my observation." Describing one such act, he wrote: "100 lashes were laid on his bare body. I stood by and witnessed the whole, without as I recollect, feeling the least compassion. So hardening is the influence of slavery, that it very much destroys feeling for the slave."

As consciousness-raising as those writings were, Gardner, Sisson, and Batchelor would have known from experience that the most unforgettable—the most morally *convicting*—testimony came first-hand from a fugitive looking you in the eye. For the whites in Waverly, the mulatto newcomer George Keys would be able to provide such flesh-and-blood testimony. The fugitives couldn't have asked for a better emissary. Keys' light complexion and ease among whites would have assuaged villagers unaccustomed to black people. Sisson was said to have described Keys as "the whitest black man, in heart and conduct, he ever knew."[19] During his years of bondage in southern Maryland, Keys apparently was a favored servant whose master kept him near at hand, so he'd learned how to behave around whites. That's according to the story that Keys' son told to a Scranton newspaper years later.[20] He said the slave-master, a doctor named John Hawkins, "mated" Keys to a slave woman and provided them with a special cabin. But hard times came and Hawkins summarily sold off Keys' common-law wife and their two infants to a planter somewhere in the Carolinas. Keys was absent at the time and never got to bid his chattel family goodbye. Instead, Hawkins handed him some money and a signed travel pass and told him to get lost up north.

That would have been George Keys' heart-wrenching testimony about being used for breeding, then having his loved ones discarded to a new plantation, never to be seen again. Keys could have added that he still wasn't safe, even in Waverly, because Hawkins hadn't legally manumitted him, and because slave-catchers were known to tear up travel passes and create bogus arrest warrants.

The Waverly whites also might have heard the testimony of Ignatius Thomas, another newcomer from Maryland. Thomas had a twin brother, Joshua. They were twice sold as a pair and always worked together in slavery. Ignatius couldn't persuade his frightened brother to run away with him. They never would see one another again.[21]

Exposure to powerful slave testimonies, along with the whites' innate piety, their proximity to the freedom routes, and the kinship networks they could summon, were four elements that laid the groundwork for greater Abington's fledgling Underground Railroad. They also enabled Waverly to move beyond serving as a way station to becoming a permanent home for fugitives, as villagers soon embarked on an even more radical experiment in self-integration.

The vanguard knew everyone wouldn't join their civil disobedience. There was always a proportion of white residents who saw slavery and the subjugation of blacks as no concern of theirs. So long as those bystanders let the support work go on unimpeded—as "negatively good" people—the activists knew that was enough, at least for the moment.

1. *Wyoming Republican* (Tunkhannock, PA), March 11, 1863, p. 2.
2. "Abolition Meeting," *Northern Pennsylvanian* (Carbondale, PA), Aug. 12, 1837, p. 3.
3. *Wyoming Republican and Farmer's Herald* (Kingston, PA), Feb. 22, 1837, p. 1.
4. Kashatus, William C. "In Immortal Splendor: Wilkes-Barre's Fugitive Slave Case of 1853," article in *Pennsylvania Heritage*, Spring 2008, p. 28.
5. *Weekly Standard* (Raleigh, N.C.), Nov. 11, 1840, p. 4.
6. Lilley, Stephen R. *Fighters Against American Slavery* (San Diego, Calif.: Lucent Books, 1999), p. 43.
7. White, Jonathan W. "A Pennsylvania Judge Views the Rebellion: The Civil War Letters of George Washington Woodward," article in the *Pennsylvania Magazine of History and Biography*, April 2005, p. 204.
8. Blockson, Charles L. *The Underground Railroad in Pennsylvania* (New York: Berkley Books, 1987), p. 131.
9. Foner, Eric. *Gateway to Freedom: The Hidden History of the Underground Railroad* (New York, W.W. Norton & Co., 2015).
10. *History of Luzerne, Lackawanna and Wyoming Counties, Pa.* (New York: W. W. Munsell & Co., 1880), p. 455.
11. Hunter, Carol M. *To Set the Captives Free: Reverend Jermain Wesley Loguen and the Struggle for Freedom in Central New York, 1835-1872* (New York: Garland Publishing, 1993) p. 224
12. Djupe, Paul A., and Olson, Laura R., editors, *Encyclopedia of American Religion and Politics* (Infobase Publishing, 2014), p. 177.
13. "Anti-SlaveryCall," *Volunteer* (Montrose, PA), Feb. 14, 1839, p. 2.
14. Gara, Larry. *The Liberty Line: The Legend of the Underground Railroad* (Lexington, Ky.: University of Kentucky Press, 1961), p. 73.
15. Lewis, William. "Underground Railroad in Abington, Pa.," (unpublished manuscript, 1944), p. 6.
16. Letter from John Raymond to William Jessup, dated Sept. 24, 1850. Holding of Susquehanna County Historical Society, Montrose.
17. Green, L.B. column in the *Scranton Republican* (Scranton, PA), Feb. 26, 1898, p. 2.
18. Kyofski, Bonclyn. "Northeastern Pennsylvania's 'Frontier Mentality' and Its Influence on the Underground Railroad," essay in *The Place I call Home: How Abolition and the Underground Railroad Shaped the Communities of Northeastern Pennsylvania* (Montrose, Pa: Center for Anti-Slavery Studies, 2009), p. 75.
19. Twining, Alfred. "Waverly an Important Station in the 'Underground Railroad,'" column in the *Scranton Times*, Oct. 3, 1916, p. 37.
20. *Scranton Republican*, Jan. 24, 1904, p. 3.
21. *Scranton Republican*, May 28, 1897, p. 7.

CHAPTER FOUR

1844–1850

Settling on Waverly

———•◦•———

ACROSS THE OLD slave states of Maryland and Virginia, runaways were managing to thread their way toward freedom in ever greater numbers. Many plantations in the upper South had been struggling, the land exhausted from decades of tobacco farming. Farmers were shifting to grain crops, which lessened the need for large field crews. As a result, "excess" slaves were frequently sold off to the industrial-scale cotton, rice, and sugar plantations that were burgeoning in recently cleared areas of the Deep South. To avoid the terrifying prospect of being "sold down the river," or of seeing one's family broken up in the process—as George Keys did—thousands of bondsmen took desperate action. They up and fled.

Some left in family groups. More often they took flight alone or in small parties. Like Keys, they tended to be males under thirty. "Many bore the marks of cruelty on their bodies, but better treatment did not necessarily prevent attempts to escape," according to historian Kenneth M. Stampp. Domestics and artisans, "the ones who supposedly had the most intimate ties with the master class—ran away as well as common field hands," Stampp writes. "[W]hile a few of them were, according to their masters, 'unruly scoundrels' or 'incorrigible scamps,' most of them seemed to be 'humble,' 'inoffensive,' or 'cheerful' slaves."[1]

Southern militias and slave patrols were on constant lookout. Most runaways were captured or gave up after a few days. Severe punishment—whippings, branding with an *R* for "runaway," even chopping off a foot— might follow as a lesson to others. Still, many tried again, refining their clandestine plans to disappear into the black communities of Baltimore or Washington, or to slip north to Pennsylvania. Most of the first fugitives who settled in Waverly had fled into Pennsylvania from the hills of western Maryland, near Frederick and Hagerstown. Census, church, and military records confirm the several folk accounts that trace that movement.

The Hagerstown newspapers were noting the escapes with alarm. In an item headlined "Oceans of Runaway Negroes," the *Hagerstown Torch Light* reported on September 17, 1846, that "fifteen Slaves, men and women, belonging to Messrs. Dall, Reichard, the Messrs. Clagetts,[2] and Dr. Rench, absconded in a body on Saturday night last. They passed through Hagerstown about half past 10 o'clock in the night, on their way to Chambersburg, mounted upon horses with which they had provided themselves. We understand that nine of the fifteen runaways were arrested and secured in the neighborhood of Chambersburg—the other six are still at large."

The next day, the *Hagerstown Herald of Freedom* reported that the fifteen had grown to seventeen. It remarked: "There is evidently a secret influence at work in this County, which, if not discovered and frustrated, will, ere ten years elapse, effect a total abolition of Slavery. – Some of our neighbors of the free States are determined to rob us of our slaves at all hazards; and hence, it behooves every friend to the laws of his State, and the rights of his fellow citizens, to be vigilant, and the officers of our County should be especially active."

Even for freedom-seekers who managed to cross the Mason-Dixon Line into Pennsylvania, the coast was not clear. The southernmost free states had become what abolitionists termed "the hunting ground of the south."[3] It was the worst along Pennsylvania's southern strip. Slave-owners frequently posted "Ran Away" notices in Pennsylvania newspapers and would come north, or hire agents, to obtain arrest warrants for individual runaways. Such arrests occurred more often in Pennsylvania than any other Northern state.[4] A number of

Runaways often were young men escaping alone. (Courtesy Library of Congress.)

Pennsylvanians joined the prowl as mercenaries angling for rewards that might top $1,000, a small fortune. "The slave catchers, loosely organized for mutual cooperation between one small-town vulture and the next north from Mason and Dixon's Line, were in business for those rewards. Less predatory citizens were not."[5]

Most fugitive slaves flared northward on their own, lying low and living by their wits without outside help. Others found their way to the homes of local sympathizers, white and free-black, who hid them in assorted barns, belfries, secret rooms, woodpiles, kilns, corn shocks, cold cellars, and other outbuildings. If the sympathizers were part of the loose-knit network that came to be called the Underground Railroad, they would guide the runaways through the brooding landscape to the next safe station. Harrisburg, home of a large free-black population and white abolitionist allies, was often a key stop.

The few remaining accounts about the Waverly fugitives describe the legs northward from Harrisburg to

Wilkes-Barre, and on to Abington. George Keys passed through Harrisburg, as did Lot Norris and Ignatius Thomas. From there they might have headed up along the Susquehanna River by foot or be hidden in wagons. Alternatively, they might have found passage on a friendly canal boat (the north branch of the Pennsylvania Canal had reached Luzerne County by the mid-1830s), knowing the water would throw hounds off their scent.

One free-black activist in Wilkes-Barre, Sampson Brown, would ride his hay wagon toward Harrisburg, "meet colored Uncle Sam halfway there, transfer a load of slaves to his wagon, hiding them under the hay," and head for home. That's according to his daughter, Essbella Brown, who was interviewed by the *Wilkes-Barre Evening News* in May 1939. Then aged 102, she recalled how her parents protected fugitives in their cellar on Northampton Street. Her mother, she said, "always kept two kettles full of hot water to throw on any slaveholders who tried to break in."

Wilkes-Barre's free-black residents, then numbering over one hundred, had an active assistance network. They also would partner with a handful of sympathetic whites, primarily the zealous William Gildersleeve.

Essbella Brown said her father would hand off fugitives to Gildersleeve for their next leg north. Gildersleeve harbored many runaways in his own home and store, recalled his great-niece, Edith Brower. "I used to hear how, if one went to his house early enough in the morning, his kitchen would often be found full of wretched hunted negroes, ragged, filthy, panic-stricken, yet drawing breath freely in this temporary refuge," Brower wrote. "All were fed and in various ways cared for, then hidden in cellars, barns, corn-cribs, smokehouse, or other buildings, to remain concealed until the following night, when one of Uncle Gildersleeve's big teams would carry them on their way to the nearest station—Tunkhannock."[6]

Two primary roads led up to Tunkhannock. The Susquehanna River shore road was the more direct way, but its remote river hamlets tended to be hostile to abolitionists. Gildersleeve more likely took the safer overland road through Providence and Leggett's Gap ("the Notch"), and on to Dalton (West Abington), La Plume, and Factoryville, where Alvinza Gardner, Rodman Sisson, and others stood by. One folk history of Factoryville says five hundred fugitive slaves were directly aided thereabouts: "Even though our town is not on the main route, it was said to be an ideal spot because it was small and out of the way of authorities."[7]

Other accounts have Gildersleeve transporting his secret cargo through the Notch and turning onto the Philadelphia-Great Bend Turnpike en route to the safe haven of Waverly. From Waverly, the freedom route might stay north on that turnpike, or dog-leg west to Dalton and turn north there en route to Montrose.[8] Gildersleeve's daughter, Mary Sayre, wrote in 1911 about the night fourteen fugitives arrived at once, all hungry and disoriented. "Father had the rigging put on the big wagon and at about 11 o'clock at night they piled in and were covered with hay and driven to Abington to a Mr. Batchelor, who had also worked with the Underground Railroad. Mr. Batchelor transferred them to his wagon, and passed them on to the next station until they finally reached Canada. . . . Once, my father took a group of slaves by night to Abington but the wagon broke down in Pittston." A neighbor lent them his big wagon, she said, and they drove off.[9]

Another recollection came from Clarks Green Baptist William Atherton. In a 1901 letter to the *Scranton Republican* newspaper, Atherton wrote, "I well remember the knock at our door at dead of night, announcing Mr.

Gildersleeve's man with a load of colored people. My mother used to get up and get supper for them. After supper they were reloaded into wagons and went to Waverly, where they were secreted during the next day by Agents Radman [sic] Sisson and Leonard Batcheler [sic] and forwarded again the next night to Montrose and thence on by relays to Canada and freedom."[10]

WAVERLY THUS BECAME A VIBRANT PART of eastern Pennsylvania's Underground Railroad network,[11] and Leonard Batchelor arose as Waverly's linchpin. His own impoverished upbringing had made him "a friend of the down trodden and oppressed," according to Batchelor family genealogist Frederick Pierce.[12] As a boy, Batchelor lost his father and a brother and saw his mother struggle to make ends meet. He "became earnest in pursuit of righteousness" both as a merchant and a committed Presbyterian, and over time "assisted scores of negroes on the way to liberty, harboring them in his own home, when to do so was at risk of life and property."

Leonard Batchelor was a key figure in Waverly's support network. ('Batchelder, Batcheller Genealogy,' by Frederick C. Pierce.)

Being Presbyterian, Batchelor had a natural connection to the Presbyterian Gildersleeve down in Wilkes-Barre and to the New Schoolers up in Montrose, which would make him a trusted conductor along the freedom line. He also was in a unique position to draw Waverly's other churches into the cause. Batchelor's 1841 marriage to Hannah Stone, daughter of a leading

Abington Baptist family, gave him stature in that congregation. Also, his fledgling Waverly Presbyterian fellowship held its worship services in the village's new Methodist Episcopal church building, which would open the door to ecumenical alliances there.

Waverly's circle of supporters had grown by the mid-1840s. It's likely that fugitives were being assisted in various ways by Batchelor, John G. Fell, Charles Bailey, William Thompson, John Raymond, William Finch, Samuel Whaling, Esther and John Stone, and an unknown number of others in or right around the village. Fell made an isolated house he owned available as a regular hiding place.[13] His large barn and other outbuildings were designated safe spots, as were certain wooded glens. Other residents may have created hidden chambers in their homes. Local lore has held that a secret chamber even existed in the home of Andrew Bedford, Waverly's ultra-conservative doctor (see box, "Unlikely Alliances"). This colorful lore is difficult to substantiate, however. Modern scholars caution that "contrary to popular legends, very few Underground Railroad stations were outfitted with secret hiding places. Most fugitive slaves were sheltered in existing rooms and spaces, such as cellars, attics, extra bedrooms, or barn lofts, to name a few."[14]

As the fugitives experienced Waverly's altruism and got to know its radical "sons of freedom" up close, some contemplated a radical notion of their own. Could the hidden future they'd been trudging toward suddenly be revealing itself? Might this close-knit, utterly white town become their town, too—not just a hideaway, but their *home*?

The world they knew was a hard place. Experience had taught them to be wary. As Harriet Tubman said, the wayward runaway was "a stranger in a strange land," terrified of being sold again. Many Underground

UNLIKELY ALLIANCES

Waverly's Andrew Bedford and John Stone were staunch Democrats in a party that trafficked in white supremacy. Bedford's signal achievement as a delegate to the state constitutional convention of 1837-38 was to introduce language that successfully stripped blacks of the right to vote in Pennsylvania. Stone was a Democratic state assemblyman in 1860 and a sales agent for the *Lackawanna Register*, a Southern-sympathizing weekly. Meanwhile, their village neighbor, Leonard Batchelor, was an outspoken abolitionist, an Immediatist on the slavery question, and a radical who had developed a deep regard for black people. He was opening doors for blacks where Bedford, in particular, had taken action to close them.

And yet the three men became protégés. According to the book *This Is Waverly*, Batchelor and Bedford opened a store together on the turnpike road in 1849. They were founding trustees of Waverly's Madison Academy and, with Stone, of Hickory Grove Cemetery.[15] They and Stone were in the inner circle that formed a temperance society and that operated the village's short-lived Temperance Hotel.

The three men certainly would have been aware of their political differences. None of them left behind personal journals, so their precise motivations and activities are not known, but it appears that Bedford and Stone came around to Batchelor's side and joined in aiding Waverly's refugee slaves. Bedford quite likely attended to the early fugitives' medical needs. His grand home on the turnpike was said to have a secret nook to hide runaways. Stone, for his part, rented land to the fugitives and sold them the plot for their church building. His and Bedford's stature as leading Democrats may have served to buffer the Waverly fugitives from any harassment by hostile locals.

Were Stone and the doctor morally changed, *convicted*, by Batchelor's evangelizing?

Perhaps. Or perhaps interactions with the freedom-seekers were what opened them to the anti-slavery cause. Bedford, as a member of the activist Methodist Episcopal Church, would have worshipped with fugitives Keys and Mason and been encouraged to see his support work as holy. (Another Methodist thus influenced might have been Waverly blacksmith Samuel Whaling, who was a Democratic leader during his party's racist campaigns—but who, upon his death, was remembered

Railroad handlers were not true friends. "Fugitives were frequently barred from entering the homes of conductors, or were forced to eat in a designated area," historian Charles L. Blockson writes. "Shackles were sometimes put on slaves to control them while they were in conductors' homes, and spies of both races would sometimes sell out escaped slaves."[18] The fugitives encountered no by Scranton's black newspaper as a friend who "did much for our race.") Stone, as a Baptist deacon, might have been influenced by John Fell and other radicals in that congregation. Stone's father-in-law was Rodman Sisson, George Keys' protector and an original abolitionist. Bedford, for his part, had business ties with two other early white activists in town, John Raymond and Gilbert Sherman, who may have worked on his conscience. And, of course, the three Democrats might have been swayed by compassionate wives and other family members.

There is another possibility as well. Stone, Whaling, and Bedford might have felt their support work didn't show a change of heart at all, but was fully consistent with their strict belief in a hierarchy of the races. Like other non-radicals of the day, they might believe black people were, at best, grown-up children unfit for the rights of citizenship and certainly not equal to whites. The three were perhaps merely condescending to help the individual runaways in front of them out of both Christian charity and class honor. They would have understood the sense of propriety that impelled a pro-slavery white woman in New Castle, Pennsylvania, to violently drive off two slave-catchers. J.C. Furnas, author of *Goodbye to Uncle Tom*, noted that the young woman acted "not from antislavery principle—she and her father were ardent 'doughface' Democrats—but because she thought slave catchers were low types and fugitives pitiable."[16]

The words of John Mann, an early president of the Anti-Slavery and Free Discussion Society, would have resonated. Abolitionism's mission, Mann said in a July 4, 1836, speech in Montrose, was "to restore the oppressed children of Africa to that niche in the architecture of society which the Great Founder designed, or in other words, which they are qualified to fill. . . . If the moral powers of the slaves have been so long and so cruelly crushed that they cannot, unaided, acquire the proper direction, it is our duty to lend the helping hand. We are morally bound, first to remove the burden, and then to assist the crippled sufferer in rising, and to support him in his feet, till he can sustain his own weight."[17]

Lending "the helping hand" could have been the shared purpose, the paternalistic *noblesse oblige* that allowed white radicals and erstwhile antagonists to transcend their differences. If nothing else, Batchelor's unlikely alliance with Bedford, Stone, and Whaling illustrated the power of interpersonal ties.

such mistreatment in Waverly. It appeared that here were righteous people with a righteous purpose. Even those whites who held back seemed to be a tolerant sort at least.

Was the concept of a black colony in Waverly formally broached, and if so, by which side and in what detail? The existing record yields no answers. Still, one can imagine the fugitives huddling to discuss the awe-inspiring prospect of setting down roots and beginning new lives in plain sight in Waverly. They would have prayed mightily for guidance. Being newborns to freedom—indigent, illiterate, road-weary, traumatized, disoriented—they knew they'd need whatever assistance they could find to get established, especially there, nearly three hundred miles short of Canada. They probably consulted with forerunner George Keys about his new life, its assets and its challenges. By then, Keys had been hired by William Thompson, a white farmer and store owner, to work the barn. Keys could have told the newcomers how at first he'd kept a pitchfork next to his bedding every night for protection,[19] but that he hadn't needed it because the slave-catchers never returned. They seemed to stay away from Waverly.

Keys could have listed Waverly's various attributes. There was steady work to be had, *paying* work, and it would be familiar: farmhands in the fields and barns, domestics in the households. Some villagers talked of setting them up with plots of land and, astonishingly, of freely providing them and their children with schooling. They were situated far enough north to make capture less likely, but not so far that trailing kin could no longer find and reunite with them. If danger should come, they would know who was trustworthy and where to hide. Waverly was relatively out of the way, so slave-hunters weren't lurking as they were in larger spots like Wilkes-Barre or Montrose, surveilling the established black communities there. (Things had gotten so uncomfortable in Montrose in 1845 that a public meeting was held "to express the indignation of the citizens against a body of armed men who have been concealed in the town for the purpose of kidnapping a number of colored persons formerly slaves, who, for several years, have resided there, leading quiet, industrious and honest lives."[20])

However safe Waverly might have seemed by contrast, some of the wayfarers still held out for Canada. Others decided to take their chances blending into the existing black communities in Towanda, Elmira, Binghamton, and even Montrose. They simply would have felt too isolated and out of place in Waverly. So those apprehensive folks moved on. But for others, little Waverly became the destination. At least one account tells of runaways departing Wilkes-Barre specifically "on their way to Abington."[21] It's said that Mary Jane Merritt arrived with fifteen children in tow.[22] Lot Norris told of escaping pursuers by hiding in the woods outside Waverly in 1845, being fed by villagers, getting work, and summoning his family, who had briefly settled in Pottsville.[23] The arrivals kept coming: the Adley family, the Johnsons, the Lees, the Lewises, the Youngs, the Randolphs, the Masons, the Snodens, and the Reets were all recorded in the 1850 census. Other fugitives were certainly among them, even if not listed openly on the census books. One can imagine the welter of emotions they felt as they settled in. As William Wells Brown wrote in his 1847 escape narrative, "The fact that I was a freeman—could walk, talk, eat and sleep, as a man and no one to stand over me with the blood-clotted cowhide—all this made me feel I was not myself."[24]

CONVERSELY, FOR THE WHITES, the influx of newcomers with their ragged appearances, dark features, and Southern drawls must have been a culture shock. Waverly was a rather clannish place, full of flinty Democrats and others who weren't necessarily the embracing sort. But in time, a truce was struck between idealist and skeptic, and the arrangement took root. Interacting with individual fugitives, hearing their stories and observing their manner, probably lessened the misgivings. As the villagers had seen with George Keys, these newcomers appeared to be gritty and resourceful. They'd had to be to get that far. Historian Larry Gara put it this way in *The Liberty Line*: "It was often, as an abolitionist wrote in his memoirs and as many witnesses of different viewpoints agreed, 'the brightest and best who were capable of surmounting all the dangers and difficulties of escape.'" Gara noted that black abolitionist William Still of Philadelphia described the fugitives he assisted as "quite smart" and "of more than ordinary shrewdness."[25]

For the open-minded villager, it helped to realize that the fugitives were pioneers, as their own families had once been, and to know that the pioneer ethic upheld the very individual liberties the runaways were now seeking.[26] Further, the blacks showed a devotion to family and seemed grateful and well-behaved—a far cry from the ogres or imbeciles they'd perhaps been led to expect. On a practical note, any opportunistic white could see that here was a ready labor pool of people accustomed to working hard. Some villagers might have gotten involved out of curiosity, seeing the experiment as a novel break from the humdrum. Others might have joined in to get right with God. Some villagers probably kept their distance, simply too burdened by their own affairs, but at least remained "negatively good" by not standing in the way. Even a hardened racist might have wagered that it was best not to fight this pet project of the insistent Mr. Batchelor and his compatriots. The activists were some of Waverly's leading businessmen and notables, after all, so why risk losing their trade and good graces?

It also should be noted that most every villager would have been pleased that the blacks were pious fellow Protestants and English-speakers—unlike the Irish

Catholic foreigners who were also beginning to arrive on the scene. The Gaelic-speaking immigrants hired onto Leggett's Gap Railroad work gangs would shock the area with outbursts of deadly internal rivalry,[27] fueling stereotypes of Irishmen as hard-drinking ruffians. As was characteristic of the era's identity politics, greater Abington's abstemious Yankees were decidedly uncomfortable with Catholic immigrants, a reality that no doubt worked to the fugitives' advantage.

The runaways knew to present an agreeable demeanor, which would smooth the transition. This was part of a slave's "double consciousness"—whatever his true feelings, he'd learned to seem harmless around whites as a survival strategy. Even in Abington, Amenzo Mumford recalled how "the Negroes were a happy lot of folks and did not appear to worry." He spoke of frequent barn dances: "The white folks would gather of an evening and the Negro boys or men would 'buck and wing' and give the plantation dances while someone patted the juba and the Negroes sang their Southern melodies."[28]

Their spiritual music was especially captivating. Old Waverly recollections refer in wonderment to the outpourings of devotional song. Indoors or out, blacks would gather together to sing. They sang to open heaven's door, to give praise for deliverance, to release their anguish. A leader would call out melodic lines and draw delicate, overlapping rhythms in response. The whites might have been privileged to witness a "ring shout," a spiritually charged form of song and movement that reached back to Africa. "Rooted in European musical traditions, whites often encountered black singing with a mixture of admiration and incomprehension," as one music historian writes.[29] For a churchgoing villager still getting used to the refugees, the might of those raised voices along with the pain and yearning they expressed could move her to see the wayfarers with new eyes, not as trespassers but as pilgrims in a biblical drama, and convert her to their side.

George Keys had already taken his influential voice into Waverly's newly erected Methodist Episcopal (ME) Church. Its fifty white congregants accepted him as a member in 1843 and another black fugitive, Benjamin Mason, in 1845.[30] On April 14, 1845, the church's supply pastor, Rev. Charles Perkins, officiated Keys' wedding to his freeborn bride from Wilkes-Barre, Hannah Fields. The easy integration may seem surprising, but was not. Methodism, a heavy presence in the South, may well have been Keys' cradle faith. The Waverly congregation Keys chose was laden with helpful whites: John Raymond, William Finch, Charles Bailey, Mary Ann Sherman, S.S. Kennedy, Mary Thompson, Samuel Whaling, Dr. Andrew Bedford, the Montrose-bred Perkins, and others to come. The national ME denomination had just split over slavery in 1844 when its Southern wing seceded. By openly welcoming black people into its fold, Waverly ME could make a timely statement to the dozen other preaching stations in its Abington Circuit.

AS THE FUGITIVES GREW MORE NUMEROUS and acclimated to living in the open in Waverly, they developed a desire to form a church of their own. There was a ready option in the African Methodist Episcopal (AME) denomination, which was sending circuit-riding preachers to outlying communities as fast as it could. Sometime in 1845, the Waverly Methodists dismissed Keys and Mason from the fold with their blessings to help organize a black church. In short order, a Waverly AME congregation was established with about twenty members. Its first pastor was Rev. William Hyatt, with Keys selected as class leader and Lot Norris, W.M. Johnson, Charles Allen, and John Mason serving with Keys as stewards.[31] It's believed that the first AME services were held in a tenement house occupied by Lot Norris and owned by Rev. Benjamin Miller, a traveling Baptist preacher and son of the renowned Elder Miller, founder of Waverly's First Baptist Church of Abington.[32]

By all accounts, most villagers accepted the new congregation in their midst. It helped to learn how much their stated values dovetailed. A Colored American Temperance Society had been formed in 1831, with AME preachers joining the crusade against liquor. Waverly had a temperance society, too, founded by Batchelor, Bedford, Stone, and Fell.

Education was another shared priority. Fugitives who'd been forbidden to read or write while enslaved knew literacy would be essential to their advancement. "African Methodist Episcopal church members believed that education would enable them to knock down the walls of discrimination in society," writes church historian Gilbert Williams. "An often-expressed idea held that 'well educated and enlightened' blacks could not be degraded because their knowledge and positive self-esteem would not allow them to sink into 'the dark cavity of oppression.' In other words, education would instill dignity."[33]

The Waverly area had a network of one-room primary schools and had just celebrated the opening of Madison Academy in 1844 on a hilltop overlooking the village. The academy provided an advanced classical education to adolescent boys and girls—and over the years would open its doors to black students. Appreciating the fugitives' eagerness to uplift themselves through education, white supporters stepped forward in an ecumenical way.

The AME denomination expected each of its churches to be self-supporting. No doubt aware that the fugitives' pockets were empty, villagers began providing material and, presumably, financial support. The Fell School, Waverly's centrally located Greek Revival gem

Waverly's old Fell School housed the fugitives' first classroom and first place of worship. (Courtesy Douglas Kerr.)

on the turnpike road, was made available for both AME worship services and for a Sunday school. The villagers were following the lead of Gildersleeve, who had organized and led a Sabbath school for fugitives in Wilkes-Barre "that they might be educated and have their minds developed."[34] Wanton Sherman, a member of the Abington Baptist church, helped to get the Waverly AME Sunday School started in the schoolhouse. One of the white teachers was his young son Gilbert, who possibly shared the very reading and writing lessons he was learning as a village youngster in that building. According to the late William Lewis of Waverly, who researched the era, Gilbert also conducted a "singing school" for the fugitives.[35] (Church-based singing schools were a common means of teaching musical literacy using the shape-note system.)

The white Methodists, who'd worshiped in the same space during their own early stage, offered continual support. In coming years, Methodist Joanna Raymond would be the superintendent of the AME Sunday school.

"FRIENDS OF EQUAL RIGHTS"

By the late 1840s, as Waverly's black settlement was sinking roots, some white allies were inspired to step into the political arena and press more openly for abolition—while area doughfaces dug in their heels. In September 1846, "a large number of friends of equal rights" in Luzerne County convened to select candidates for office under the Liberty Party banner. The Liberty Party was a religiously motivated protest party with "but one object," its members declared that day: "the abolition of Slavery."[36] Its Luzerne County leadership included familiar names: William Mason of Abington was named county president, and William Gildersleeve of Wilkes-Barre and Alvinza Gardner of Abington vice presidents. The candidates for row offices included the Abington trio of Gardner, Rodman Sisson, and Isaac Tillinghast. Norval Green, who later moved to Waverly, hosted the meeting. The following year's Liberty slate included Gildersleeve,

Tillinghast, and Sisson. They barely made a public dent, however. In 1847, for instance, Sisson drew a paltry 28 votes for county sheriff compared to the Democratic victor's 2,120 and the Whig's 1,868.[37] The Liberty Party would soon fragment. By 1848, many members, including all of the above-named men, had moved to the Free Soil Party, whose issue was stopping the spread of slavery into the western territories. Free Soil county leaders included Waverly activists Leonard Batchelor and Samuel Stone.

Meanwhile, the ruling Luzerne County Democrats stuck to their guns. In 1849, under the presidency of Waverly's Dr. Andrew Bedford, the party declared that each state and territory had the constitutional right to practice slavery—and it denounced "the fanatic ravings of the abolitionists."[38] Paradoxically, 1849 was the same year Bedford and abolitionist Batchelor opened a store together in Waverly.

The Methodists would sometimes join the fugitives in worship, an easy fellowship since the AME had a similar order of worship and common doctrine. The bond held for decades; on Christmas 1865, the Methodists would present a church Bible inscribed to "the Colored Congregation of the ME Church, Waverly, Pa."[39] In other words, even though the black church was officially AME, Waverly's white Methodists continually regarded it as a daughter congregation of their own.

The importance of the black church cannot be overstated. For escaped slaves, it was what has been called "a rock in a weary land." It not only ministered to their souls, but was the heart of their social life, serving as a safe place for meetings and free discussion. It was their *own* space, a symbol of their emerging liberty and self-determination. And for refugees still coming up the line, it served as a magnet. The presence of a viable black church meant a community of their people awaited, ready to baptize them into freedom. Congregants would feed and shelter the newcomers, and circuit-riding ministers were able to notify other black churches about movements up and down the line. "The A.M.E. church was the trail fugitives followed," says Sherman Wooden, head of the Center for Anti-Slavery Studies in Montrose. The church would bring them in quietly, and arriving safely "was like being saved. It was a spiritual moment, with celebration and happiness."

It's not certain where all of Waverly's new arrivals were able to live in those first years. Some may have found lodging in tenement houses as Lot Norris did, or been invited to occupy surplus space in the homes of white sympathizers. Others may have simply doubled or tripled up in haylofts, outbuildings, or rooms above the village stores. But at some point in time, a land tenancy arrangement developed that proved as significant to their viability as forming a church had been.

On a high point at the northeast corner of Waverly was a stretch of available land. It lay along the road to Carbondale, just beyond the last row of village houses. A protective stand of pines known as Fell's Woods rose behind it to the north. A long block to the south stood Madison Academy, a few frame houses, and acres of open pasture and rolling farmland. John and Esther Stone owned that undeveloped stretch along the Carbondale road. The Stones had already built their lone home there, a short walk from the academy boarding house where Esther served as the matron. Somewhere around this time, the Stones began to divide the rest of

Esther Sisson Stone and John Stone provided land to establish Colored Hill.
(This Is Waverly, by Mildred Mumford.)

the property into parcels and accepted fugitive families as their neighbors. It seemed to be a long-term rent-to-buy arrangement. According to William Lewis, the Stones "sold lots to Negroes on the installment plan or as they could pay (some never finished paying) and the Negroes built little homes on their lots." Lot Norris is said to have been the first, erecting a saltbox house barely larger than a southern slave hut from recycled timbers to house his growing family. Records at the Luzerne County Recorder of Deeds office show the Stones eventually transferring titles to a few families. The only stipulation was that the occupants "build, maintain and keep in repair all the fences," presumably to keep the chickens and other yard animals from wandering.

The fugitives did their best to improve their parcels, putting up fences, coops, privies, and outbuildings; sinking vegetable patches and planting a fruit tree or two; and adding rooms, catch-as-catch-can, as the need arose and families grew. They took in boarders from among the stray newcomers and set up a system to hide other freedom-seekers who were passing through.

This became their new corner of the world. It was where they'd eventually plant their church building. It became known locally as Colored Hill.

The cluster of cabins was in easy proximity to the surrounding farms where the men found work plowing, tilling, threshing, clearing land, building walls, chopping wood, cleaning barns, and tending the animals. Others became handymen for merchants and families down in the village. The women hired themselves out as housekeepers, nannies, and laundresses. The steady income allowed the families to make their payments to the Stones, and maybe put a little aside for the church building fund. It is a telling fact that by 1850, these fugitives felt secure enough to divulge both their names and their Southern origins to the white census-takers. In the unlikely green pastures of Colored Hill, they were able to restore one another and shake off the stigma of bondage.

Then came the Fugitive Slave Act and a new round of danger.

1. Stampp, Kenneth M. *The Peculiar Institution: Slavery in the Ante-Bellum South* (New York: Vintage, 1956), pp. 110-111.
2. The slave-owner Clagetts named in the article may be the "Clickett" that Waverly fugitive Ignatius Thomas identified as his former master in western Maryland. A search of land and census records from that region found no Clickett but a number of slave-owning Clagetts.
3. Siebert, William H. *The Underground Railroad From Slavery to Freedom* (New York: Macmillan, 1898), p. 240.
4. Ibid., p. 240.
5. Furnas, J.C. *Goodbye to Uncle Tom* (New York: Sloane, 1956), p. 206.
6. Brower, Edith. *Little Old Wilkes-Barre As I Knew It* (Wilkes-Barre, PA: Fowler, Dick & Walker, 1923), pp. 1944-45.
7. Derr, Allean F. "Factoryville: The Hollow in the Beech Woods" (unpublished manuscript, in the holdings of Keystone College Library), p. 37.
8. Lewis, William. "Underground Railroad in Abington, Pa.," (unpublished manuscript, 1944), p. 4.
9. Moss, Emerson I. *African-Americans in the Wyoming Valley, 1778-1990* (Wilkes-Barre, PA: Wilkes University Press, 1992), pp. 36-37.
10. Atherton, William. "Wilkes-Barre of Old," article in the *Scranton Republican* (Scranton, PA), Jan. 31, 1901, p. 3.
11. Schuelke, Frieda. "Activities of the Underground Railroad in Oswego County," Journal of the Oswego Historical Society (Oswego, N.Y.: Palladium-Times Inc., 1940), p. 5.

12. Pierce, Frederick Clifton. *Batchelder, Batcheller Genealogy* (Chicago: W.B. Conkey Co, 1898), p. 523.
13. Lewis, William. "Waverly and the Underground Railroad (unpublished manuscript, 1952), p. 2.
14. Blight, David W., editor *Passages to Freedom: The Underground Railroad in History and Memory* (Washington, DC: Smithsonian Books, 2004), p. 109.
15. *Scranton Republican*, Jan. 2, 1891, p. 2.
16. Furnas, op. cit., p. 212.
17. *Spectator and Freeman's Journal* (Montrose, PA), July 14, 1836, p. 2.
18. Blockson, Charles L. *The Underground Railroad* (New York: Prentice-Hall, 1987), p. 229.
19. Swallow, Rev. Silas C., article in the *Harrisburg Telegraph* (Harrisburg, PA), Dec. 18, 1924, p. 8.
20. "Slave Hunting," *Wilkes-Barre Advocate* (Wilkes-Barre, PA), Jan. 8, 1845, p. 2.
21. Parke, Rev. Nathan G., quoted in the *Pittston Gazette* (Pittston, PA), April 12, 1902, p. 4.
22. Wooden, Sherman. *The Place I Call Home: How Abolition and the Underground Railroad Shaped the Communities of Northeastern Pennsylvania* (Montrose, PA: Center for Anti-Slavery Studies, 2009), p. 25.
23. Lewis, op. cit. "Underground Railroad in Abington, Pa.," p. 5.
24. Brown, William. *Wells Narrative of William W. Brown, an American Slave, Written by Himself* (London: Charles Gilpin, 1850), p. 102.
25. Gara, Larry. *The Liberty Line: The Legend of the Underground Railroad* (Lexington, Ky.: University of Kentucky Press, 1961), p. 44.
26. Kyofski, Bonelyn. "Northeastern Pennsylvania's 'Frontier Mentality' and Its Influence on the Underground Railroad," essay in *The Place I call Home: How Abolition and the Underground Railroad Shaped the Communities of Northeastern Pennsylvania* (Montrose, Pa: Center for Anti-Slavery Studies, 2009), p.75.
27. Hitchcock, Frederick L., and Down, John P. *History of Scranton and Its People, Vol. 1* (Scranton: Lewis Historical Publishing Co., 1914), p. 42.
28. Lewis, op. cit., "Underground Railroad in Abington, Pa.," p. 6.
29. Sacks, Howard L. and Judith R. *Way Up North in Dixie: A Black Family's Claim to the Confederate Anthem* (Champaign, Ill.: University of Illinois Press, 2003), p. 71.
30. Lewis, William. "Colored Settlement at Waverly" (unpublished manuscript, undated), p. 3.
31. *History of Luzerne, Lackawanna, and Wyoming Counties, Pa.* (New York: W.W. Munsell, 1880), p. 459.
32. Lewis op.cit., "Colored Settlement at Waverly," p. 3.
33. Williams, Gilbert Anthony. *Christian Recorder: Newspaper of the African Methodist Episcopal Church* (Jefferson, N.C.: McFarland & Co., 1996), pp. 78-9.
34. Wedlock, Narria. "A Wilkes-Barre Abolitionist," 1963 paper cited by wbwilliamcgildersleeve.blogspot.com, online.
35. Lewis, op. cit., "Colored Settlement at Waverly," p. 3.
36. *Republican Farmer and Democratic Journal* (Wilkes-Barre, PA), Sept. 30, 1846, p. 3.
37. *Republican Farmer and Democratic Journal* (Wilkes-Barre), Oct. 20, 1847, p. 3.
38. *Republican Farmer and Democratic Journal* (Wilkes-Barre), Sept. 19, 1849, p. 3.
39. Lewis, op. cit., "Colored Settlement at Waverly," p. 4.

CHAPTER FIVE

1850–1861

"With Loaded Pistols"

———◆———

A S IT HAPPENED, the houses flanking the turnpike
at the southern entrance into Waverly were all occupied by abolitionists. Nighttime arrivals of fugitive
slaves had the good fortune to be met by men like John
Raymond. He was clearly a deep sympathizer. Over the
years, Raymond had gotten to know George Keys and
other black newcomers through his church. Raymond's
son Orlando would work among them in the fields. Three
of his daughters attended school with the children of
runaways. Raymond was alert to their situation—and
by late September 1850, he sensed tensions brewing.
Other white sympathizers had caught wind of it, too.
They met and decided to issue a public call to action.

Raymond agreed to put it in writing. Being a businessman, he was used to composing formal correspon-
dence. So on September 24, he penned a letter to Judge
William Jessup in Montrose, one of the region's foremost
abolitionists. "Mr. Jessup sir," his letter began,

> There seems to be a desire amongst some of the people that
> there should be a rally made or a convention of the sons of
> freedom in Northern Pennsylvania so that the people may
> know that the spirit of freedom is not entirely gone amongst
> us.
>
> There was a line from a freewill baptist preacher living in
> Jackson sent here to Abington upon the subject two weeks

since. And now sir whilst the collored friends go to their work with their pockets filled with loaded pistols and trembling with excitement with a look of anguish in their eye shall we not meet and do something for them.

We have written to Mr. Gildersleeve that if it might be thought best to have a call for a convention at Montrose the fifteenth of Oct. if this should meet your mind you will probably get as many names as possible as a call for a convention published in Montrose paper.

Raymond added that Judge Jessup "might safely make use of the following names" from Abington: "Rodman Cisson, Alvinza Gardner, Wm Mason, Isaac Tillinghast, Lenord Batchelor, J. Raymond," and from Benton, "Wm Green, Lyman Green, Wm Seamons, Anson Reynolds". He closed the letter with "Yours for the oppressed, J. Raymond."

The appeal was timely. Just one week earlier, Congress had imposed a dark new reality on the North with passage of the Fugitive Slave Act. The South, as part of the so-called Compromise of 1850, agreed to allow California to be admitted as a free state, but in return was granted far tougher federal rules on pursuing runaways in the North. The law now required Northern authorities to apprehend and turn over all suspected fugitive slaves in their jurisdictions, and it ordered citizens to aid in the capture or face heavy fines and even jail time. In response, an untold number of black people uprooted their families and fled to Canada. "While the law was a terror to the free [black], it was still a greater terror to the escaped bondman," observed Frederick Douglass. "Asleep or awake, at work or at rest, in church or market, he was liable to surprise or capture."

Raymond's appeal to the judge bore fruit. On October 24, the *Montrose Democrat* newspaper reported that activists had convened at Montrose's Baptist church

With this 1850 letter, Abington's "sons of freedom" convened a regional meeting in response to the Fugitive Slave Act. (Courtesy Susquehanna County Historical Society, Montrose, PA.)

"and unanimously adopted a resolution denouncing the Fugitive Slave Law and pledging sympathy." Its words were pained: "Resolved, that we tender the unhappy fugitives from the house of bondage our warmest sympathies—we know not how to advise them amid their deep trials—above all we pity those helpless women and children. We repeat we know not how to advise. Society and law have made war on the colored man; they disown and outlaw him, and afford him no protection; and if in this war he throws himself upon the rights of manhood and defends himself and his family, when no one else will defend, who can blame him!—and if the pursuer falls in the conflict, whom has he to blame but himself!"[1]

Two important facts came to light with those words. First, the region's white activists had no doubt that the Fugitive Slave Law represented a dangerous turning point in the sectional conflict with the South. Second, and more importantly, the whites were signaling that however incensed the new "war on the colored man" made them, if push came to shove, they would not become brothers in arms. They'd stand by while the fugitives obtained deadly weapons. They might even help provide the firearms. But, perhaps at the behest of their own worried families, they wouldn't join the fight. Any physical resistance to capture would be left to the fugitives themselves.

That was the case across most of Pennsylvania. Front-line protection against kidnappers was a role that free-blacks had long borne and that runaways in Waverly and elsewhere were now willing to take on as part of their emerging self-determination. As the *New York Independent* newspaper remarked at the time, Southerners would find that "men, however abject, who have tasted liberty, soon learn to prize it, and are ready to defend it."[2]

"Vigilance committees" had been in place in many Northern black communities since the 1830s, initially to protect free-blacks from kidnapping and later to help fugitive slaves as well. Scholars credit the vigilance system with laying the groundwork for the Underground Railroad. The advent of the 1850 Fugitive Slave Act spurred black men in self-reliant "Maroon" enclaves and other places to organize paramilitary companies, with or without white support. There were reports of the extralegal groups marching in formation in Harrisburg and Reading as a show of force. It wasn't mere show. Members were skilled at jumping into action when word came that "the wind was blowing from the south." They would quickly mob and menace slave-catchers, spring fugitives from abduction, disable vehicles, and employ other methods of resistance. Slave-hunters were said to be "amazed by the speed with which news of their presence in the area spread and by the determination of the crowds to resist their efforts."[3] In 1851, the *Jeffersonian* newspaper of Stroudsburg reported an incident near Pottsville in which a black crowd prevented two Maryland officers from entering a home where a fugitive hid. "She afterwards affected her escape, in company with several other colored persons."[4] The state's official fugitive slave commissioner was repeatedly harassed, and his Harrisburg office was targeted for arson.[5] In the sensational 1851 incident known as the Christiana Riot, more than fifty black activists surrounded a Maryland slave owner, shooting him dead and wounding two whites in his posse.

Defiance also was evident in northeastern Pennsylvania. Blacks in Bradford County declared in the abolition organ the *Liberator* that "before we will submit to be dragged in Southern bondage by the man-stealers of the South, we will die in defense of our right to liberty."[6] In October 1850, two Southern slave-catchers

The bloody "Christiana Tragedy" of 1851 was a renowned example of resistance in the North to slave-catchers. ('The Underground Railroad,' by William Still.)

encountered open hostility in Honesdale, Wayne County, which had a number of resident abolitionists and blacks. The Southerners were hunting for "a beautiful creole" runaway, the *Star of the North* newspaper reported—but added, "it will hardly be possible for them to take her, the feeling is so strong against them."[7] That same month in Montrose, a slave owner was said to have come in search of a certain fugitive. According to a recollection in the *Scranton Republican*, one evening the man "passed a couple of negroes who were carrying a bushel basket, which must have contained nearly a hundred pistols of the old-fashioned type used before the invention of the Colt revolver. He noticed that the men bearing the weapons went down in the direction of the portion of the town where most of the black men resided. He made no further search for his 'property,' but he quickly returned to his hotel, and the next morning took the first stage out of the place. That, I believe, was the last attempt that was ever made to capture a runaway slave in old Abolition Montrose."[8]

And in the erstwhile safe eddy of Waverly, loaded pistols were suddenly being carried for protection. One story held that "a band of farmers" drove off slave-catchers who'd come to Waverly to nab Lot Norris. According to an old-timer's account, the abductors were Southern slaveholders while Norris's defenders, presumably black men from Colored Hill, were "armed with guns, pitchforks, etc."[9] It's not known exactly where or when the confrontation took place, but the armed farmers might well have been some of Waverly's future black soldiers: George Keys, John Mason, Richard Lee, and others. In a 1904 article in the *Scranton Republican*, Keys' son, George Jr., mentioned the ad hoc vigilance efforts in the course of explaining his surname: "The colored people, through force of circumstances, were occasionally compelled to change their names. This was done during the slavery days to avoid falling into the hands of kidnappers who infested Pennsylvania during those times and, finding the fleeing slaves, by force took them back to their masters and received rewards. Mr. Keys states that at Waverly, the slaves banded together and drove the kidnappers away. Then they chose new names. George's father happened to have a door key in his hand and seeing it, their leader named him Key, and from Key it was changed to Keys."[10]

Another incident took place on the outskirts of Waverly. According to a column in the *Scranton Times,* Benjamin Champlain, a white farmer who lived just north of the village, encountered slave-catchers one day. "Mr. Champlain was quite a joker," wrote columnist Alfred Twining, "and when four of the fugitive hunters got as far as the Fell woods—now owned by Mahoney & Parker— Mr. Champlain was asked if he has seen any runaway n**s within a day or two. 'Yes,' said Mr. Champlain, 'the abolitionists, through their underground system, heard you were coming, and the negroes were notified. The latter were permitted to help themselves to guns, and they are hiding in Jerry Knight's woods at Wallsville, waiting for you. You follow this road to a turn to the right, and you'll find them all right.' Of course Mr. Champlain wanted to send the slave hunters on a wild goose chase, and put a scare into them. Suffice to say, after some tall cursing the slave hunters turned back toward Waverly."[11]

Would-be abductors apparently learned their lesson. Abington's Amenzo Mumford, son of abolitionist Archa Mumford, said it became clear that "the 'system' was so scattered over so big a territory and so well perfected, that it was a useless expense to look for fugitives in this section."[12] Similarly, the *Scranton Republican* reported in 1897, "So far as is known no fugitive slaves were ever captured and returned to slavery under the fugitive slave law in old Lackawanna Valley."[13]

In the southern end of Luzerne County, animosity to black rights was pronounced, and the populace included a number of mercenary slave-catchers.[14] Characteristically, doughface Democrats convened a public meeting in Wilkes-Barre in November 1850, to *celebrate*

Below is the opening stanza of a long poem written by Montrose abolitionist L. P. Hinds. It appeared in the *Susquehanna Register* on November 14, 1850, a month after the Montrose gathering that Abington activists had initiated in response to the new Fugitive Slave Act.

THE SLAVE HUNTER

See him!
The tyrant has come, as the thief in the night,
Like the robber of graves, he shuns the daylight;
And his minions gleaming with pistol and steel,
Cry down with Jehovah—to us lowly kneel:
From the sluices of vice, and houses of game,
The black hearted hunter comes covered in shame;
Commanding a people, whose trust is on high
To scent keenly the breeze that carries a sigh—
See! Hirelings of slavery here from the South,
With law on their lips, a curse in their mouth.

the Fugitive Slave Act. Presiding was E.W. Sturdevant, who'd led the constitutional push to disenfranchise Pennsylvania blacks back in 1838. The doughfaces issued resolutions endorsing "obedience to righteous law" and calling "the man who encourages resistance to law a traitor to his country, and an enemy to mankind."[15]

In September 1853, that hard line was suddenly challenged when a federal marshal and his two gun-wielding deputies confronted a suspected fugitive and tried to strong-arm him into custody. The incident took place in public view, first in the Wilkes-Barre restaurant where the hunted man worked, and then at the Susquehanna River, where he plunged in a frantic effort to escape. Some whites in the gathering crowd were said to have shouted, "Don't hurt him!" and "Shame!" while a group of blacks chased the officers away. According to historian William C. Kashatus, the bloodied black man, William Thomas, "eventually found refuge in Canada. The Federal officers were arrested for 'inciting a riot,' but their prosecution was overturned by a Federal circuit court that rejected the prosecution's claim of state sovereignty."[16]

THE INCIDENT AND ITS AFTERMATH revealed a measure of public unease with the long arm of the fugitive law, even in a Democratic bastion like Wilkes-Barre. One of the city's leading lawyers, George R. Bedford—son of Waverly physician Andrew Bedford—recalled it this way: "One effect of the attack on Thomas was to completely change the politics of some who witnessed it. Certain of them who were pronounced Democrats and in favor of the fugitive law were so impressed with the brutality incident to the law's enforcement that they became at once active Abolitionists, and thereafter aided fugitive slaves to make good their escape."[17] While Sturdevant and his partisans continued their vehement support of the slave-hunters, other whites were feeling a new sympathy for fugitives and resentment at how the law encroached on their own autonomy. "Northern whites, usually the most respected members of their communities, suddenly found themselves, and their fine homes, subjected to search and seizure, clearly a violation of a free man's personal rights."[18]

On a lecture tour in Pennsylvania in 1851, abolitionist Jermain Loguen sensed the change: "I never saw the time during the last ten years that I have been in the antislavery field when the public ear was so ready and willing to hear on American Slavery."[19]

As the decade wore on, further developments awakened many Northerners to the anti-slavery message. *Uncle Tom's Cabin*, the heartrending novel about runaways, caused a sensation when it was released in 1852. *Twelve Years a Slave*, the exposé about a free-black's abduction from the North, came out in 1853, followed by Frederick Douglass' *My Bondage and My Freedom* in 1855. The turmoil in "Bleeding Kansas" and other border states raised alarm about Southern demands that slavery be guaranteed in the western territories by federal fiat. The Supreme Court's infamous 1857 Dred Scott decision worsened tensions by declaring slaves property and forbidding Congress from regulating slavery.

Meanwhile, the arrest of suspected fugitives continued in Northern states—over two hundred by 1856, most frequently in Pennsylvania—but the stories of false arrests, summary proceedings, and the threat of arbitrary searches of white homes fueled a resentment that the forces of Southern "slavocracy" had literally gone too far. According to Dickinson College historian Matthew Pinsker, there was "a general reluctance across the North to encourage Federal intervention or reward southern power. In other words, it was all about states' rights—northern states' rights."[20] Pennsylvania and other states had passed "personal liberty" statutes to try to protect their free-blacks from being kidnapped. Even though the US Supreme Court overturned the protections, some defiant Northern juries kept invoking them, including one to absolve abolitionists in the Christiana Riot killings. "These northern legislatures and juries were, for the most part, indifferent to black civil rights," Pinsker writes, "but they were quite adamant about asserting their own states' rights during the years before the Civil War."

Pennsylvania's combative Jacksonian Democrats fought back hard. A struggle for political supremacy ensued between hard-line Democrats and "Free Soil" Whigs. Governor William Johnston, a Whig, refused to enforce the Fugitive Slave Law—and was narrowly defeated in 1851 by Democrat William Bigler, who insisted on enforcing it. In 1854, Bigler was ousted by James Pollock, the candidate of the Whigs and "Know-Nothings." Democrats rebounded in 1856 with the election of Bigler as US senator and pro-slavery Pennsylvanian James Buchanan as president.[21] And their candidate for governor, William Packer, swept into office the next year. The political gyrations continued for years, reflecting the polarization in Pennsylvania's body politic. The Luzerne County Democratic party argued that the very soul of the country was at stake: "Shall the noble structure handed down to us stand in all its beauty and grandure [sic], or shall the fell spirit of black abolition reign amidst the ruin it is attempting to create," the party declared in a 1856 resolution. "This is the issue—and this alone."[22]

DURING THIS PERIOD, Waverly remained an anomaly. The village had its share of avowed Democrats—Andrew Bedford had even formed a Buchanan and Breckinridge

Waverly's old AME church was in use from 1855 to 1923. (This Is Waverly, by Mildred Mumford.)

Club in Waverly during the 1856 campaign[23]—yet they evidently were accustomed enough to the black people in their midst to not bring trouble upon Colored Hill. The presence of pistol-toting blacks also helped to keep danger away. As a result, during a decade when many Northern white communities took steps to exclude black people from their limits,[24] Waverly continued to absorb them. Census records show the black population of the village and surrounding township grew from 38 in 1850 to 67 in 1860. White sympathizers continued to nurture and support the black church. The Baptists opened their churchyard, the present Hickory Grove Cemetery, to black burials. Perhaps boldest of all, the one-room schoolhouses in and around Waverly integrated without a ruckus. This flew in the face of white sentiment elsewhere in the state, where districts were setting up segregated schools with government sanction. By the turn of the decade, according to the 1860 census, fifteen Colored Hill youngsters were being formally educated. For many of their parents—forbidden to read or write

Colored Hill is shown at left center in this detail from an undated drawing of Waverly on display in the township building.

in slavery and still hobbled by illiteracy—having white classrooms freely open the doors to their children must have seemed miraculous.

More of their prayers were answered in 1855 when the brand-new Waverly AME church building opened its doors on Colored Hill. The wood-frame sanctuary was small and rough-hewn, but stood as a proud sign of their permanence. The *Christian Recorder*, the official AME publication in Philadelphia, reported on February 1, 1855: "In Abington, they are finishing off a beautiful little house of worship, for which they will owe three hundred and thirty-five dollars at the time of its completion." John Stone deeded the plot to the church trustees the next year for $30, and congregants presumably paid down the debt through collections and continuing white largesse. In 1856, abolitionist John Raymond's daughter Joanna, just 22, was installed as the AME Sunday School superintendent. The church's membership had swelled to about thirty people, but they always made room for curious whites who would occasionally join their prayer meetings or attend the big winter revivals and summer camp meetings out back in Fell's Woods.

In addition to prayers and songs of praise, the sanctuary would have reverberated with emotional sermons against slavery and the fugitive law. Congregations like Waverly's were customarily pastored by "book preachers," educated men who stayed abreast of current events and would read aloud from the newspapers for their unlettered congregants. The Colored Hill church's founding pastor, Rev. James Hyatt, was an outspoken cleric who co-authored an AME leadership resolution in 1854 that denounced slavery's "villainies," and resolved "that until our voices are heard no more we will wage a life-long and sleepless warfare with the principles of slavery in all its varied forms."[25] Another of Waverly's early black pastors, Rev. Thomas M. D. Ward, a renowned orator who rose to become an AME bishop in 1868, was the freeborn child of parents who'd escaped Maryland. Another, Rev. William Johnson, had fled Virginia to claim freedom. Ever since 1850, the denomination had observed the last Friday in June as a day of fasting and prayer for the abolition of slavery.

Some white churches in the vicinity also were taking public stands. The activist Factoryville Baptist Church led the way in December 1850, when it formally denounced the Fugitive Slave Law and demanded its repeal.[26] Then, in 1854, the Abington Baptist Association broke its long collective silence on slavery. The nation's Baptists had severed nine years earlier when the Southern Baptists broke away to protest anti-slavery activism by Northern congregations. The Abington association spanned from Pittston to Nicholson, and few of its churches were as progressive as Factoryville's.

Rev. Thomas M. D. Ward, later a bishop, was one of Waverly AME's first pastors. (Courtesy Union Theological Society; University of North Carolina at Chapel Hill University Library.)

The association had managed to avoid the divisive topic until Rev. Edward L. Bailey of Carbondale introduced a resolution at the annual Baptist convention in Benton, in September 1854. "The body, though moderately anti-slavery, had not, up to this period, expressed a decided opinion on that exciting question," Bailey wrote years later. "At this session, however, the Association passed the following brief but comprehensive resolution, which was published in the minutes of this and two subsequent years: 'Resolved, that we believe the system of Slavery as it exists in the United States, to be a great and growing evil, and that we pledge our interest and influence to prevent its extension and promote its extinction.' To this was added in 1856, 'And that the time for action has now come.'"[27]

Also in 1854, Waverly's First Presbyterian Church of Abington joined with the thirty other churches in the Montrose Presbytery to unanimously denounce Congress' Nebraska-Kansas Bill because it removed federal restrictions on the spread of slavery into the western territories. (Rev. Burr Baldwin, the radical stated clerk of the Presbytery of Montrose, had organized the Waverly church in April 1850. Baldwin, who had integrated his flocks in Newark, New Jersey, and Montrose, worked with Judge Jessup and Leonard Batchelor to keep the Waverly church out of the hands of the anti-abolitionist Old School Presbyterians in Wilkes-Barre.[28])

The region's Methodist Episcopal churches began taking public stances in 1857. The thirty-two congregations in the Wyoming Conference, meeting in Waverly in May 1857, adopted a resolution to "pledge ourselves to the friend of the slave, in the Church and the State, on the border and distant from it, both North and South, to the religious, literary and political world, that we are bound to stand by the slave till his shackles fall and he enjoys the boon of freedom as fully as ourselves."[29] The next year, the conference added a call for its Sunday school literature to denounce slavery. In 1859, it adopted anti-slaveholding language proposed by Rev. DeWitt Clinton Olmstead, who would become Waverly's outspoken wartime pastor.

Sometime during the 1850s (the date is not certain), a hotel in Scranton's Hyde Park section hosted what was said to be the first anti-slavery convention in Luzerne County. According to a *Scranton Republican* column from 1893, the hotel keeper for the "memorable convention" was Norval Green of Waverly. Greater Abington was well-represented, with Green, Leonard Batchelor, Rodman Sisson, "Alvinzy" Gardner, and William R. Finch among the participants.[30]

The open support had to hearten Waverly's black residents. It stood in stark contrast to the intensified hostility they would experience from other quarters. As the nation crossed into war, doughfaces near and far would rail against their rights, rail against their allies, even rail against their courage, and scapegoat them for the nation's crisis.

---

1. *Montrose Democrat* (Montrose, PA), Oct. 24, 1850, p. 2.
2. Jackson, Kellie Carter. "At the Risk of Our Own Lives: Violence and the Fugitive Slave Law in Pennsylvania," essay in *The Civil War in Pennsylvania: The African American Experience*, edited by Samuel W. Black (Pittsburgh: John Heinz History Center, 2013), p. 59.
3. Blackett, R.J.M. *Freedom, or the Martyr's Grave: Black Pittsburgh's Aid to the Fugitive Slave* (Pittsburgh: University of Pittsburgh, 1997), pp. 129-130.
4. *Jeffersonian* (Stroudsburg, PA), Feb. 27, 1851, p. 3.
5. Cooper, H.C. Jr. *The Twentieth Century Bench and Bar of Pennsylvania, Vol. 2* (Chicago: Brown & Cooper, 1903), p. 770.
6. Jackson, op. cit., p. 54.
7. *Star of the North* (Bloomsburg, PA), Oct. 10, 1850, p.2.
8. "Stroller's Notebook" column, the *Scranton Republican* (Scranton, PA), March 17, 1913, p. 6.
9. Morris, J.M. letter cited in "Underground Railroad in Abington, Pa." (unpublished manuscript by William Lewis, 1944), p. 4.
10. "The Son of a Former Slave," article in the *Scranton Republican*, Jan. 24, 1904, p. 3.
11. Twining, Alfred, "Waverly an Important Station of the UGRR," article in the *Scranton Times* (Scranton, PA), Oct. 3, 1916, p. 37.
12. Lewis, William, "Underground Railroad in Abington, Pa." (unpublished manuscript, 1944), p. 6.
13. *Scranton Republican*, May 3, 1897, p. 8.
14. *Pittston Gazette* (Pittston, PA), April 12, 1902, p. 4.
15. *Appendix to The Congressional Globe, Vol. 112*, (Washington, DC: Blair & Rives, 1856), p. 505.
16. Kashatus, William C. "In Immortal Splendor: Wilkes-Barre's Fugitive Slave Case of 1853," article in *Pennsylvania Heritage*, Spring 2008, p. 25.
17. "Some Early Recollections, by George R. Bedford," in *Proceedings and Collections of the Wyoming Historical and Geological Society, 1918* (Wilkes-Barre: E.B. Yordy Co., 1919), p.26.
18. Freeman, Aileen Sallom. *Lincoln: The Northeastern Pennsylvania Connection* (Paupack, PA: Fosi Ltd., 2000), p. 166.
19. Jackson, op. cit., p. 56.
20. Pinsker, Matthew "The Underground Railroad and the Coming of War," essay in *History Now*, online.
21. "Abraham Lincoln and the Politics of the Civil War: Pennsylvania Democrats," Pennsylvania Historical and Museum Commission online essay, 2011, at explorepahistory.com.
22. *Luzerne Union* (Wilkes-Barre, PA), Sept. 17, 1856, p. 2.
23. *Luzerne Union* (Wilkes-Barre, PA), Aug. 6, 1856, p. 2.
24. Gara, Larry. *The Liberty Line: The Legend of the Underground Railroad* (Lexington, Ky.: University of Kentucky Press), p. 63.
25. Payne, Daniel A. *History of the African Methodist Episcopal Church* (Nashville, Tenn.: AME Sunday School Union, 1891), p. 136.
26. "History of Factoryville Baptist Church," item in *Minutes of the 87th Session of the Abington Baptist Association* (Scranton: Koehler Printers, 1894), p. 45.
27. Bailey, Edward L. *History of the Abington Baptist Association: From 1807-1857* (Philadelphia: J.A. Wagenseller, 1863), p. 63.

28. Osmond, Jonathan. *History of the Presbytery of Luzerne, State of Pennsylvania* (Presbyterian Historical Society, 1897), pp. 258-9.
29. *Minutes of the Wyoming Conference, 1857* (Owego, N.Y.: Gazette Power Press, 1857), p. 10.
30. Green, L.B. "Waywise Wanderings" column, The *Scranton Republican*, April 10, 1893, p. 6.

CHAPTER SIX

1860–1862

Pennsylvania's "Inner Civil War"

———◦•◦———

BY 1860, THE NATION was spinning apart. Confrontations of the prior decade had remade the political landscape in drastic ways. The Whig Party imploded. The Republican Party emerged, its chief goal to keep slavery in check. The Republicans drew in old anti-slavery Whigs and even some disenchanted Democrats willing to coalesce behind presidential candidate Abraham Lincoln. The Democrats, meanwhile, split in two. Their Southern wing demanded that slavery spread to the western territories and be enforced by the federal government, states' rights be damned. The Northern Democrats stopped short of that, preferring that each new territory decide it own status. Dueling presidential tickets were assembled—Lincoln for the Republicans, John Breckinridge for the Southern Democrats, Stephen Douglas for the Northern Democrats, John Bell for the accommodationist Constitution Union Party—and one of the bitterest campaigns in US history ensued.

In northeastern Pennsylvania, many citizens took up the Republican cause. They'd grown weary of the slavocracy's aggressive ways, and fearful that slave labor in the territories would undercut the new wage economies there. Farmers especially liked that the new party embraced area Congressman Galusha Grow's homestead law allotting 160 western acres free to any man willing to till it. A Republican campaign cry

Harper's Weekly *engraving of Wide-Awake torchlight rally in New York, October 1860. (Courtesy Library of Congress.)*

became "free labor, free soil and free men!" The Lincoln campaign spawned a youth phenomenon known as the "Wide-Awakes." At mass rallies across the region, young men in Wide-Awake Clubs would turn out in black satin capes to strut in torch-lit marches. The *Pittston Gazette*, a Republican-leaning weekly, reported on campaign rallies in Scranton, Pittston, and White Haven, running this statement by the White Haven club: "*Resolved, that while the Southern fire-eaters (tacitly encouraged by a bogus democracy of Northern dough-faces) are continually committing overt acts of Treason, we will be 'Wide-Awake.'*"[1] The clubs at the Scranton march (headlined "Grand Republican Rally! Scranton in a Blaze!") represented Wilkes-Barre, Plymouth, Pittston, Hyde Park, Scranton, Carbondale, and Clarks Summit.[2]

The region's supporters of Breckinridge—a Kentucky slaveholder—countered with rallies at which they raised and festooned enormous "hickory poles" in homage to "Old Hickory" Andrew Jackson. A Democratic

An 1860 political cartoon, titled "Dividing the National Map," depicts the four vying presidential candidates. From left: Lincoln, Douglas, Breckinridge, and Bell. (Courtesy Library of Congress.)

newspaper in Bloomsburg, Columbia County, reported that campaign rallies in August and September drew "ever-faithful Democrats of that section of the country," including groups from neighboring Luzerne County.

Breckinridge easily captured Columbia County on Election Day. Luzerne County went for Lincoln, although not by much. A single "Fusion" ticket representing the three anti-Republican slates took 48 percent of the Luzerne vote, reflecting how profoundly split the county was over slavery and the war that was to come.

Luzerne Republicans celebrated Lincoln's victory in the national vote and looked ahead with a naïve hope. On November 15, the *Pittston Gazette* dismissed talk of secession as "too absurd to be treated gravely . . . Although it is only natural that certain madmen in South Carolina should, as usual, bully and bluster, we have an abiding conviction that the sober second thought of every portion of the South will cause their love of the Union to triumph over any temporary feeling of vexation."[3]

The slavocracy and its Northern allies would yield no ground, however. One of the top firebrands was Pennsylvania Supreme Court Justice George Washington Woodward of Luzerne County. The doughface Woodward had been an anti-black delegate to the 1837-38 constitutional convention, and characteristically had electioneered for Breckinridge in 1860. On December 13, a month after Lincoln's win, Justice Woodward was a featured speaker at a mass rally outside Philadelphia's Independence Hall

One of the Democrats' leading pro-slavery figures in 1860 was George Washington Woodward of Luzerne County. (Courtesy Library of Congress.)

that called for accommodating the South. Slavery benefited every citizen, Woodward told the crowd, citing the value of slave-grown cotton to the national economy.

"The Providence of that Good Being who has watched over us from the beginning, and saved us from external foes, has so ordered our internal relations as to make negro slavery an incalculable blessing to us," Woodward declared, in remarks reprinted for circulation. "[T]o intrude our opinions upon the people of sovereign States concerning their domestic institutions would be sheer impertinence. But do you not see and feel how good it was for us to hand over our slaves to our friends of the South—how good it was for us that they have employed them in raising a staple for our manufacturers—how wise it was to so adjust the compromises of the Constitution that we could live in union with them and reap the signal advantages to which I have adverted?"[4]

A week later South Carolina leaders, convinced that the Republican administration was hell-bent on abolition, held a secession convention and voted unanimously to break away from the Union. They urged fellow Southern states to form "a great slaveholding confederacy, stretching its arms over a territory larger than any power in Europe possesses." In mid-April 1861, the nation plunged into the War Between the States.

On Sunday, April 14, two days after Confederate cannons fired on Fort Sumter, anti-secession emotions were running high at Scranton's First Presbyterian Church. Rev. Thomas P. Hunt, a New School abolitionist, minced no words in his sermon: "Oh! Thou God of nations, Thou hast seen that the accursed minions of slavery have dared to fire upon the sacred flag of this country which Thou hast created. This great free Republic which Thou hast ordained to be the asylum of the oppressed of all nations they are seeking and threatening to destroy through their hellish ambitions to propagate and perpetuate the damnable institution of slavery. They would destroy the best government Thou hast given to man! We pray thee stay their wicked hands, already imbued with the blood of freedom; and curse them! Curse them!! We pray Thee, oh Lord, curse them!! Send them to the Hell to which they belong! And save, oh save, our beloved country!"[5]

Reverend Hunt's jeremiad was recorded by Col. Frederick Hitchcock in his *History of Scranton and Its People*. Hitchcock (who went on to lead both white and black troops during the war) noted that Reverend Hunt was a Virginia native who had freed his inherited slaves and become "a stalwart in the ante-bellum agitation" against slavery. Hitchcock was in the pews that Sunday and recalled that "we in the crowded audience responded in our hearts, 'amen! and amen!'" He called this "the spirit of the North" at the time.

It certainly was the spirit of the Republicans and their loyalist compatriots. They rallied round the flag—in fact, many of them gathered to erect new flagpoles and raise the Stars and Stripes in grand displays of patriotism. That spring and summer, the *Pittston Gazette* recorded liberty pole ceremonies in Kingston, North Kingston, Exeter, Wyoming, Orange, Pittston, Hughesville, Greenfield, and East Benton. Swept up in "war fever," loyalist fathers and sons began volunteering for what they were sure would be a swift, glorious military victory. On the propaganda front, many Republicans took the very slur that doughfaces had long used against abolitionists—*"DISUNIONISTS!"*—and turned it against the secessionists and their Northern brethren.

Both sides dug in and the rancor increased. According to Lock Haven University historian Robert Sandow, "divided loyalties pitted neighbor against neighbor and Pennsylvania witnessed its own 'inner civil war.'"[6]

ONCE SECESSION CAME, Democrats in the North separated into either "War Democrats" or "Peace Democrats." The former type, sometimes called Union Democrats, were willing to work with Republicans toward a shared goal of subduing the Southern rebellion quickly and by force. The latter faction wanted no part of that and held rallies across the state to sue for peace, for "reunification with slavery intact." According to the Pennsylvania Historical and Museum Commission, some of the more radical doughfaces cheered the secession and actually suggested that Pennsylvania join the Confederacy.[7] Such shows of defiance were tantamount to treason, critics cried.

On June 15, "the peace loving men" of Northern Luzerne gathered in Fleetville to raise a hickory pole and rally against Lincoln's "despotism and destruction," according to a report in the *Gettysburg Compiler*.[8] The

County Judge Edward Merrifield (left) was a doughface leader. Doughface Aaron A. Chase (right) was publisher of the Scranton Times. *(Courtesy The* City of Scranton and Vicinity and Their Resources.*)*

lineup of speakers included Benton Township Democratic leader Theron Finn, county judge Edward Merrifield, and Fleetville lawyer Aaron A. Chase, a Madison Academy graduate who went on to become publisher of the *Scranton Times.* "The genuine spirit of unterrified Democracy is fully aroused in Luzerne," the *Compiler* remarked. In Susquehanna County, the *Montrose Democrat* reported that "peace meetings" were being conducted by Democrats in Lenox "who are known to be in sympathy with Jeff. Davis & co., and opposed to our Government."[9]

Waverly provides a good example of the churn in public attitudes. The prior autumn, the village's Democratic bloc had gone for David R. Randall, a Democrat, over incumbent Republican George W. Scranton for Congress. But when war broke out and Randall emerged as prosecession, Waverly turned against him. In a June 1861 special election necessitated by Congressman Scranton's sudden death, Waverly rejected Randall and voted overwhelmingly instead for Hendrick Bradley Wright, a War Democrat.[10]

Left: Congressman Hendrick B. Wright went from being anti-abolition to anti-secession. Center: New York Senator Dickinson, a renowned orator, was a guest speaker in Waverly. Right: Rep. Galusha Grow was an influential local congressman. (Courtesy Library of Congress.)

Wright was a prototypical War Democrat. The *Luzerne Union*, a Democratic paper in Wilkes-Barre, commented that Wright (one of William Fogg's courtroom antagonists back in 1836) "labored for years to ward off the natural result of the sectional abolition party—civil war—but when the first blow was struck at the National flag, and the war had actually begun, no man in private life contributed more to strengthen the hand of President Lincoln in putting down rebellion."[11]

Three months after winning the special election, Congressman Wright was in Waverly as a featured speaker at a large anti-Confederacy rally. Six to ten thousand people attended the September 25 event, held as part of the Northern Luzerne Fair on the edge of town. Wright told the crowd how he had attempted to have Luzerne Democrats form a "Union ticket" but was thwarted by inflexible doughfaces including Benton's Theron Finn. The *Pittston Gazette* noted that Wright's swipe at the doughfaces "was warmly endorsed by the masses."[12] The Waverly rally also featured addresses by Congressman Galusha Grow and, most prominently, by former Binghamton mayor and New York senator Daniel S. Dickinson, an orator known for his eloquence on the stump. Dickinson, who stayed at Dr. Andrew Bedford's stately Waverly home for the occasion, had been a supporter of Southern states' rights, but flipped to become a staunch War Democrat once the South seceded. (In fact, he would later be in the running as Lincoln's bipartisan ticket mate in 1864.) Dickinson made dozens of speeches with soaring rhetoric such as this:

"When the timid falter and the faithless fly, when the skies lower, the winds howl, the storm descends, and the tempest beats, when the lightnings flash, the thunders roar, the waves dash, and the good ship Union creaks and groans with the expiring throes of dissolution, I will cling to her still as the last refuge of hope from the fury of the storm and if she goes down I will go down with her, rather than survive to tell the story of her ignoble end. I will rally round the star-spangled banner so long as a single strip can be discovered, or a single star shall shimmer from the surrounding darkness."

By the time of the Waverly fair and its calls to patriotism, the first Pennsylvanians had already gone south to fight. After Sumter, Lincoln had called for seventy-five thousand troops for three months, and soon expanded that to forty thousand more volunteers for three years and twenty-five thousand regulars for five years. He got a robust response. The first contingent of area troops left Wilkes-Barre on April 18, 1861. In early May, two dozen men from Tunkhannock linked up with a unit in Factoryville and departed by train for Harrisburg.[13] In time, they would be joined by ten regiments, each one thousand strong, that Luzerne County provided in whole or part. A year later, Pennsylvania had more men in uniform than New York, even though its population was one million less.

But it must be noted that no black man was welcome in the federal ranks. The Northern states turned away all volunteers of color until 1863, driven by the blind prejudice that blacks would be cowardly and un-disciplined. While some white recruits were progressive abolitionists, at least as many others were indifferent to the anti-slavery cause. Many were offended by the very notion of serving alongside men they considered racially inferior. To keep the recruits coming, military officials needed to stem the rumor that the war had a secret purpose: to free the South's estimated four mil-lion slaves and let them roam the country at will. To that end, Rev. N.G. Parke, of Pittston, remarked years later, "When Northern troops were first called for in Pittston as elsewhere there was no reference to slavery. They were called to save the nation."[14]

The spurned black community salvaged its dignity as best it could. The AME newspaper the *Christian Recorder* commented that for black men to try to enlist any more would be "to abandon self-respect and invite insult." In-stead, it called on black people to deploy another power at their disposal, as it said on May 25: "Yes, ye proscribed Americans, though disenfranchised in the North, and enslaved in the South, you can now wield a power more terrible than the rifle, the revolver, or the howitzer – *it is the effectual fervent prayer of the righteous man.*" The *Weekly Anglo-African*, meanwhile, urged readers to orga-nize paramilitary companies and drill in the event con-ditions changed, and in the meantime to demonstrate their patriotism by sending supplies to Union soldiers.[15]

Northern doughfaces, newly branded as copper-heads—snakes that strike without warning—intensified their race-baiting to stoke opposition to Lincoln and the war. Wilkes-Barre historian Sheldon Spear notes that the *Luzerne Union*, a Democratic organ, engaged in "un-relenting anti-black, racist vocabulary" that reflected "the prevailing prejudice of many northern whites, who hated blacks and who rejected the radical notion of the war as a crusade for their freedom."[16] In Tunkhannock,

THE COPPERHEAD PARTY.——IN FAVOR OF *A VIGOROUS PROSECUTION OF PEACE!*

The propaganda war between loyalist forces and the dissident Northerners known as copperheads was bitter and even violent. (Courtesy Libary of Congress.)

the *North Branch Democrat* warned of blacks coming north to live as "paupers, thieves and beggars," and said emancipation would be an offense to the pocketbook: "[T]he loss of production to the world by freeing the negro is enormous. In the item of groceries alone . . . the North is now paying *Forty Millions of dollars* more for them that she ought to do, because their high price is occasioned by the idleness of the negro."[17]

WHEN THE LIKELIHOOD OF A MILITARY DRAFT came in 1862, the state's inner civil war only worsened. Battle casualties had been mounting, yet the War Department was confident a military surge could defeat the Confederacy. In July, Lincoln called for three hundred thousand fresh troops. He gave each state a quota and instructed that men be drafted from any state that fell short. Pennsylvania's quota was twenty-one regiments, for three-year terms.

Hundreds of loyalist sons of Luzerne answered the call, enough so that the county opened its own training facility, Camp Luzerne, outside Wilkes-Barre. The one full regiment that mustered there, the 143rd Pennsylvania Infantry, included many young white men from greater Abington. Asher and George Fell, Lysander Jordan, George Nicholson, Pardon Smith, Milo Stone, Charles Finch, George Perry, Aaron Von Storch, Jeffrey Brundage, Augustus Atherton, James and John Miles, Levi Miller, and Avery Harris, among others, gathered that August 1862 in Waverly, headed to Dalton, and shipped out to Camp Luzerne, where they were grouped in the 143rd's Company B.

Avery Harris, then 22, was a budding abolitionist who cursed slavery as "a travesty and blot upon that grandly sublime declaration of our rights." To his dismay, few other recruits in the training camp shared his zeal. Harris wrote in his journal that some were "negro-haters" while most of the rest "simply tolerated" slavery as an institution that "must eventually be wiped out."[18]

Lincoln loyalists in the area did their part to encourage more sign-ups. In August, one group of them held an enlistment rally in Milwaukee, Ransom Township—where, one week earlier, Democrats had erected a hickory pole and demonstrated against the "black Republican war."[19] The defiant loyalists erected a liberty pole and gave speeches that ended with a call for "a thorough annihilation of all the causes which have led to this unhallowed Rebellion."[20] In September, Factoryville Baptist Church leaders adopted a resolution declaring that "this rebellion will never be put down until its cause, slavery, is removed." The resolution called on "all able bodied men to form military companies" and added a wish "that men should be put in command of our Armies who have no sympathy with slavery."[21]

But not everywhere was Lincoln-leaning. The county assessors assigned to visit towns to record the names of draft-eligible men learned that the hard way. Across much of rural Pennsylvania, farm families were already complaining about the higher taxes and inflation caused by a war they didn't much support. If drafted, many a struggling farmer couldn't afford to pay for a "substitute" conscript the way others could. And if he lost a farmhand to the draft, his own costs were sure to rise because laborers, ever scarcer, were raising their fees. Workers in the coalfields, many of them recent immigrants, were leery of both their Republican mine bosses and the consequences of black abolition. Scores of draft-eligible men clamored for disability or hardship exemptions. Others went into hiding. As one reader of the *Wyoming Republican* of Tunkhannock remarked, "The Underground Railroad to Canada has lately been crowded with a new class of passengers. Men heretofore opposed to the road were the first to seek its facilities for escaping—not from the horrors of slavery—but from the bare prospect of serving their country in its hour of need."[22] The county draft assessors were frequently harassed, sometimes violently, prompting Lincoln to crack down. On September 24, the president suspended the writ of habeas corpus and made draft resistance a federal crime.

The dissidents raged all the more. One of the worst confrontations occurred in late September on the Blakely-Archbald border, a poor section outside Scranton heavily populated by refugees of the Irish potato famine. In a breathless report on the incident, the loyalist *Pittston Gazette* said the enrollment officer that day, Charles Roesler of Scranton, was set upon "by angry women and children" in Shanty Hill and took shelter in a building. A group of men broke down the door with a battering ram and Roesler tried to flee. "About 500 wild Irishmen stood in the way; but he determined to cut his way through," the *Gazette* reported, "emerging from the crowd with blood streaming from his head, he ordered his friends to fire. They did so, with effect, at the same time retreating towards their wagon, which they reached amid flying stones and clubs, with bloody hands and bruised bodies."[23]

The draft deadline came with Pennsylvania still short of its enlistment quota. On October 16, 1862, the draft began. Conscripts were drawn from each district and ordered to their county seats to board trains to Harrisburg. More grassroots resistance erupted. Five hundred miners prevented a train from leaving Pottsville. Their leaders traveled among the collieries to organize a mass protest. "From this rebellious group," writes journalist Jim Zbick, "emerged a secret band of terrorists known as the Buckshots, later known by a more infamous name—the Molly Maguires."[24]

The next day, October 17, was worse. The scene of violence was again Blakely, where soldiers opened fire on rioters, killing at least one bystander (some reports said two) and injuring about a dozen others. It was among the nation's worst outbreaks of draft resistance up to that point. Only when the draft commissioner returned with an armed squadron and a cannon did the Blakely dissidents stand down. Flare-ups also were reported in Scranton, Carbondale, and isolated patch towns in Schuylkill County.

On October 23, a worried Governor Curtin sent a cable to Secretary of War Edwin Stanton. "Notwithstanding the usual exaggerations, I think the organization to resist the draft in Schuylkill, Luzerne, and Carbon Counties is very formidable," Curtin telegraphed. "There are several thousands in arms, and the people who will not join have been driven from the county. They will not permit the drafted men, who are willing, to leave, and yesterday forced them to get out of the cars. I wish to crush the resistance so effectually that the like will not occur again."

Though Curtin was denied extra troops to hunt the resisters, Pennsylvania was able to proceed with its draft. By year's end, the state had conscripted about twenty thousand men and sent three-quarters into military service.

ON THE POLITICAL FRONT, the aggressive draft was a disaster for the Republicans. State and congressional elections were held that very October, amid the turmoil, and the opposition Democrats capitalized. The war casualties, the draft, the crackdown on dissenters, the tax hikes, plus a newly released, preliminary version of the Emancipation Proclamation, had all aroused the Democrats' base. They also were helped by the copperhead Woodward and fellow conservative court justices who issued a ruling that disallowed federal soldiers from voting absentee while deployed in the field.

The Democrats' 1862 election slogan—"The Constitution as it is; the Union as it was; the Negroes where they are"—carried the day. Republicans lost control of the Pennsylvania House of Representatives and lost four congressional seats in 1862. Their governors were defeated in New York and New Jersey; they lost legislative majorities in New Jersey, Illinois, and Indiana; and they lost thirty-four seats in Congress.

As the war ground on, so did Pennsylvania's fractious inner civil war. While loyalists kept faith with the president, copperheads kept up their public agitations. In Philadelphia, "the disloyal element openly expressed joy over Confederate victories in the faces of their patriotic neighbors."[25] Farther north, dissident miners continued to interfere with recruiting, encourage desertions, and menace loyalists.[26] Hundreds of draft resisters and deserters hid out across rural northern Pennsylvania—and black men remained sidelined.

In Waverly, Colored Hill stayed out of harm's way. Its numbers had grown steadily, helped by the fact that enforcement of the Fugitive Slave Act had ceased with the advent of the war. By 1860, census records show, sixty-seven people of color resided in Waverly and adjacent Abington Township. In the mix by then was a smattering of freeborn adults from Northern states: Paige and Christiana Wells, Thomas Williams, Jackson Clark, John Sampson, John Lee, Amitas Thomas, Catherine Mason, and others. The integrated schooling of the black children continued. The men found their labors ever more valuable as white workers went off to war. In November 1861, AME Bishop Willis Nazrey paid an ecclesial visit to the region and reported spending two days among Waverly's "good-hearted people; finding them in possession of good church property."[27]

During that period, the little AME sanctuary must have rung with prayers for the Union's righteous cause. News of Lincoln's emancipation plan would have brought mighty hallelujahs. That September, fresh from the Union victory at Antietam, the president had warned the Confederacy to end its rebellion by January 1, 1863, or he would declare their slaves free and under federal protection. While the bold plan certainly thrilled the Colored Hill fugitives, they must have been dismayed to learn that it didn't cover the four slaveholding border states, including Maryland, from where so many had escaped.

Would they never be able to reunite with lost family and friends? Their men stood ready to join the fight. Might they help the president break slavery's iron grip? They would soon learn that the door to their enlistment would indeed open in the coming year. Unfortunately, that also would provoke more white spite, in the military ranks and on the home front.

1. *Pittston Gazette* (Pittston, PA), Sept. 13, 1860, p. 3.
2. *Pittston Gazette*, Oct. 11, 1860, p. 2.
3. *Pittston Gazette*, Nov. 15, 1860, p. 2.
4. *Speech of Hon. George W. Woodward, delivered at the Great Union Meeting in Independence Square, Philadelphia, December 13th, 1860* (Philadelphia: Age Office, 1863), pp. 9-10.
5. Hitchcock, Col. Frederick L. *History of Scranton and Its People* (New York: Lewis Historical Publishing Co., 1914), p. 261.
6. Sandow, Robert M. *Deserter Country: Civil War Opposition in the Pennsylvania Appalachians* (New York: Fordham University Press, 2009), p. 101.
7. " Abraham Lincoln and the Politics of the Civil War: Pennsylvania Democrats," PHMC online essay, 2011, at explorepahistory.com.
8. *Compiler* (Gettysburg, PA), July 8, 1861, p. 1.
9. Adleman, Debra. *Waiting for The Lord: Nineteenth Century Black Communities in Susquehanna County, Pa.* (Rockport, Me.: Picton Press, 1997), p. 48.
10. Randall lost the special election but went on to be named Luzerne County's District Attorney in 1864.
11. *Pittston Gazette*, June 27, 1861, p. 2.
12. *Pittston Gazette*, Oct. 3, 1861, p. 2.
13. Bradsby, Henry C. *History of Luzerne, Lackawanna, and Wyoming Counties, Pa: With Illustrations and Biographical Sketches of Some of Their Prominent Men and Pioneers* (New York: W.W. Munsell & Co., 1880), p. 98.
14. *Pittston Gazette*, April 12, 1902, p. 4.
15. Davis, Hugh. *"We Will Be Satisfied With Nothing Less": The African American Struggle for Equal Rights in the North During Reconstruction* (Ithaca, N.Y.: Cornell University Press, 2011), p. 11.
16. Spear, Sheldon. *Wyoming Valley History Revisited* (Jemags & Co.,: Shavertown, Pa, 1994).
17. "Free Negroism and the Failure of Emancipation," *North Branch Democrat* (Tunkhannock, PA), June 18, 1862, p. 2.
18. Tomasek, Peter, editor. *Avery Harris Civil War Journal* (Wilkes-Barre: Luzerne National Bank, 2000), p. 1.
19. *Pittston Gazette*, Aug. 22, 1861, p.2.
20. *Pittston Gazette*, Aug. 28, 1862, p. 2.
21. Wooden, Sherman. *The Place I call Home: How Abolition and the Underground Railroad Shaped the Communities of Northeastern Pennsylvania* (Montrose: Center for Anti-Slavery Studies, 2009), p. 118.
22. Letter to the Editor. *Wyoming Republican* (Tunkhannock, PA), Sept. 3, 1862, p. 2.
23. *Pittston Gazette*, Oct. 2, 1862, p. 2.
24. Zbick, Jim. "Pennsylvania's 'Perfect Hell,'" article in *America's Civil War Magazine*, January 2013, p. 55.
25. Taylor, Frank H. *Philadelphia in the Civil War, 1861 1865* (Philadelphia: City of Philadelphia, 1913), p. 239.
26. Ibid., p. 55.
27. *Christian Recorder*, Dec. 28, 1861, in Accessible Archives, online.

CHAPTER SEVEN

1863

"Black Soldiery" and Home Front Strife

------◦•◦•◦------

O N NEW YEAR'S DAY 1863, with the South fighting on despite an ultimatum to desist, President Lincoln issued his threatened executive order. All slaves held in Confederate jurisdictions, he declared, "shall be then, thenceforward, and forever free" and entitled to federal protection. Though the Emancipation Proclamation reverberates in history, its scope was actually limited and its terms legalistic. According to Lincoln scholar Harold Holzer, the president avoided "celebratory hallelujahs" so as not to alienate the four slaveholding border states that had not seceded, or to provoke conservative factions in his military "where opposition might foment insubordination and worse."[1] Black observers in the North reacted with disappointment. "It was not a proclamation of 'liberty throughout the land, unto all the inhabitants thereof,' such as had hoped it would be," wrote Frederick Douglass. The *Christian Recorder* noted the order's limited reach yet expressed hope "that Congress will do something for those poor souls who will remain in degradation" in unaffected parts of the slaveholding states.

Confederate President Jefferson Davis nonetheless found it intolerable. On January 5, he shot back with a proclamation of his own: all free-blacks in Confederate territory, including children, would be enslaved as of February 22, and any black people captured in free states would be placed into bondage. In addition, he announced, captured Union officers could expect to be held as criminals for "inciting servile insurrection."[2]

Many of Pennsylvania's War Democrats, who had forged a loose alliance with the Republicans, felt betrayed by Lincoln's sweeping new course of action. Luzerne County Congressman Hendrick B. Wright complained angrily that "if you make this a war of slave emancipation, as God is my judge, I believe that this Government is irretrievably gone. There is no war for slave emancipation, it is to put down rebellion and treason."[3] Similarly, Democrats in Pike County issued a dissent "that we believe the war, as now prosecuted, is a war for the negro, a crusade against slavery, and that the present course of the Administration is fast deadening and paralyzing the patriotic sentiment of the loyal North."[4]

For many Northern whites, Lincoln's proclamation also aroused a dread that newly freed Southern slaves would descend upon them to "rape, pillage and fill charitable poorhouses."[5] The *North Branch Democrat* of Tunkhannock warned of proposals for "taking the bread from the mouths of thousands of white widows and orphans to buy feed and clothes [for] worthless vagabond negroes."[6] Rural districts petitioned their state legislators to ban the migration of blacks into Pennsylvania and to legislate against interracial marriage. The restrictions passed the Democratic-controlled assembly but died in the Republican-led state senate. Loyalist Republicans countered with a mocking bill to prohibit the immigration of redheads,[7] and presented a committee report recommending that freed slaves be welcomed "for every slave we wrest from treason, we take one soldier."

The Emancipation Proclamation did indeed raise the likelihood of black men in federal uniform. Among its clauses was that freed slaves "of suitable condition, will be received into the armed service of the United States to garrison forts, positions, stations, and other places, and to man vessels of all sorts in said service." Lincoln knew that as his armies pushed deeper into the South, black military service was ever more necessary, come what may. Within a month, the US Congress took up Republican legislation to allow "black soldiery."

The bill faced a barrage of condemnation from Democrats. One of its staunchest foes was Congressman Wright of Luzerne. In a lengthy account of the floor debate in Washington,[8] the *Wayne County Herald* of Honesdale reported that Wright claimed the bill

THE NEGRO ON THE FENCE.

Harken to what I now relate,
  And on its moral meditate.
A wagoner, with grist for mill,
Was stalled at bottom of a hill;
A brawny negro passed that way,
So stout he might a lion slay.
"I'll put my shoulder to the wheels
It you'll bestir your horse's heels!"
So said the African, and made
As if to render timely aid.
"No," cried the wagoner, "stand back!
I'll take no help from one that's black!"
And, to the negro's great surprise,
Flourished his whip before his eyes.
Our "darkey" quick "skedaddled" thence,
And sat upon the wayside fence.
Then went the wagoner to work,
And lashed his horses to a jerk;
But all his efforts were in vain
With shout, and oath, and whip, and rein.
The wheels budged not a single inch,
And tighter grew the wagoner's pinch.
Directly there came by a child
With toiling step and vision wild;
"Father," said she, with hunger dread,
"We famish for the want of bread."
Then spake the negro: "If you will,
I'll help your horses to the mill."
The wagoner, in grievous plight,
Now swore and raved with all his might,
Because the negro was'nt white,
And plainly ordered him to go
To a certain place that's down below.
Then rushing came the wagoner's wife,
To save her own and infant's life,
By robbers was their homestead sacked,
And smoke and blood their pillage tracked.

Here stops our tale. When last observed,
The wagoner was still "conserved"
In mud at bottom of the hill,
But bent on getting to the mill,
And hard by, not a rod from thence,
The negro sat upon the fence.   —*Ev'ng. Post.*

In April 1863, amid the debate on "black soldiery," the Pittston Gazette *published this parable in verse about narrow-minded whites. (Courtesy the* Pittston Gazette, *Newspapers.com.)*

"would produce demoralization, for soldiers of the army had said to him, that if black men were sent to them they would regard it as a condemnation of their conduct, and leave the service if they could." Congressman Edward McPherson, a Gettysburg Republican, remarked that officers in both the Revolution and the current war "were in favor of negro allies," the *Herald* reported. "Mr. Wright, resuming, said the white Anglo Saxon race was capable of taking care of itself. But if it had not power to maintain our position negroes could not help us out of the difficulty. They were not reliable in military service. He believed that by the reconstruction of the Cabinet and the restoration of [sacked General-in-Chief George]

McClellan to the army the country could be saved. Applause broke forth in a heavy volume from the galleries, manifested by the stamping of feet and the clapping of hands." Wright concluded by thundering: "Abandon the proposition to bring negroes into the army, or we are lost!"

Wright and Philip Johnson, Wayne County's Democratic congressman, opposed the black-soldiery legislation, but the bill cleared the House, 85-55, on its way to adoption. In late May, the federal government issued General Order Number 143 establishing the Bureau of the United States Colored Troops. State and local officials in Pennsylvania refused to set up a training camp for the new USCT troops, however, so the federal military had to act quickly on its own. Camp William Penn was created outside Philadelphia as the first and largest of the segregated training camps. In time it would induct 10,500 black recruits. Ten would be from Waverly.

In Tunkhannock, the *North Branch Democrat* had a growling response. Its editor, future Wyoming County judge Harvey Sickler, ran an item from the *New York Herald* that suggested outfitting black soldiers in loudly colored uniforms. "It is perhaps the best way to get rid of them. Those who are not killed in battle, or fail to die from exposure, will probably be taken prisoner, in which case they will be summarily disposed of by being shot or sold into slavery and sent away beyond the reach of the proclamation."[9]

Furious as the Lincoln-haters might have been, many in Pennsylvania's rival populace felt otherwise by then. As the war dragged on and casualties mounted, the notion of arming black soldiers—once widely considered "lunacy"[10]—had become acceptable to an increasing number of Lincoln loyalists and War Democrats. In early March, for instance, an audience at Pittston's Lyceum lecture hall heard an impassioned debate on black soldiery and then cast a floor vote in favor.[11] Militant abolitionist Henry C. Wright of New York noticed the new openness during his spring 1863 lecture tour that went through Luzerne County. "Last fall," he wrote in the *Liberator*, "multitudes insisted that the only cure was to hang the Abolitionists and the Negroes." But by spring, "Not a voice, scarcely, do I hear in this region, raised against [arming blacks] now. Rather than be damned as a nation, the people are willing to be saved by the Negro. As the Republic feels itself sinking in an ocean of blood, it calls to the outcast, outraged and enslaved Negro –'save, or I perish!' What a testimony in favor of the despised, insulted and branded Negro it will be, in the future, that he forgot and forgave the wrongs inflicted on him, and came forward and encountered mutilation and death to save his deadliest enemy; for to the Negro this Republic has been his most bloody and inhuman for ever since it had an existence."[12]

WHEN THE OPPORTUNITY CAME, black men from the North and South did answer the Union's call to arms, approximately one hundred eighty thousand by the end, organized into one hundred sixty regiments. The indignities they would face were manifest—no $300 enlistment bounty as per white recruits, monthly pay one-quarter less, equipment often inferior, commanders all white—and still they came. In spring of 1863, even before Camp William Penn was erected on the outskirts of Philadelphia, as many as fifteen hundred men from Pennsylvania (including one who would later live in Waverly) had headed off to New England to join the 54th Massachusetts and other black regiments that formed at that state's initiative.

Many African American pastors and community leaders were exhorting their men to volunteer for the USCT's three-year enlistments. "This is our golden moment," a widely distributed circular in Philadelphia declared.

This patriotic handbill was issued by the Supervisory Committee for Recruiting Colored Regiments, based in Philadelphia. (Courtesy Library Company of Philadelphia.)

"We appeal to you! By all your concern for yourselves and your liberties, by all your regard for God and humanity, by all your desire for citizenship and equality before the law, by all your love of country, to stop at no subterfuges, listen to nothing that shall deter you from rallying for the army. Strike now and you are forever and henceforth Freemen!" In Waverly, AME Pastor William Johnson said each man bore a transcendent duty "to fight for God and his country."[13] He was joined by

Leonard Batchelor, the town's leading abolitionist, who championed recruitment "especially among the colored people."[14]

Secretary of War Edwin Stanton directed that the first black enlistees from eastern Pennsylvania be mustered into three USCT infantry regiments. In early July, as the Battle of Gettysburg was raging, a young trio from Waverly—John Sampson and brothers Joshua and Peter Norris—headed off to Philadelphia to take their place in the 3rd USCT. It was the first regiment to be trained at the brand-new Camp William Penn.

Sampson, the oldest of the three at 21, was a freeborn New York native and an unwed, live-in laborer for a white farm family. Peter Norris, 20, and his brother Joshua, 18, also were unwed laborers. More significantly, they were the freeborn sons of Lot Norris, one of Colored Hill's leading lights. Lot Norris had become a lay preacher, so his home and the adjacent AME church must have resounded with heavenly petitions as he and wife Mary—both illiterate fugitives from bondage—and their five other children sent Peter and Joshua back down South to fight the slave power.

For the three small-town striplings, simply heading to metropolitan Philadelphia would have been thrilling enough. But it also happened that immediately after they'd reported to boot camp, the regiment received an illustrious visitor—Frederick Douglass, the black orator and hero of his race. White and black onlookers came to the camp from around the area to hear the famous man's words. According to the *National Anti-Slavery Standard*, Douglass presented the regiment with "an elegant silk flag, the handiwork of the ladies of the city,"[15] then congratulated the recruits "on being at last recognized in the rights of manhood by the country of their birth."

The Norris brothers took the military oath and were mustered into Company C, and Sampson into Company

Black recruits stand in formation at Camp William Penn. (Courtesy Charles L. Blockson Afro-American Collection, Temple University Libraries, Philadelphia, PA.)

The 3rd USCT regiment's battle flag played on patriotic sentiment. (Courtesy Library of Congress.)

Major Louis Wagner, an abolitionist, commanded the training camp.

The orator Frederick Douglass addressed troops at Camp William Penn. (Courtesy National Portrait Gallery.)

D. All thousand men of the 3rd were outfitted in Union blue and assigned combat gear, including smoothbore muskets and bayonets. Peter Norris was also selected to be a company bugler. For an intensive month, the recruits drilled and took target practice under the exacting eye of Major Louis Wagner, the camp's white commanding officer. Wagner, who had been badly wounded at Second Bull Run, was a loyalist of strong anti-slavery sentiments—a blessed contrast to the many other white officers who would scorn their own USCT troops. In a speech that winter, Wagner voiced his regard. "They come to the camp, many of them, ragged and dirty," he remarked. "But when they put on the uniform, they feel that they are men, and that they can hold up their heads among men."[16]

The 3rd regiment would receive a unique battle flag that captured the recruits' swelling pride. Designed by Frederick Douglass' cousin, artist David Bustill Bowser of Philadelphia, the flag depicted the mythic figure of Columbia and a handsome black soldier clasping the American flag together. Above them streamed the motto *Rather Die Freemen, Than Live to Be Slaves.*

As their camp training drew to a close, the assembled troops were addressed by another of their advocates, white abolitionist lawyer George H. Earle. "Though your regiment is called on at the close of the fight, may your conduct be the reverse of that which your enemies predicted would characterize you," Earle hailed. "You will go forward into battle in a great and holy cause, to sustain a noble government, and fight for the right and for human freedom. May you always sustain that cause with courage and honor; may your strong arms hasten the day of peace; may God, who looks, I trust, approvingly on this scene, keep you in his holy keeping, and preserve this country for a future of liberty, freedom and righteousness."[17]

When it came time to head south by transport ship, Wagner made preparations to have the men parade in full uniform and weaponry through downtown Philadelphia to the Delaware River docks. That would allow the public to behold the state's first black regiment and loved ones to see their men for, in many cases, "the last time in this world."[18] The march was abruptly canceled, however, when the mayor persuaded the USCT bureau's commander that the street parade might "provoke a riot" by hostile whites.[19] Philadelphia still had considerable commercial and social ties to the South and no shortage of residents who despised black people; Douglass had termed Philadelphia "one of the most disorderly and insecure cities in the Union" for blacks. Heeding the mayor's warning, the commander diverted the troops directly to the Poplar Street wharf. Families and well-wishers managed to crowd down to the wharf and sent their men off from there with loud hurrahs. The 3rd regiment steamed down the coast to Morris Island, South Carolina, to join the ongoing assault on the Rebel-held Fort Wagner. Two rugged years of duty would follow.

BACK HOME IN ABINGTON that summer of 1863, the whites were on edge. Lee's threat to invade Pennsylvania was a shock. To prepare, Governor Curtin called for fifty thousand "emergency men" to defend the state on a short-term basis. Volunteers quickly joined from Waverly and environs, and were mustered into the 30th Pennsylvania Infantry, also known as "Col. Money's Tigers." (They included abolitionists Amenzo Mumford and Lyman B. Green of Abington,[20] John Seamans of Benton and Gilbert Sherman of Waverly, as well as a mulatto man from Waverly named Wesley Baptiste.)

July brought Lee's invasion and the bloodbath at Gettysburg. The 30th Infantry engaged the Rebels in

DECENT BURIAL

George O. Fell of Waverly, teenage son of abolitionist John G. Fell, joined the 143rd Pennsylvania Infantry in 1862 as a private serving under his older brother, Lt. Asher Fell. George had risen to sergeant by the time his company was thrown into battle at Gettysburg in July 1863. In the early action, probably on July 1, young Sergeant Fell was mortally wounded. His death and its aftermath were movingly recounted years later by J. Howard Wert, who had been a teenager living near Gettysburg during the battle.

"Severely wounded in the hip, young Fell was left upon the field within the enemy's lines," Wert eulogized in 1907. "He was found two days afterwards in a private residence, placed there, probably by the enemy, and was made as comfortable as circumstances would allow.

"His father, who repaired immediately to the battlefield, had only the melancholy satisfaction of finding a mess of corruption, wrapped in a soldier's blanket, with a few inches of earth over it, but recognized it by marked articles of clothing as the body of his son. Unable to remove the body, and the National Cemetery being not yet planned, he secured for it decent burial in the grass-grown and ancient graveyard attached to the German Reformed Church, on High street, Gettysburg.

"This was but one case of tens of thousands, at the same moment, darkening all the land and filling it with lamentations. Of a fine person and brilliant accomplishments, just ready to enter Yale College, with glittering prizes for honor and success opening before him and beckoning him onward, he dropped all, thrilled by his country's need, and at the age of eighteen, volunteered beneath the Stars and Stripes in the company in which his elder brother, who went unhurt through the fires of Gettysburg, was a lieutenant."[21]

Gettysburg author Gregory A. Coco quoted Wert's account in a book *Killed in Action*. Coco noted that Sergeant Fell's body was eventually moved to the Pennsylvania section of the Soldiers' National Cemetery, where Wert eulogized him.

The senior Fell returned to his grieving family in Waverly that summer of 1863. A memorial stone tablet honoring his fallen son was placed at Hickory Grove Cemetery where it remains today, flat on the ground alongside his father's resting place. And in 1883, eight years before John Fell died, Waverly's war veterans named their new Grand Army of the Republic fraternal organization the Sgt. George O. Fell GAR Post 307. It would become one of the few racially integrated GAR posts in Pennsylvania.

skirmishes near the state border. Then news arrived that the Luzerne boys of the 143rd were in the thick of the Gettysburg fighting—and that twenty-one of them had died, including locals George O. Fell and James L. Miles. (See box, "Decent Burial," above.)

Also, the area was in the throes of more turmoil over the draft. A comprehensive federal conscription law had been enacted that spring to keep the military supplied with fresh reinforcements. Under the new system, enrollment officers again went into communities to compile lists of eligible men. Each draftee was given ten days and three official options: report for duty; supply a substitute in his stead; or pay a $300 "commutation fee" to escape service and stay home. Resisters, deserters, and anyone harboring them risked stiff fines and jail time. Cries of unfairness ensued, with the protests tending to fall along class and ethnic lines.

"The most serious problems of all occurred in the coal mining regions," historian Arnold Shankman writes. "The miners, many of whom were Irish, had no desire to fight for the Negro, and peace men easily convinced them that emancipation was the sole aim of the war. Uneducated, overworked, underpaid, and exploited, they saw no reason to leave their families and risk their lives to take up arms against southerners who had never bothered them."[22] Democratic newspapers accused the enrollment officers of secretly working for coal operators, while Republicans called the predominantly Irish labor leaders disunionists. Anti-draft rioting broke out in Schuylkill and Carbon Counties. A coal executive was murdered for supposedly feeding information about his employees to draft officers. In Carbondale's "lower wards," women and children pelted enrollment officers with sticks and stones. Army troops were sent to Scranton and Williamsport to guard government property and prevent the sort of murderous rioting that broke out in New York City. During a subsequent draft-resistance trial, the defendant admitted he'd been part of a plot to overpower troops guarding Carbon County coalfields, seize their guns, and march to Scranton to attack soldiers stationed there. The brazen plan was to raise a miner-led militia and assist Lee's invasion of Pennsylvania.[23]

In a move rich with irony, copperheads unsuccessfully sought the protection of a new round of "personal liberty laws"—the very sort of laws they'd denounced when Northern states had enacted them to resist the Fugitive Slave Act. The earlier laws, the *Pittston Gazette* remarked, "were intended to protect anti-slavery white men, as well as the free colored people, against oppression. Now they are sought as a protection for traitors and sympathizers with the rebellion. The slave hunt has ceased, and the hunters are themselves in danger."[24]

The *Gazette*, a Republican-leaning weekly, attempted to chronicle copperhead activities in Luzerne County that year. It asserted that county Democrats were organizing chapters of the Knights of the Golden Circle, a shadowy pro-slavery organization, "in every county, township and borough." According to the paper, the groups were functioning as a secret fifth column, "banding themselves together under a solemn oath to do all in their power to cripple the administration, embarrass the war power, discourage enlistments, and by armed force to resist the draft and protect deserters."[25] In January, the *Gazette* claimed that rogues in Newton and Falls Township had stolen guns, blankets, robes, whips, and food from loyalists for "defense against the draft, and other property to compensate for taxes paid to carry out a d—d Abolition war." The miscreants were summoned to Clarks Green to answer a complaint. After making bail, they returned to Newton and were welcomed by more than one hundred armed supporters "threatening vengeance on Black Republicans and Abolitionists."[26] The outcome of the legal case is not known.

In July, trouble broke out at Buttermilk Falls in Falls Township when an enrollment officer was fired upon and driven off by hostile men who believed a secret, rigged draft was afoot. The *Lackawanna Register*, a new Democratic weekly based in Scranton, termed the showdown "The Falls War." The enrollment officer returned with a squad of soldiers and was met by an armed and angry crowd. Local Democratic leaders were summoned to calm the situation. According to the *Register*, the party leaders told the protesters that "as good citizens, especially as Democrats, they must obey the laws; it was bad enough that Abraham Lincoln and his men break the law, but for them, in all things lawful, it was proper to yield a willing obedience." Another draft officer was brought in, and the enrollment proceeded.[27]

Whether Democratic leaders counseled obedience or resistance to the conscription law was a point of sharp contention. The *Register* and Democrats insisted that their dissent did not extend to law-breaking, although evidence suggests that there was a pattern of dissuading people from military service.[28] Luzerne County's copperhead district attorney, Ezra B. Chase, gave a speech in which he "advised his hearers not to go to war but to stay at home and go to the polls" to elect defiant Democrats.[29] Military authorities arrested Chase for treason as a result (but the case was never prosecuted). Many local men were indeed clamoring to escape service. In Scranton, 49 men were "held for service" by October, while 225 others were exempted (primarily on claims of disability, sole family support, or underage status). In addition, 29 men furnished substitutes, 42 paid the commutation fee—and 124 failed to report altogether.[30]

AS THE OCTOBER GUBERNATORIAL ELECTION approached, Democratic leaders in Northern Luzerne tried to capitalize politically on the discontent. A string of anti-Lincoln rallies was organized in June, July, and August in Greenfield, Scott, Lenox, Harford, Dundaff, Fleetville, Nicholson, Meshoppen, Monroe, and Tunkhannock.

The *Lackawanna Register* ran jubilant reports on what it termed the "outpourings of the people." In Greenfield, "the enthusiasm was beyond all precedent." Hundreds came by buggy, horseback, and on foot to cheer as copperheads Charles Silkman of Scranton and County Judge Edward Merrifield denounced Lincoln's "despotic power" and abolition "fanaticism."[31] At the Scott rally, the *Register* said, "We learn that score and hundreds are being cured of 'n** on the brain,' in the upper town-ships of this County, and also in many townships in Susquehanna." Silkman "peels the wool and abolition hide right off some of the Beachwoods [Abington] n**-humanity-folks."[32] In Harford, several thousand people heard more of Silkman's slanders. According to the *Register,* "the 'Negro Equality' doctrine, in connection with the Abolition policy of the Administration, received the largest share of his satire—the tremendous volleys of which frequently call out the most enthusiastic demon-stration." (Great cheering and applause, in other words.) The paper noted that forty to fifty "Black Republicans and Abolitionists" also showed up that day and "were a little disposed to make a disturbance, but seeing the de-termination of the sturdy yeomanry present to preserve order, and defy threats, these men let prudence direct their conduct and thereby saved a chastisement."[33]

Fleetville hosted perhaps the largest rally. It took place on July Fourth—the same day the Norris brothers and John Sampson were entering the service at Camp William Penn. "MORE THAN 6,000 PRESENT!" The *Register's* Fleetville headline shouted. "THE GREATEST ENTHUSIASMS PREVAILED." A manifesto was read to the crowd that bore the signatures of many Democratic leaders in attendance. One was the document's author, Waverly lawyer Thomas Smith, a former Democratic state legislator who had a son in the Union army. Other signatories were Uriah Gritman, one of William Fogg's

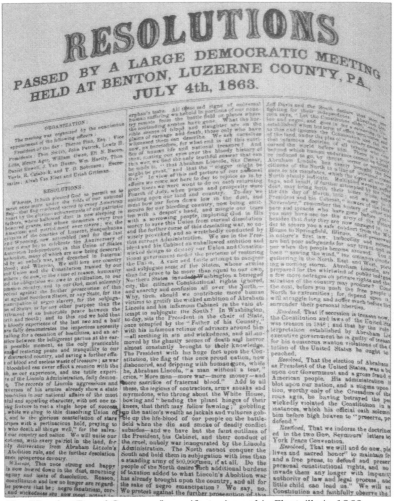

The *"Cracker Barrel Congress"* manifesto, issued in Fleetville in 1863,
denounced Lincoln's *"Abolition rule."* (Courtesy Lackawanna Historical
Society, Scranton.)

nemeses in 1835; Benton farmer Theron Finn, who
had a son on the draft list; Benton farmer Alvah Van
Fleet; Ransom farmer Lewis H. Litts, a former county
commissioner who was on the draft list himself; Wyoming County farmer Henry Ager, also on the draft list;
Nicholson justice of the peace Eli N. Bacon, whose son
was on the draft list; and Daniel Howell, J. Van Husen,
William Hartly, Thomas Voyle, R. Cataback, and T. O.

Robinson, all copperheads from Benton and Newton. Finn, who presided over the event, told his listeners that "today is not a day of joy and gladness, but one of sadness."[34] The manifesto, said to have been composed in the back room of Finn's store at Wallsville Corners, was presented to the crowd. It was a long, angry screed that denounced the federal government's "negro fanaticism" and called for "a speedy deliverance from Abraham Lincoln's bloody Abolition rule." Further, it declared the president guilty of treason and said that "for his numerous wanton violations of the Constitution of the United States he ought to be impeached."

"When the speeches ended," The *Register* reported, "a committee of two hundred ladies presented the gentlemen who addressed them with a most beautiful bouquet." Teams of horses then departed, "loaded down with the iron-hearted Democracy and converted Republicans, of Northern Luzerne and Susquehanna Counties."

In the hotbed of Newton, open dissent continued. A loyalist writer from Abington (identified only as "Union League") told the *Pittston Gazette* that Newton copperheads were haranguing the Methodist and Presbyterian parsonages with cries of "Come out, you G-d d-d black old Abolitionist!" According to the writer, rogues broke into the Presbyterian church, "ornamented it with hickory," stole bibles, hymnals, collection boxes, and Sunday school books, and set up a "Copperhead Sunday School" next door.[35]

It's not clear what a copperhead Sunday school would teach, but it might have included the writings of John Henry Hopkins, an Episcopal bishop whose tracts of pro-slavery apologia were circulating through the North. In September, an old Abington Democrat, farmer Walter Joyce, informed the *Lackawanna Register* that he and others had received copies of Bishop Hopkins' pamphlet, *A Scriptural, Ecclesiastical, and Historical View of Slavery,* and were enthusiastically digesting its message that slavery "was recognized, protected and even taught in the Old Testament, and recognized, and protected and even taught in the New." The pamphlets, Joyce wrote, "are opening the eyes of a great many who were taught to believe in the sin of Slave-holding. It is very seldom we old farmers get hold of any such plain, matter of fact argumentations, so easily understood. The circulation of this letter has put several itinerant abolitionist preachers in a perfect panic."[36]

One of those preachers, in Joyce's mind, might have been Rev. Dewitt Clinton Olmstead, the Methodist minister assigned to Waverly that year. The New York native had been an early abolitionist in his denomination—and his outspokenness in Waverly was miffing Democrats. "A minister of the Gospel who will vilify his neighbors and members by opprobrious epithets such as 'secessionists, 'copperheads,' and 'traitors,' on the street and elsewhere, simply because they differ from him in political sentiment, is unworthy of high calling, and unworthy of the respect due to ordinary men," declared the *Register* (which was masterful at opprobrious epithets itself).[37]

Reverend Olmstead and his progressive brethren would not be silenced. In Hyde Park, an anti-Lincoln soldier on leave complained to the *Register* that he'd attended a Methodist service there and endured the abolitionist preacher's prayer "thanking God for bloody victories . . . He saw in it the wiping out of the 'abominable and damnable institution slavery.'"[38] Also, the Rev. Thomas P. Hunt, the pastor of Scranton's First Presbyterian Church, formally rose up to rebut Bishop Hopkins' pamphlet. In a long public lecture at Phoenix Hall in Wilkes-Barre, Reverend Hunt asserted among other things that slaves in biblical times could actually be heirs to a master's property, "but he thought such doctrine would not suit Southern slaveholders even if preached by Bishop Hopkins," the *Gazette* reported. "His lecture was full of argument drawn directly from the Bible, and was interspersed with glowing wit and the most scorching sarcasm, which repeatedly brought down the house."[39]

PASTORAL ORATORY WAS NOT THE ONLY WAY Lincoln loyalists responded to the copperhead agitations that year; sometimes it came to blows. When rogues entered a hotel in Orange, a village near Buttermilk Falls, and began a "hurrah for Jeff Davis," loyalists cleared them out, "whipping two or three of them soundly."[40] In the Abington area, the Glenburn Hotel was a meeting place for loyalists and featured a liberty pole on the adjacent green. "This symbol was apparently anathema to the Benton Copperheads," according to the late Dalton historian Norm Brauer. "[A]rmed with a sense of righteousness and bolstered by fellow Newton Township Copperheads, on one summer night they stealthily burned the Liberty Pole." Union supporters "retaliated

The old Glenburn Hotel, where Union loyalists met. (Courtesy Mimi Cutler Archives.)

so forcefully," Brauer writes, that the copperheads never returned.[41]

In late July, Abington area loyalists gathered for a "Union Mass Meeting" in Benton Centre (Fleetville). Among its leaders were John G. Fell and Reverend Olmstead, both of Waverly. Congressman Galusha Grow gave a long speech defending the conscription act and denouncing the copperheads. Resolutions were adopted pledging support for the Lincoln administration and the Emancipation Proclamation, and against foes who "are striving to prejudice the weak minded and uneducated portion of our citizens, against said government and its legally elected representatives, and by the encouragement thus given to our enemy at the south."[42]

As the election season heated up, loyalists were urged to form Union Leagues, also known as Loyal Leagues, and show the colors. Their primary political target was Justice George Washington Woodward, the Luzerne demagogue whom Democrats had nominated for governor as part of a multi-state drive to put copperheads in governors' seats. At a Republican rally in Wilkes-Barre in early October, Congressman Grow gave another long speech lashing out at the copperheads and saying a Woodward victory "would rejoice the Southern fire-eaters." The next day, an estimated ten thousand people showed up for a Republican parade in Scranton that featured the incumbent governor, Andrew Curtin. The *Pittston Gazette* said the procession "was nearly a mile in length and displayed numerous banners. Col. Monie's Tiger Regiment was a distinguishing feature of the occasion, and the competition for the flag which had been promised to the largest company present was quite spirited. Co. D, of Bailey Hollow [Dalton] and Factoryville, took the prize."[43] Then, a final round of "Grand Union Republican Mass Meetings" was mounted in late September and early October in Scranton, Wilkes-Barre,

Pittston, Peckville, Carbondale, Blakely, Tompkinsville, and Waverly.

Democrats, meanwhile, urged their rank-and-file not to waver, but to remember what was at stake in the election. The *Lackawanna Register*, by then one of the best-read papers in the county, put it this way: "Democrats are in favor of the Constitution as it is, and the Union as it was, and in favor of continuing this government as framed by their fathers—a government of whites for the benefit of themselves and their posterity forever. The Republicans are opposed to the Constitution and the Union unless the slaves are all made free. They are in favor of making the negroes equal with the whites in this government, in favor of improving the black race by amalgamation, in favor of enslaving the Irish and Catholics and giving to negroes the right of suffrage."[44]

THE ELECTION RESULTS revealed the state electorate's utter polarization. Curtin edged Woodward by a mere 16,000 votes out of 500,000 cast statewide. Woodward carried Luzerne County by a lopsided 9,808-7,022, and locally he swept Benton (157-113) and Newton (132-77). Curtin easily won Abington (308-137), Greenfield (124-69), and Scott (172-81). Waverly Borough went for Curtin, but by only 33 to 28.

On the legislative front, the election left the Harrisburg statehouse nearly deadlocked. The Republicans held a 17-16 advantage in the state senate and a 52-48 edge in the House. (Luzerne's senator and three House members were all Democrats.) Pennsylvania's inner civil war would not abate.

On Colored Hill, residents no doubt were distressed by the endless wrangling of the whites. Their landlord, John Stone, was selling the vituperative *Lackawanna Register* at his store down in the village, and the literate among them could keep folks abreast of the paper's white-supremacist rhetoric. They'd know about the Loyal Leagues and about the copperhead rallies nearby. The men of Colored Hill might have increased Waverly's turnout for Curtin had they been able to vote—but all of them, even the free-blacks living among them, were still barred from the franchise.

How did they feel about having nearly half of their longtime white neighbors vote for Woodward, a man who scorned black people and lauded slavery as a blessing? The record is silent on the matter. But it is known that the men of Colored Hill kept faith with the Union cause and continued to depart the safety of their adopted home to sign up for combat. As they did, their loved ones replaced the old fear of capture with a new anxiety about battle.

On October 19, Richard Lee reported to Camp William Penn and was mustered into the 25th USCT. He was 32 at the time, a laborer and a Maryland-born fugitive. Lee left behind his wife and their freeborn infant son.

Three days before Christmas, fugitives John Mason, William Bradley, and John Washington left their wives and freeborn youngsters and reported to camp in Philadelphia. They went with the blessings of Reverend Olmstead's Methodist congregants, Batchelor and his Presbyterians, and Sisson's Baptists. In the AME church, where John Mason was a founding trustee, congregants must have supplemented the holiday hymns with petitions that their departing recruits be girded with spiritual armor.

At camp, Mason, Bradley, and Washington were assigned together to Company D of the 22nd USCT. The three, all Colored Hill farmers, were relatively old, at 40, 34, and 38, to be raw recruits. Thrown quickly into action, they and Richard Lee would suffer war injuries that hobbled them for the rest of their lives.

1. Holzer, Harold. "America's Second Declaration of Independence," article in *America's Civil War*, January 2013, pp. 34-35.
2. "Time of War" chart, *America's Civil War*, January 2013, p. 28.
3. Lewis, William V. Jr. *Lincoln: Luzerne County Friends and Foes* (Wilkes-Barre: Luzerne County Historical Society, 2015), p. 71.
4. *Wayne County Herald* (Honesdale, PA), Feb. 26, 1863, p. 2.
5. Kashatus, William C. "Draft Resisters Sought Refuge in Columbia County During Civil War," article in the *Citizens' Voice* (Wilkes-Barre, PA), May 26, 2013.
6. *North Branch Democrat* (Tunkhannock, PA), March 4, 1863, p. 1.
7. Sandow, Robert M. *Deserter Country: Civil War Opposition in the Pennsylvania Appalachians* (New York: Fordham University Press, 2009), p. 74.
8. *Wayne County Herald* (Honesdale, PA), Feb. 5, 1863, p. 2.
9. "The Negro Uniform," *North Branch Democrat*, Feb. 18, 1863, p. 3.
10. Glatthaar, Joseph T. *Forged in Battle: The Civil War Alliance of Black Soldiers and White Officers* (New York: Free Press, 1990), p. 1.
11. *Pittston Gazette* (Pittston, PA), March 12, 1863, p. 2.
12. *Liberator* (Boston), May 8, 1863, p. 2.
13. *Christian Recorder* (Philadelphia), March 18, 1865.
14. Pierce, Frederick C. *Batchelder, Batcheller Genealogy* (Chicago: W. B. Conkey Press, 1898), p. 522.
15. *National Anti-Slavery Standard* (Philadelphia), July 11, 1863.
16. *Liberator*, Jan. 15, 1864.
17. "Flag Raising at Camp William Penn," *Christian Recorder*, Aug. 1, 1863, Accessible Archives, online.
18. *Christian Recorder*, Aug. 8, 1863.
19. Telegram to Maj. Louis Wagner from Maj. Charles W. Foster, commander, Bureau of US Colored Troops, July 31, 1863 (in 3rd USCT Regimental Order Book, E112-115, National Archives and Records Administration, Washington DC).
20. Green, L.B. "Musing of the Rambler," *Scranton Republican*, Jan. 2, 1895, p. 2.
21. Coco, Gregory A. *Killed In Action* (Gettysburg, PA: Thomas Publications, 1996), pp. 92-93.
22. Shankman, Arnold "Draft Resistance in Civil War Pennsylvania," article in *Pennsylvania Magazine of History and Biography*, April 1977, p. 197.
23. Holzer, op. cit., p. 59.
24. *Pittston Gazette*, Jan. 22, 1863, p. 2.
25. *Pittston Gazette*, July 9, 1863, p. 2.
26. *Pittston Gazette*, Jan. 22, 1863, p. 2.
27. *Lackawanna Register* (Scranton), July 16, 1863, p. 2.
28. Lewis, op.cit., pp. 60-61.
29. Neely, Mark E. *The Fate of Liberty: Abraham Lincoln and Civil Liberties* (Oxford Paperbacks, 1991).
30. *Pittston Gazette*, Nov 12, 1863, p. 2.
31. *Lackawanna Register*, June 11, 1863, p. 2.
32. *Lackawanna Register*, June 25, 1863, p. 2.
33. *Lackawanna Register*, July 2, 1863, p. 1.
34. *Lackawanna Register*, July 16, 1863, p. 2.
35. *Pittston Gazette*, Aug. 6, 1863, p. 2.
36. *Lackawanna Register*, Sept. 24, 1863, p. 2.
37. *Lackawanna Register*, Dec. 31, 1863, p. 2.
38. *Lackawanna Register*, Aug. 13, 1863, p. 2.
39. *Pittston Gazette*, Jan. 7, 1864, p. 2.

40. Brabsby, Henry. *History of Luzerne, Lackawanna, and Wyoming Counties, Pa.* (Scranton: W.W. Munsell & Co., 1880), p. 267.
41. Brauer, Norm. *Revisiting Bailey Hollow: A History of Dalton* (copyright Norm Brauer, 1988), p. 27.
42. "Union Mass Meeting in Benton," *Wyoming Republican* (Tunkhannock, PA), July 29, 1863, p. 2.
43. *Pittston Gazette*, Oct. 8, 1863, p. 2.
44. *Lackawanna Register*, Aug. 13, 1863, p. 2.

CHAPTER EIGHT

1863–1864

Scars & Stripes

———•◦•———

BY THE START OF 1864, Waverly's first black recruits, John Sampson and the Norris brothers, had already undergone a baptism by fire. Their 3rd USCT regiment had been rushed down to Folly Island, South Carolina, on the southern rim of Charleston Harbor, in August 1863. The area was a hot war zone. One month earlier, a Union force led by the all-black 54th Massachusetts had stormed Fort Wagner, one of the main cannon batteries guarding the mouth of Charleston Harbor. That ferocious assault failed, and the 54th, while gaining acclaim for bravery (as dramatized in the 1989 Hollywood film *Glory*), lost nearly half of its ranks. The eager recruits of the 3rd suddenly found themselves among a mass of white Union soldiers encamped on narrow Folly Island, helping to press the assault on the Rebel fort and the strategic port city beyond. [*See Map 3, "Assault on Fort Wagner" on xvii.*]

The 3rd regiment got an assignment that was both perilous and arduous: to help dig a series of trenches through the sand and dirt toward Fort Wagner. Under the dark of night, the black troops were ferried over to Morris Island, the next barrier island toward Charleston. The Union held the lower half of the four-mile-long island, the enemy cannons of Wagner still looming at the upper end. In between, scores of explosive canisters known as torpedoes lay hidden in the sand. Rebel sharpshooters waited with high-powered Whitworth rifles that were accurate from a half-mile away. For several weeks, the black men, armed only with shovels and spades, inched the trenches forward toward the Rebel ramparts—alert to the booby traps, staying low to avoid sniper fire and incoming artillery barrages, keeping their focus even when others were hit. They might be joined by sappers and reconnaissance teams on forward patrol. It was a "memorable trial of skill and endurance," Samuel P. Bates wrote in his military history. Bates told how Union sappers came upon a dead body one night and knew to approach carefully. "A small string was discovered attached to its leg, which led away to the trigger of a torpedo buried in the sand. Such was warfare which this command was called to meet."[1]

During the day, the men of the 3rd helped to construct gun batteries to pound the Rebel defenses. In addition, they were assigned to haul timber, gather sod from nearby tidal marshes and swamps, erect fortifications of wood and sod, and unload shipments from supply vessels. The unbroken, lowly fatigue duty rankled. Inspired by Frederick Douglass' personal call to arms, they'd arrived at the front, yearning to prove their manhood; "we Expected to be Treeated as men but we have been Treeated more Like Dogs," wrote one. When some white officers actually tried to use them as personal man-servants, a complaint went up to the general in charge, who twice had to order that "colored troops will not be required to perform any labor which is not shared by the white troops." The racial pay disparity also arose as an issue. Not only did a black soldier earn $10 a month to a white's $13, but the white also got a $3 monthly allotment for equipment, whereas the black had the $3 deducted from his. This was a particular irritant at Morris Island, as the 3rd regiment's commander, Col. Benjamin Tilghman, explained in an

appeal to the US Senate.[2] His men's shoes and clothing were quickly destroyed by the mucky conditions of
their daily fatigue duty—causing them to spend fully
four-fifths of their pay on replacement uniforms. New
clothing should be provided without charge as a matter of "simple justice," Tilghman wrote. (Congress did
equalize the troops' pay arrangement, but only five
months later.)

Compounding their ill treatment was ill health. The
southern heat, bad water, poor sanitation, and gruel-
ing labor took its toll. Intestinal ailments were rampant,
especially among the black troops.[3] But throughout, the
men stuck to their hard duty. On trench detail one night
in late August, a corporal of the 3rd regiment was digging toward Fort Wagner when he struck a torpedo. The
blast killed him instantly and hurled his body through
the dark onto the plunger of another torpedo.[4] The luck-
less fellow would be one of six men from the regiment
to die on Morris Island, along with a dozen wounded.
Their comrades pressed forward to the ramparts until,
on September 7, the Rebels abandoned Wagner and the
nearby Fort Gregg. The Union force occupied all of Morris Island and intensified the siege of the Rebel city.

Sgt. Henry Harmon of the 3rd, a freeborn sailor from
Philadelphia, expressed hope that his black comrades
got due credit for their part in the fort's capture. Harmon penned a letter from Morris Island telling how
his men "with spades and shovels dug up to the very
parapet of the rebel fort under a heavy fire of grape
and canister shell from rebel batteries Gregg, Wagner,
Sumter, and James Island. In those trenches our men
distinguished themselves for bravery and coolness,
which required more nerve than the exciting bayonet
charge. . . . When you hear of a white family that has
lost father, husband, or brother, you can say of the colored man, we too have borne our share of the burden.

Harper's Weekly *in August 1863 printed this image of black troops digging trenches toward Fort Wagner.*

We too have suffered and died in defense of that starry banner which floats over free men."[5]

As Union troops strengthened their positions, the enemy responded with bombardments from Fort Moultrie, across the mouth of Charleston Harbor. Federal casualties during this phase included Privates Joshua and Peter Norris. A bursting shell felled Joshua in late November. According to his postwar disability application, the explosion buried him in the sand with his head wrenched painfully between his legs. He was sent to the field hospital for treatment, returned to action, and reinjured his back carrying railroad ties at Fort Wagner in early 1864. At about that time, his brother Peter herniated his abdomen while laboring to pull a siege cannon up the beach. The siege cannons were enormous—weighing up to fourteen tons—and required hundred-man teams to drag them more than two miles to the gun batteries.

Although the siege of Charleston would continue for another year, a large infantry force was no longer needed, so the 3rd USCT was shipped down to Florida in late January 1864. Their contributions on Morris Island did not go unnoticed. Officers from white regiments that had mingled with the USCT men gave favorable reviews; one went so far as to observe that "blacks had a great appreciation of their duty and tended to work harder and longer than the white soldiers."[6] The brigade commander, Brig. Gen. George H. Gordon, recommended that black troops had earned the right to be used in all capacities in future actions.

Despite their injuries, the Norris brothers were able to join their company and ship out to northern Florida, where the 3rd regiment would remain until after the war. Pvt. John Sampson of Waverly did not join them, however. In February, he was sent to Hilton Head Island, the command base sixty miles southwest, to be an attendant at its busy central hospital. The assignment made sense: Sampson was a company bugler, a role with the side duty of stretcher-bearer, and he had been reassigned as a hospital nurse earlier in January so he'd already had experience assisting the wounded. Clara Barton, founder of the American Red Cross, spent months attending soldiers and sailors at both Morris Island and Hilton Head, but it is doubtful Sampson ever worked alongside her. The Union practice, acceding to white norms, was to segregate military patients by race. The black ward might be termed the contraband section in facilities like Hilton Head that accommodated the newly freed "contraband" slaves who stayed near federal protection. Care in the contraband wards was uniformly second-rate, the sanitation worse, and the mortality rates higher.[7] Sampson would have found himself working among indifferent white doctors and untrained, undersupplied nurses who were frequently female volunteers from the contraband slave camps.

Once in Florida, the rest of the 3rd was assigned to garrison several forts around Jacksonville. Over the coming months, the regiment sent out numerous raiding parties to destroy Rebel property and liberate slaves. In effect, they became marauders. Sgt. Thomas Rockhold of Company D, Peter Norris's unit, wrote a dispatch to the *Christian Recorder* describing their exploits.[8] During a surprise midnight raid on a Rebel camp ten miles outside Jacksonville, Rockhold wrote, "we had the pleasure of liberating some of our flesh and blood. There were about two hundred slaves at that place." The next day, February 9, his patrol moved on to another camp, "had a little skirmish," and captured four pieces of artillery. The men of Companies G and D pushed on to Barber's Station, fifty miles from Jacksonville. "We found, there, ten of our wounded soldiers, and two wounded rebels," Rockhold recounted. "One of them [the Confederates] died while we were there, and we buried him with pleasure; although we were convinced in our own minds, if it were us, they would not even give us a drink of water. But we had a Christian spirit in us."

Setting their people free—hundreds of them—and hearing their testimonies of bondage must have been profoundly moving, even cathartic, for freeborn sons of fugitives such as the Norris brothers. Alas, the accomplishments were not without cost. Sometime in early April, Joshua lost his hearing during an unspecified action in Florida. In addition, a medical certificate lists him as contracting malaria and scurvy, two banes of camp life. A doctor's report lists Peter as suffering from "ague" (malaria). The two soldiered on as the 3rd USCT was moved around the state until being discharged in October 1865.

THE BLACK RECRUITS OF 22ND USCT, meanwhile, completed their month of intensive training back in Pennsylvania and paraded out of Camp William Penn in mid-February 1864. Unlike the men of the 3rd, they were granted permission to march through central Philadelphia en route to the city wharf. It was an occasion to display their bold new regimental standard, a banner depicting a victorious black soldier poised with bayonet over an astonished Rebel officer. The ranks now included six farmers from Waverly. John Mason, William Bradley, and John Washington had been joined in January by George Keys, son George Jr., and Francis Asbury Johnson. The six—now proud infantry privates—shouldered their prized muskets and joined the march through downtown. They were met by a mix of stirring martial music, applause from well-wishers, and "some ignorant and dirty slang" hurled by white hecklers.[9] Their lives of collective indignity left many recruits spoiling for a fight, and the catcalls could only sharpen their resolve.

After being reviewed by Gen. George Gordon Meade, the commander of the Army of the Potomac, the men filed onto waiting steamers bound for Virginia and the Eastern Front. They went first to Yorktown and then down to Hampton Roads and the famous citadel known as Fortress Monroe, at the mouth of the James River. There the 22nd USCT was attached to the Army of the James and became part of the historic Overland Campaign of 1864. The crucial objective of the Army of the James was to cripple the Confederate capital, Richmond, and force its surrender by choking off its supply lines from the south. That would be accomplished by capturing Petersburg, the Rebels' vital communications and transit center twenty-five miles due south of

Richmond. [*See Map 4, "Petersburg Campaign 1864" on page xviii.*]

To prepare, Union troops and supplies would be moved up the James River to a massive staging area east of Petersburg. From there, they were to mount a coordinated land assault on Petersburg's defense lines. The Army of the James commander, Maj. Gen. Benjamin Butler, knew he'd need strong outposts along the James River to keep his ship traffic safe from enemy attack. Butler entrusted the task to his black troops, reasoning that "they would fight more desperately than any white troops in order to prevent capture" and its brutal consequences.[10] Just three weeks earlier in Tennessee, Rebels had methodically tortured and massacred scores of USCT soldiers who were trying to surrender their fort, an atrocity that scandalized the North. As Butler would see, the "Fort Pillow Massacre" left his own black soldiers hungry for retribution.

In early May, the 22nd and a regiment from the District of Columbia, the 1st USCT, took their places together at a strategic landing on the James known as Wilson's Wharf, sixty miles upriver from Hampton Roads. "The sight of former slaves coming ashore at Wilson's Wharf must have worried local planters," writes historian Leonne Hudson. "Many of the troops had once been held in bondage in the surrounding region."[11] On a bluff above the landing, the black troops set to work felling trees, piling up earthwork fortifications, and digging defensive trenches. The cannon bastions and rifle pits were positioned facing inland to protect the river from overland attack. The zigzag earthworks were christened Fort Pocahontas in tribute to the legendary Indian maiden from nearby Jamestown. A few miles upriver, two other USCT regiments stood guard at Fort Powhatan, named for the great chieftain who was Pocahontas's father.

The 22nd comprised mostly New Jersey men. In their midst, the Waverly crew was able to tent together: John Mason, William Bradley, and John Washington in Company D; Francis Asbury Johnson and George Keys Sr. and Jr. in Company F. The elder Keys, at age 44 the oldest of the six, could take pride watching his 18-year-old son practice his new role as company bugler. He could also keep a protective eye on young Asbury Johnson, the Colored Hill preacher's son, a pup of 15 who'd listed himself as 18 so he could join up. Encamped now deep in enemy territory, the fugitives could school the younger ones on Southern realities.

The troops of the 1st and the 22nd drilled together, swapped stories and tunes, and did their best to bond for the rigors ahead. By all accounts they felt an easy rapport with the 22nd's new regimental commander, Col. Joseph Kiddoo, a battle-hardened Pittsburgh lawyer. The same went for the top commander at Fort Pocahontas, Brig. Gen. Edward Wild of Massachusetts. Wild was a gruff Harvard grad and abolitionist who had lost an arm in battle. His faith in his black troops—known as Wild's African Brigade—was matched only by his hatred of the Confederacy and slavery.[12]

Wild made their presence known by immediately sending out foraging parties from the fort to pillage nearby plantations and cause panic and flight. As was the case with the 3rd regiment in Florida, the raiders marauded the countryside dispensing rough justice. A few white land-owners who resisted were gunned down on the spot. Furniture and other loot were plundered, including from the slave plantation of former US president John Tyler. At the Tyler estate, said a member of one 22nd raiding foray, "We took all the slaves & ordered them to take a reasonable amount of clothing bedding &c whereupon they walked very deliberately into the best room took the best bed pillows. . . . I never saw a

The black troops erected two forts like this one at strategic spots on the James River, then defended them against Confederate attack. (Courtesy Library of Congress.)

The 22nd USCT's battle flag gave a new meaning to the Virginia state motto, Sic Semper Tyrannis *("Death to All Tyrants"). (Courtesy Library of Congress.)*

Left: Col. Joseph Kiddoo, the popular commander of the 22nd USCT (Courtesy Massachusetts Commandery, Military Order of Loyal Legion of US) Center: Brig. Gen. Edward Wild, whose troops were called "Wild's African Brigade." (Courtesy Library of Congress.) Right: Maj. Gen. Fitzhugh Lee, whose Rebel cavalry was twice repulsed by the black soldiers. (Courtesy Library of Congress.)

happier lot [of] human beings than were those slaves when they were on their way to freedom."[13] They were among numerous slaves liberated and taken to Fort Pocahontas for protection.

On one memorable occasion, a wealthy local planter ran into trouble when he went to Wilson's Wharf to take an oath of allegiance to the Union. The man, William Clopton, claimed to have treated his twenty-five slaves well. That brought a loud challenge from several contraband women present at the fort. They said Clopton had been their "massa"—and had beaten them brutally. It also came out that Clopton once owned one of the men who by then was a soldier at the fort. An inflamed Wild had Clopton tied to a tree and ordered that same soldier forward to lash the planter's bare back "Cheers echoed through the African Brigade" at the sight of the black soldier "bringing blood from his loins at every stroke, and not forgetting to remind the gentleman of the days gone by," wrote a sergeant who was present. "After giving him some fifteen or twenty well-directed strokes, the ladies, one after another, came up and gave him a like number, to remind him that they were no longer his, but safely housed in Abraham's bosom, and under the protection of the Star Spangled Banner."[14] For Waverly fugitive soldiers John Mason, William Bradley, John Washington, and George Keys Sr., the blood-letting must have stirred bitter personal memories. They would not have questioned Wild's term for the whipping: "poetical justice."[15]

In mid-May, the 22nd regiment was rotated upriver to guard the twin fort, Powhatan. Within days, Kiddoo's infantrymen got their first taste of combat there. A division of Rebel cavalry descended on Powhatan on May 21, in response to planters' indignation that black patrols were still "pilfering and depredating in every direction."[16] The cavalry commander, Maj. Gen. Fitzhugh Lee, Robert E. Lee's nephew, was confident his mounted assault, backed by artillery fire, would overwhelm the black troops. He was mistaken. Kiddoo's fighters kept their composure and held their positions. The horsemen were beaten back by what Kiddoo termed "well-directed shots from our guns." The *Pittsburgh Gazette*, already following the accomplishments of native son Kiddoo, ran an excited report on the victory. According to the *Gazette*, the Powhatan engagement ended with eleven of Lee's horsemen dead and sixty wounded, while the 22nd had two soldiers captured and one wounded. The injured black fighter, the correspondent wrote, "stood his ground on picket against the attack of six cavalrymen. One he shot, the rest he guarded off with his bayonet, and with that implement he disposed of two more. Thus he defended himself until one of the three survivors gave the brave fellow a stroke across the face. He fell, and the enemy left him for dead; but he came to after a while, and crawled back into the fort, bringing his musket with him. . . . The soldier was made a sergeant on the spot."[17] (Three days later, Fitz Lee tried his luck down at Wilson's Wharf, where the USCT men repulsed his repeated assaults and caused more than 200 Rebel casualties. Lee later conceded that his men "found a foe worthy of their steel."[18])

The rousing victory at Powhatan gave the men of the 22nd a bolt of confidence, and they would need it. Three weeks later, their courage under fire would be tested again and again on a monumental day at Petersburg that twice saw the Waverly soldiers at the center of the bloody action.

IN LATE MAY, THE 22nd REGIMENT moved farther up the James River toward Petersburg with orders to prepare for a direct assault on the city's outer defenses. Wednesday, June 15, was chosen as the day of attack. Some 16,000 Union soldiers were mobilized. In the pre-dawn hours, a division of 3,500 USCT troops including the men of the 22nd set off southwestward along one of the major roadways to Petersburg. Their objective was to pierce the near end of the Rebels' Dimmock Line, a ten-mile-long string of cannon batteries and infantry trenches that curved across hilltops and farm fields. Fewer than 3,000 Confederates were in place to defend Petersburg that day. Though badly outnumbered, the Rebels would fight hard.

As the morning light rose, the roadway became clogged with civilians, white and black, rushing in the other direction to escape the coming battle. Union cavalrymen pressed through them, under orders to screen the black division's movement. The advancing column soon arrived near a place called Baylor's Farm. There, at about 6 a.m., the force suddenly confronted Rebel horsemen. The column also began taking fire from the woods. These were not the Dimmock guns, still two miles distant. Instead, the cavalry reported that they were encountering an isolated forward emplacement that guarded the roadway. The Rebel defenders were entrenched on rapidly rising land and obscured by trees. Behind their rifle pits and earthworks were four cannons and several hundred infantrymen. To subdue them, the USCT troops would have to cross a half-mile of overgrown terrain.

The troops, known now as "Duncan's black brigade," were ordered to form battle ranks, fix bayonets, and prepare to attack. They took positions on both sides of the road, the 5th regiment on the right, the 22nd at right center, the 4th at left center, and the 6th on the left. With a command from George Keys Jr. and the other buglers, the front line moved out, the back line following a few paces behind. From the rear, Union artillery began sending a deafening cannonade over their heads in support. The battle was under way.

The enemy took aim and unleashed a ferocious fire from the woods. The 4th took the brunt of it, losing the first of what would be 120 dead or wounded that day. Many in the 5th Massachusetts Colored Cavalry broke and ran, having no experience fighting on foot. The rest, including the 22nd, fell back from the fusillade and regrouped. Then, to another round of bugle blasts and cries of "Remember Fort Pillow!" the soldiers said their prayers and charged ahead, over the fallen bodies and back into the kill zone. Among them was Sgt. Charles R. Douglass of the 5th Cavalry, the son of Frederick Douglass. The next day, the young sergeant told his father how it went. "Our regiment was in the second line of battle," he wrote. "As we came through the second piece of woods, the enemy opened on us with shot and shell. We kept on, however, until we reached the next piece of woods. Then we were only about a quarter of a mile from the enemy, they being drawn up in line of battle behind their breastworks. All this time we were under a withering fire from the Rebel batteries . . . the first line of battle fell back upon us under a galling fire, which killed several of our men in the second line."[19] A sergeant from the 5th added that "we rallied, and after a terrible charge, amidst pieces of barbarous iron, solid shot and shell, we drove the desperate greybacks from their fortifications, and gave three cheers for our victory."[20]

The breakthrough stunned the field correspondent from *Frank Leslie's Illustrated Newspaper*.[21] "The majority of the whites expected that the colored troops would run, but the sable forces astonished everybody by their achievements. With a wild yell that must certainly have struck terror into the hearts of their foes, the 22d and 5th U. S. colored regiments, commanded by Cols. Kiddoo and Conner, charged, under a hot fire of musketry and artillery, over the rebel ditch and parapet, and drove the enemy before them, capturing a large brass

The cannon that the men of the 22nd USCT captured is paraded before cheering white troops at Baylor's Farm, in an engraving from Harper's Weekly.

fieldpiece, and taking entire possession of their works, its defenders . . . seeking safety in rapid flight, leaving their dead and wounded in the works."

Edward G. Longacre, a historian of the Petersburg Siege, noted that most of the Rebel defenders had been redeployed to the other flank by then, leaving the position lightly manned. Still, he termed this "the first successful charge by African-American soldiers in the eastern theater of operations."[22] The victors "tossed caps into the air and shouted at the tops of their lungs. Members of the 22nd USCT capered about the cannon they had seized as though it were a trophy beyond price." They wheeled the fieldpiece around and fired its remaining shells toward the fleeing Confederates. Then, a group from the 5th Massachusetts, elated and pulsing with adrenaline, carted the cannon away to show off to white infantrymen nearby.

In 1892, French illustrator Andre Castaigne immortalized the June 15 frontal assault by the black infantrymen at Petersburg—including six soldiers from Waverly. His painting, The Charge of the 22nd Regiment, *hangs today in the US Military Academy's West Point Museum. In 2014, the US Postal Service chose the image for a commemorative stamp marking the sesquicentennial of the Petersburg Siege. (Courtesy West Point Museum Collection, United States Military Academy.)*

The 22nd had shown its bravery for all to see. Its standard-bearer was the first to breach the Rebel works. The assault left at least twenty of its men wounded. Company F, which included the Keyses and Johnson, had one of its corporals, 19-year-old James Dunwood, shot dead and an officer, Second Lieut. McKendree Shaw, wounded. Colonel Kiddoo, not wanting to lose the momentum, ordered his men to prepare themselves for more action. "No time was lost," wrote a *New York Tribune* correspondent. Dunwood "was sadly buried where he fell, and the boys shouldered their muskets and moved on."[23]

It was only eight a.m. Ahead lay the Dimmock Line and twelve more hours of battle.

WHILE STRETCHER-BEARERS loaded the fallen onto wagons, the able-bodied remainder of Duncan's black brigade soon fell into line and moved out toward the Dimmock batteries two miles beyond. By early afternoon, they had marched within about eight hundred yards of the guns and came under heavy fire again, from both front and flank. They were trapped in what became a shooting gallery. A correspondent for the *Pittsburgh Daily Commercial* described the scene: "The men could move but a few rods before the rebels got range, when they were obliged to lie down and wait an opportunity. Soon they would rise, push forward a few rods further, and again lie down. At about half-past one they gained the designated locality, and then for five mortal hours lay exposed to the strain of constant apprehension from the ceaseless shelling."[24] The correspondent said veteran officers told him "there can be no severer test of soldiers, particularly for green troops, as were Duncan's entire brigade. That after a long strain upon their nerves they should be able to rise, move against such a formidable line of works, and carry them triumphantly, is irresistible proof that black troops can and will fight."

At about six p.m., white troops fighting to the right of Duncan's brigade swamped one of the key Rebel batteries, Number 5, and rushed southward along the exposed Dimmock Line. The USCT got the order to press the advantage. Bugles sounded, sending the black infantrymen surging across the field and uphill into the face of more punishing grapeshot, canister, and musket fire. The 22nd targeted Battery 7. To its immediate right, the 1st regiment charged Battery 6. "Nothing less than the pen of horror could begin to describe the terrific roar and dying yells of that awful yet masterly charge and daring feat," wrote Rev. Henry Turner, regimental chaplain of the 1st. "The rebel balls would tear up the ground at times, and create such a heavy dust in front of our charging army, that they could scarcely see the forts for which they were making. But onward they went, through dust and every impediment, while they and the rebels were both crying out – 'Fort Pillow!' . . . Soon the boys were at the base of the Fort, climbing over abbatis, and jumping the deep ditches, ravines, &c."[25]

The 1st and a white brigade captured Battery 6 together. The 22nd achieved quick success at Battery 7. Colonel Kiddoo said the men of his Company D, which included Waverly's Bradley, Mason, and Washington, broke through from the rear and seized "two 12-pounder howitzers and one iron piece."

Kiddoo turned his sights to the next battery before them, Number 8. It was about six hundred yards away, well situated on a promontory high above a dank ravine littered with fallen timber. His men would have to attack across that difficult stretch and uphill to take the fort. With dusk gathering, Kiddoo ordered his exhausted troops forward one more time. Some men from the 1st joined in support. "The charge was made across a deep and swampy ravine," Kiddoo's battle report stated. "The enemy immediately ceased firing his artillery and took the parapets of the fort and rifle-pit as infantrymen. My men wavered at first under the hot fire of the enemy, but soon, on seeing their colors on the opposite side of the ravine, pushed rapidly up and passed the rifle pits and fort." In their flight, the outmanned Confederates abandoned a 12-pounder howitzer. The attackers immediately turned the gun against nearby Battery 9. The defenders began to fight back from Battery 9. Kiddoo decided not to respond this time. It was nearly dark, and his men were low on ammunition.

The regiment also needed to collect its fallen. Kiddoo assigned an officer to care for the wounded and bury the dead. The report back: eleven men buried, forty-three

"THE HIGHEST COMMENDATION"

The well-witnessed valor of the Waverly soldiers and their brethren on June 15 changed many minds. "The gallant style in which the colored troops made the [evening] charge as well as their general conduct throughout the day, elicited the highest commendation," a *Philadelphia Inquirer* correspondent remarked. The *Pittsburgh Daily Commercial* put it this way: "In the thickest of the fight, and under the most trying circumstances, they never flinched. The old Army of the Potomac, so long prejudiced and so obstinately heretical on this subject, stand amazed as they look on the works captured by the negroes, and are now loud and unreserved in their praise."

Not everyone was sold, of course. Some attributed the success to the troops' white officers, others to the relatively thin Rebel defenses. The writer for *Frank Leslie's Illustrated Newspaper* could only explain it by crediting "the Southern aristocratic blood in the veins of many of these colored troops."

But others who had seen the USCT in action were filled with praise. A white New Hampshire officer present that day said, "Negroes will keep on their feet, and move on, with wounds that would utterly lay out white men." The commander of the assault, Maj. Gen. William "Baldy" Smith, sought out his black troops on the field the next day. According to a reporter who was there, Smith "went to thank them, and tell them he was proud of their courage and dash. He says they can't be exceeded as soldiers, and hereafter he will send them in a difficult place as readily as the best white troops."[26]

The chaplain of the 4th regiment, Rev. William Hunter, declared June 15 "a day long to be remembered by the entire colored race on this continent. It is the day when prejudice died in the entire army of the U.S. of America. It is the day when it was admitted that colored men were equal to the severest ordeal. It is the day in which it was secured to us rights of equality in the army and service of the Government of the United States."[27] Reverend Hunter was referring to legislative action taken that same day. As historian Edward G. Longacre has written, "Fittingly on this day, Congress addressed the implications of what one of Smith's white troops called blacks' 'equal value' in battle. . . . Heeding the words of commanders such as Butler ('the colored man fills an equal space in ranks while he lives, and an equal grave when he falls'), legislators passed a pay equalization bill, retroactive to January."[28]

The accomplishments of the 22nd at Petersburg grew in luster over the years, becoming seen as black soldiery at its best. In 1892, French illustrator Andre Castaigne immortalized the men in a painting, *The Charge of the 22nd Regiment*. The original hangs today in the US Military Academy's West Point Museum. In 2014, the US Postal Service chose the image for a commemorative stamp marking the sesquicentennial of the Petersburg Siege.

wounded. The 22nd's final count for June 15 would be eighteen killed in action, including an officer from Company D, one hundred forty-three wounded including five officers, and one man missing.

The Waverly contingent had been spared death, but not maiming. During one of the day's assaults, a minié ball slammed into Pvt. John Mason's right hand. An examining doctor said the gunshot "fractured the first phalanx of right thumb, entered the palm, and made exit at the base of metacarpal bone of little finger," leaving Mason's hand "totally incapacitated." Shrapnel from a bursting shell tore into Pvt. William Bradley's torso "in the left side near the spine." He spent a painful night lying exposed on the battlefield until he was carried away the next day to have the wounded dressed. Cpl. John Washington sustained shell wounds as well, his to the head and side. The impact left a dent in Washington's skull and troubled him for the rest of his life.

Approximately three hundred Rebels fell into Union hands on June 15. It's believed that some were cut down on the spot by wrathful black soldiers, and that white troops had to step in to protect others.[29] Chaplain Henry Turner of the 1st USCT wrote openly that some captives "held up their hands and pleaded for mercy, but our boys thought that over Jordan would be the best place for them, and sent them there, with a very few exceptions."[30] Kiddoo was silent on whether the 22nd was party to any vengeance. His report said simply "my regiment, both officers and men, behaved in such a manner as to give me great satisfaction and the fullest confidence in the fighting qualities of colored troops." (See box, "The Highest Commendation.")

BY THE NEXT MORNING, the mile and a half stretch of the Dimmock Line between Batteries 3 and 11 was in Union hands. The commander in charge of the June 15 operation, Maj. Gen. William "Baldy" Smith, was urged by his field officers to thrust farther, but he instead ordered a full withdrawal. "Smith's Pause" is considered one of the great miscalculations of the war because it allowed the Confederates to gather reinforcements and harden their defenses. The long Siege of Petersburg ensued. Both sides dug warren's nests of tunnels and earthworks, skirmished periodically, and endured a ten-month plague of mortar fire, snipers, dust, sun, and sickness.

In particular, the daily sniper fire put everyone on edge. A white officer from Scranton, Adj. William B. Phillips, wrote home from the trenches about how the snipers "like the wicked, are never at rest . . . Those confounded sharpshooters have a particular spike on my headquarters, and the dust flies all over from their shots, fired onto my embankments . . . There goes another. Phiz, bang."[31]

Phillips wrote that letter on July 4, 1864—the same day one of the "confounded sharpshooters" felled George Keys Sr. of Waverly. According to the injury report, Keys had just left cover on a water detail. Water was a constant concern along the Petersburg siege lines, enough so that cease-fires were arranged to enable both sides to safely access water sources. The truce did not extend to black soldiers, however. Their very presence was an irritant to the Rebels, their June 15 victory galling. That day, the Fourth of July, the Rebel sniper who spotted Keys may have felt extra spite because military bands from the Union side had been blasting the "The Star-Spangled Banner" for all to hear.

The gunshot struck Keys in his right thigh, up near his hip. Caused by a minié ball, it would have been an ugly, shattering wound. The report doesn't specify where the shooting happened or how Keys got back to safety. He presumably wasn't with his son at the time.

Buglers were high-value targets, meaning George Jr. would have had standing orders to stay back. But Keys was probably with Asbury Johnson because he'd been watching over the preacher's boy—and because young Johnson was shot that day as well. Their short stature, 5-foot-5, didn't protect them from the snipers. Johnson's injury report doesn't describe his wound, but it also turned out to be a bad one. Whether or not the two soldiers sensed it, their war was over.

Bradley and Washington, wounded on June 15, would recuperate enough to return to duty with the regiment. Later that year, they underwent more bruising combat—and setbacks this time—north of Petersburg. The most intense action was in late September at the Battle of Chaffin's Farm and New Market Heights. The 22nd had a lead position in the storming of Confederate forces atop the heights. The attack was foiled, and the regiment sustained eleven men dead, four wounded, and eight missing. In the heat of the action, not all of the men performed admirably. Kiddoo, in fury, called out a sergeant and twenty-two privates by name. His field order[32] said the men "Straggled and Skulked and played the coward in the late battles and some of them actually ran away while their brave comrades were fighting the enemy. These cowards shall not share the honors so gallantly won for the Regiment [in late September]. All good soldiers should frown upon them with that contempt due to their cowardly conduct. It is therefore ordered that these men be placed in the rear in a camp by themselves called the Camp of Skulkers and Cowards and that they do all the fatigue duty of the Regiment till it again moves against the enemy when an opportunity will be given them to retrieve their lost honor."

Their opportunity came a month later, at the Second Battle of Fair Oaks. The 22nd assaulted Rebel

A contraband camp of escaped slaves. The military often placed its black hospital wards near these camps. (Courtesy National Archives and Records Administration, Matthew Brady Collection.)

entrenchments "with great steadiness and courage, but was again repulsed with heavy slaughter," with more than one hundred killed or wounded.[33] Regimental records show that two of the "skulkers" were among the wounded.

Kiddoo also was hit that day at Fair Oaks, struck in the back while charging across the field with his men. The wound was serious, and he was sent downriver to the brick hospital for officers inside Fortress Monroe. The wounded Keys and Johnson were there, too, but in nearby Hampton, relegated to the tents of the contraband ward.

Rev. Amos Billingsley, a white Presbyterian cleric from western Pennsylvania, was a military hospital chaplain who made the Hampton tents part of his ministry that year. In an 1872 memoir, *From the Flag to the Cross*, Reverend Billingsley described watching government steamers regularly arriving from the front to unload hundreds of mangled soldiers. On his visits to the contraband wards, he saw black patients "very low with disease," in need of clothing, and "a good deal neglected" spiritually. Having no resident chaplain or chapel, the black soldiers would hold impromptu prayer meetings at their beds, he wrote: "Speaking right from the heart, they frequently became very eloquent and powerful, reaching the heart and stirring the soul of every listener. It was a privilege to hear them."[34]

Death was a constant. One day, Reverend Billingsley buried ten soldiers "all in old graves out of which dead bodies had been exhumed and taken home." Another time, at the Gangrene Camp, he found "one suffering colored soldier, in the last stages of life, covered all over with perspiration. Pointing him to the all-compassionate Saviour, and commending him to the God of all grace, with prayer and exhortation, we bid him a last farewell."[35]

Gangrene-causing bacteria would have been rife in the hospital tents, often spread by the hands and dressings of unwitting caregivers. Keys and Johnson also risked infection from the nature of their wounds. The minié ball was a devilish weapon whose soft lead casing and greased grooves gave it an extra payload of germs. If the shattering wound didn't lead to amputation, it could bring on ulcerations, runaway fever, tetanus, and gangrene.

Asbury Johnson soon developed what the military generically termed "camp fever." When his condition didn't improve, he was transferred up to Washington where, sometime that winter, he asked to be sent home to the care of his family. Johnson wouldn't have known it, but in November 1864, Waverly compatriot John Mason also was released from the service. Doctors at a military hospital near New York City felt they couldn't do any more for Mason's ruined hand and discharged him on a disability certificate. Meanwhile, George Keys Sr. would hang on for several more months in Hampton.

BACK IN LUZERNE COUNTY, familiar scenes were playing out in 1864. The year had begun with a new military draft. Abington and Waverly were among the first places to fill their quotas (13 and 4, respectively), while elsewhere, men clamored for exemptions. The county commissioners began providing a $300 bounty to volunteers as a way to avoid conscriptions. Commissioner Uriah Gritman, the Fleetville copperhead, was the county board's lone dissenting member. He complained that "he would sooner pay the three hundred dollars for each volunteer to stay at home, and further that he did not believe the North could put down the rebellion."[36]

The *Lackawanna Register*, the copperhead newspaper in Scranton, kept up its invective. It warned white soldiers not to fight alongside blacks, "for if you get killed, some African gentleman, in his long tall blue, may take your widow or marry your sweetheart for you.

The 1864 Democratic platform played on hostility to black rights. (Courtesy Division of Rare and Manuscript Collections, Cornell University Library.)

It will be pleasant to die on the field of battle, knowing this is the best government the sun ever shone upon; and that for the life you gave up, some darkey will come in your place to warm his shins at your fire, to sleep in your bed, to eat at your table, to ride in your carriage, to father your children, and to shine as odiforously in your mansion as a rotten mackerel."[37]

Politically, the Lincoln-haters were hardly in retreat and the state's electorate remained torn down the middle. The presidency was up for election that year, a race that pitted Lincoln against Democratic Gen. George McClellan, a Pennsylvania native and foe of abolitionism. Lincoln carried Pennsylvania, but by only 20,000 votes, on his way to re-election. He might have lost Pennsylvania had the state constitution not been amended to allow soldiers to vote from camp. Despite his overall victory in the state, the president took a drubbing in Luzerne County, where the tally was: McClellan, 10,045; Lincoln, 7,645.

On Colored Hill, families would spend the year holding their distant soldiers in prayer. Perhaps some of them received precious letters from the front. They could keep up with war news from dispatches in the AME's weekly *Christian Recorder*. The *Lackawanna Register* also was available at John Stone's store, though they'd have to suffer its insults. Fortunately, there were cordial whites in the village to commiserate with and swap news about the fighting. The all-white 143rd Pennsylvania Infantry, laden with local boys, was heavily involved in the Overland Campaign and other battles that year. Colored Hill could share the sorrow over the death of Lysander Jordan of Benton, cut down at Petersburg just ten days after Keys and Johnson were shot. The disabled John Mason would return to his family from the war, perhaps even in time for the winter holidays, and was certainly swarmed with sympathy and questions.

During that melancholy season of 1864, Colored Hill families could take heart from one especially prominent source of white support. The Abington Baptist Association, at its annual convention, issued a declaration that, "It is absolutely necessary to destroy the true cause of the present formidable rebellion—slavery . . . [The nation] is like a man with three arms! The two of the three that are natural and necessary are liberty and law; the one that is unnatural and superfluous is slavery. And the nation is now being subjected to a grand surgical operation in the amputation of this monstrous third arm."

---

1.   Bates, Samuel P. *History of Pennsylvania Volunteers, 1861-5* (Harrisburg: B. Singerly, State Printers, 1871), p. 925.
2.   Col. Benjamin Tilghman letter to Senate Military Committee, Jan. 14, 1864 (in 3rd USCT Regimental Order Book, E112-115, at National Archives and Records Administration, Washington, DC).
3.   "The Civil War's Black Soldiers: Medical Care," National Park Service article at NPS.gov e-library, online.
4.   Wise, Stephen R. *Gate of Hell: Campaign for Charleston Harbor, 1863* (Columbia, S.C.: University of South Carolina Press, 1994), p. 180.
5.   Redkey, Edwin S. *A Grand Army of Black Men: Letters from African-American Soldiers in the Union Army 1861-1865* (Cambridge, England: Cambridge University Press, 1992), pp. 35-36.
6.   Wise, op. cit., p. 215.
7.   "The Civil War's Black Soldiers: Medical Care," op. cit.
8.   *Christian Recorder* (Philadelphia), June 25, 1864 (Accessible Archives, online).
9.   *Christian Recorder* (Philadelphia), Feb. 13, 1864 (Accessible Archives, online).
10. Harwood, Jameson M. "No Danger of Surrender: An Historical Archaeological Perspective of the Civil War Battle of Wilson's Wharf, Charles City County, Virginia," 2001 article for National Park Service, at fortpocahontas.org.
11. Hudson, Leonne. "Valor at Wilson's Wharf," article in *Civil War Times Illustrated*, March 1998, p. 48.
12. Harwood, op. cit.
13. Dobak, William A. *Freedom by the Sword: The U.S. Colored Troops, 1862-1867* (Washington DC: Center of Military History, US Army, 2011), p. 346.
14. Hudson, op. cit., p. 48.
15. Wild's raiders also were suspected of killing two civilians, for which Wild was court-martialed and convicted. Butler later reversed the conviction.
16. *Charleston Mercury* (Charleston, SC), May 16, 1864 (Accessible Archives, online).
17. *Pittsburgh Gazette* (Pittsburgh), July 9, 1864, p. 3.
18. Hudson, op. cit., p. 52.
19. Douglass, Charles, "Letter From a Son of Frederick Douglass," reprinted in the *New York Times*, June 26, 1864.

20. Redkey, op. cit., pp. 98-99.
21. "Siege of Petersburg. Storming of the First Line at Baylor's Farm," in *Frank Leslie's Weekly*, July 9, 1864 (Accessible Archives, online).
22. Longacre, Edward G. *Army of Amateurs: General Benjamin F. Butler and the Army of the James, 1863-65* (Mechanicsburg, PA: Stackpole Books, 1997), p. 145.
23. *Pittsburgh Gazette*, June 28, 1864, p. 1.
24. *Pittsburgh Daily Commercial* (Pittsburgh), June 21, 1864, p. 1.
25. *Christian Recorder* (Philadelphia), July 9, 1864.
26. *Pittsburgh Daily Commercial* (Pittsburgh), June 21, 1864, p. 1.
27. *Christian Recorder*, July 16, 1864, p. 2.
28. Longacre, op. cit., p. 146.
29. Howe, Thomas J. *The Petersburg Campaign: Wasted Valor, June 15-18, 1864* (Lynchburg, Va.: H.E. Howard Inc., 1988), p. 35.
30. *Christian Recorder* (Philadelphia), July 9, 1864 (Accessible Archives, online)
31. Letter 1282, posted at soldierstudies.org, online.
32. General Order 24, issued by Col. Joseph B. Kiddoo, Oct. 9, 1864 (RG 94: Records of the Adjutant General's Office, 22nd USCT, E112-115, National Archives and Records Administration, Washington, DC).
33. Bates, op. cit., p. 992.
34. Billingsley, Rev. Amos S. *From the Flag to the Cross: Or, Scenes and Incidents of Christianity in the War, The Conversions . . . Sufferings and Deaths of Our Soldiers, on the Battle-field, in Hospital, Camp and Prison; and a Description of Distinguished Christian Men and Their Labors* (Philadelphia: New-World Publishing Co., 1872), p. 282.
35. Ibid., p. 269.
36. *Pittston Gazette* (Pittston, PA), March 10, 1864, p. 2.
37. *Lackawanna Register* (Scranton), Jan. 14, 1864, p. 2.

CHAPTER NINE

1865–1866

A Fitful Peace

⎯⎯⎯•◆•⎯⎯⎯

NEW YEAR'S OF 1865 found Pvt. Francis Asbury Johnson in crippling pain. He'd just turned 16 and was back north, fighting for his life.

The teenager had been severely wounded at Petersburg the previous July. When his condition steadily worsened, military doctors granted his wish to be shipped home. Waverly was the only home Asbury knew, but by 1865 his family was living in Kinderhook, New York, near Albany. While he had been away at war, his father was transferred to Kinderhook to pastor its Bethel AME church. Rev. William M. Johnson and his wife Eliza, both slave-born fugitives, took in their stricken young soldier and did what they could to nurse him through the long New York winter. Infection wracked Asbury's body, most likely leading to septic shock.

Death came on February 3. Reverend Johnson assumed the painful task of eulogizing his firstborn son. His March 18 tribute in the *Christian Recorder* may have been Waverly's first awareness of the terrible loss. This "young and faithful follower of Jesus" felt a duty "to fight for God and his country," the pastor wrote. "His sufferings were great. When a strong man Death was about to take him, he bade us all good-by, laid his head in his mother's arms, and stepped into the chariot which bore him to the skies. He sleeps in Jesus, beloved and mourned by many friends."[1]

It so happened that Asbury Johnson died on the very day a high-level peace conference was being held on a steamship at Hampton Roads, near the contraband ward where he'd languished, and where Pvt. George Keys Sr. still lay wounded. President Lincoln's shipboard negotiation with Confederate officials proved fruitless, and the war would grind on. In coming weeks, the remaining comrades of the 22nd USCT found themselves at the center of history again.

The 22nd, including the trio still left from Waverly, had been entrenched for months around Petersburg and Richmond, helping to keep pressure on the depleted Rebels. A camp letter in March from W. A. Freeman of the 22nd expressed their determination: "Of the men who once comprised this regiment, numbers sleep 'neath the clods of the valley, on Southern soil; some lie wounded in hospitals, while the remnant that survives those heroes and patriots are still at the front—ready on the altar of their country—ready to assist in striking the last blow at this accursed rebellion."[2]

April brought a cascade of events. On April 2, the Richmond defenses broke. Rebel forces evacuated after first setting their capital city ablaze. News of the evacuation caused jubilation in the Union trenches, camps, and even hospital wards. Federal troops quickly marched into the burning city. The 22nd USCT was one of the first units in, and its men immediately set about extinguishing the flames. They were there on April 4 when President Lincoln entered the ruined capital, accompanied by black cavalry and cheered by liberated slaves who jammed the streets to see the great emancipator and touch his carriage.

The South surrendered at Appomattox on April 9—but then, on Saturday, April 15, came devastating news out of Washington: an assassin's bullet had killed the president. Plans were hastily made to move Lincoln's

President Lincoln, touring the newly occupied city of Richmond, is hailed by liberated slaves. (Courtesy Library of Congress.)

body to the White House and, on the following Wednesday, to march the casket up Pennsylvania Avenue to the Capitol where the body would lie in state. On April 16, Commanding General Ulysses S. Grant, a supporter of black soldiery, cabled his generals to immediately dispatch "one of the best regiments of colored troops you have, to attend the funeral ceremonies . . . One that has seen service should be directed." The reply came the next day. The singular honor would go to the 22nd USCT "on account of its excellent discipline and good soldierly qualities."[3] Its men were being summoned from the field.

Regimental records indicate that Company D, which included William Bradley and John Washington, and Company F, with George Keys Jr., arrived in Washington in the nick of time, on April 19. The lines of marching

Abraham Lincoln's funeral cortege heads up to the Capitol. The men of the 22nd USCT, including three from Waverly, were selected to represent the Union's black troops, and marched at the head of the procession up Pennsylvania Avenue. (Courtesy Library of Congress.)

dignitaries, military units, and mourners black and white already extended for several miles along Pennsylvania Avenue. The 22nd wheeled itself into place—at the very head of the solemn national cortege. "One noticeable feature of the procession," correspondent Noah Brooks wrote, "was the appearance of the colored societies which brought up the rear, humbly, as was their wont; but just before the procession began to move, the Twenty-Second United States Colored Infantry (organized in Pennsylvania), landed from Petersburg and marched up to a position on the avenue, and when the head of the column came up, played a dirge, and headed the procession to the Capitol. The coffin was taken from the funeral car and placed on a catafalque within the rotunda of the Capitol, which had been darkened and draped in mourning."[4]

Two days later, Lincoln's body was moved to a waiting train to begin its slow, circuitous journey home to Illinois. As the funeral train pulled away, bells tolled and

The black soldiers were sent into these marshlands of Charles County, Maryland, to hunt for Lincoln's assassin. (Courtesy Jim Remsen.)

several thousand soldiers presented arms. "A portion of the soldiers in line near the depot were two regiments of U.S. Colored Troops," historian J. C. Power wrote in 1872. "They stood with arms reversed, heads bowed, all weeping like children at the loss of a father. Their grief was of such undoubted sincerity as to affect the whole vast multitude. Dignified Governors of States, grave Senators, and scar-worn army officers, who had passed through scenes of blood and carnage unmoved, lost their self control and were melted to tears in the presence of such unaffected sorrow."[5]

The next day, the 22nd was on the move again—assigned this time to quickly join the manhunt for Lincoln's killer, John Wilkes Booth. The men were deployed down to Charles County in lower Maryland. One of them, George Keys Jr., may not have realized it, but his father had escaped from that very county twenty years earlier. It was still an inbred land of tidewater plantations and Confederate sentiment. (Keys' white owner, Hawkins, had sold land there in 1834 to a man whose

The 22nd USCT took part in the hunt for Lincoln's assassin, John Wilkes Booth, who was fatally shot in a barn. (Courtesy Library of Congress.)

son, Samuel Cox, attained a measure of infamy for assisting the fleeing Booth.[6]) After four days of scouring the marshes and seeking tips from local blacks, the soldiers got word that Booth had been cornered and shot dead in a barn down in Virginia.

The 22nd might have been deployed back to Richmond at that point, but for the churning politics of race. By war's end, nearly half of the federal forces in and around Richmond were black—and white Virginians were complaining loudly about having the all-black 25th Corps occupy their capital and hold sway over them. There also were reports that some black soldiers were in communication with roving black militants who hoped to form separatist communities in the South.[7] Henry Halleck, the occupation commander, was leery of USCT troops anyway, and decided to minimize his problems. Over the dissent of his corps commanders, Halleck engineered a move to have the entire black corps, including the 22nd regiment, sent to the far reaches of Texas.[8] The 22nd would spend its final six months of service patrolling the Rio Grande border, fighting mosquitoes and thirst while on the hunt for any Rebel holdouts.

THROUGHOUT THIS PERIOD, meanwhile, the 3rd USCT remained on duty in Florida, six hundred miles south of Washington. The dangerous raids into the bayous continued, including a notable one in early March 1865. Samuel Bates, in his history of the Pennsylvania volunteers, says a twenty-nine-man patrol "proceeded sixty miles up the St. John's River in boats, rowing by night, and hiding in the swamps by day . . . and gathered fifty or sixty contrabands, besides several horses and wagons, burned store-houses and a distillery belonging to the rebel government, and returned bringing their recruits and spoils safely into camp." The expedition won praise from the general commanding the Department of the South. In his commendation, Maj. Gen. Quincy Gillmore noted, "When returning they were attacked by a band of over fifty cavalry, whom they defeated and drove off with a loss of more than thirty to the rebels. After a long and rapid march they arrived at Saint Augustine on March 12, having lost but 2 killed and 4 wounded. This expedition, planned and executed by colored men under the command of a colored non-commissioned officer, reflects great credit upon the brave participants and their leader."

Following the Confederate surrender, the Norris brothers and their comrades in the 3rd assumed a new role as occupying authorities, encountering open scorn from Southern whites. Many of the soldiers, by then combat-hardened and testy, would shock the whites by meeting their contempt head-on. Pvt. William B. Johnson, of Philadelphia, described an ugly face-off that occurred in May as the regiment's troop train was en route to Tallahassee. "The cars stopped for wood, when the platforms of the cars were immediately crowded with white and colored persons, all eager to catch a glimpse of the 'black soldiers,'" Johnson wrote to the *Christian Recorder*. "Some deep dyed villain made the remark that all the n**s should be in—(a place of not very moderate temperature.) A moment afterward, twenty guns were pointed at his heart; and one man, more angry and revengeful than the rest, discharged his piece, the ball grazing the speaker's cheek; and if it had been a little closer, Johnnie would have been no more, and would, in all probability, have received a through-ticket for the locality which he named."[9]

A Union officer told the man to be gone "lest a worse evil came upon him." The Southerner was learning that new rules were in force, and they didn't include kowtowing. Private Johnson noted with satisfaction that another white man from the vicinity who had given an enslaved boy three hundred lashes the day before had been hauled in to await trial, while a third was arrested for stabbing a black man.

Much the way black veterans of World Wars I and II would bristle at the Jim Crow conditions that awaited them back home, many proud USCT soldiers by 1865 had lost tolerance for their people's mistreatment. The anger sometimes boiled over, and in Jacksonville that October, it led to a mutiny. Some troops of the 3rd "rioted after seeing a comrade tied up by his thumbs as punishment for an offense that the court-martial records never clearly specified but was probably insubordination," writes historian Donald R. Shaffer. "White officers quickly suppressed the mutiny, and several of the ringleaders were executed after being convicted in swift courts-martial. Yet Jacksonville was merely an extreme example of the fact that, with the war over, black soldiers were less tolerant of punishments that offended their manhood."[10]

A "GRAND REVIEW" OF THE VICTORIOUS UNION ARMIES was held in May 1865, in Washington. More than one hundred fifty thousand servicemen paraded through the capital, yet no black troops were included. While the volatile issue of race may have played a role in the omission, it was also the case that few USCT soldiers were available. Their three-year enrollments had yet to expire, and many of their units remained on duty in the South, like the 3rd and the 22nd, enforcing order and safeguarding emancipation.

The black community of Harrisburg rectified the situation six months later, on November 14, by holding a special grand review and ball for black troops. Many USCT regiments had been mustered out of service by then, so men from more than twenty-five states were able to take part. Harrisburg was a busy transit point

The USCT Grand Review was re-enacted in Harrisburg in 2010, shown here, and commemorated again in 2015. (Courtesy Yulanda Burgess.)

for the military, making it well-situated to host what became the only national event honoring the USCT. The festivities included a procession before cheering onlookers and dignitaries, including Lincoln's first secretary of war, Simon Cameron, an early advocate of black soldiery. Leaders of the new black Equal Rights League heralded the returning servicemen as heroes and said their sacrifices in combat ought to merit greater legal rights for their people—including a restoration of voting rights in Pennsylvania. A parade banner underscored the point, declaring "He who defends liberty is worthy of all its franchises."

In an optimistic report on the event, the loyalist *Cleveland Daily Leader* said the accolades "illustrate completely the wonderful progress which we have made as a nation toward the recognition of equal rights, during the last five years. That such an ovation could have been held at all in a Northern city—that it should call out popular sympathy, instead of riot and disorder— that it should be participated in by men high in social, political and military life—that it should be indorsed by our most distinguished generals, in letters written to a committee of colored men—that, indeed, there should be any colored soldiers to greet—are all evidences of the great change which the war has wrought upon the national conscience and heart."[11]

It's not known if any of the Waverly vets were present in Harrisburg that day, but they certainly could have been. The 22nd USCT had men in the procession, and their commander, the indefatigable Joseph Kiddoo, by then an official for the Freedman's Bureau, was called forward to address the crowd. There were also contingents from three other regiments—the 3rd USCT, the 54th Massachusetts, and the 11th US Colored Heavy Artillery—whose ranks included men who would live out their days in Waverly.

This undated photo, titled Return of Colored Troop, *shows a formal procession outside the courthouse in Montrose. (Courtesy Susquehanna County Historical Society, Montrose, PA.)*

By mid-November 1865, John Sampson and the Norris brothers of the 3rd had been mustered out in Jacksonville, while George Keys Jr., John Washington, and William Bradley of the 22nd had been demobilized in Brownsville, Texas. Individuals from other black units also were able to begin solo journeys to Waverly: Richard Lee, injured in Florida while serving in the 25th USCT; Samuel McDonald, disabled in Louisiana while with the 11th Colored Heavy Artillery; and Samuel Thomas, a cook in the famous 54th Massachusetts, who was mustered out in Charleston.

There is no evidence of Waverly's organizing a public ceremony to honor its returning soldiers, white or black. (A ceremony for black troops was held in front of the courthouse in Montrose, while the white vets of the 143rd Pennsylvania "were received with great honors" in Wilkes-Barre in June.) It would have been left to the churches of Waverly and environs, along with families and neighbors, to welcome back their servicemen with open arms, one by one. The Colored Hill community must have been overjoyed to see its men again. Villagers often said the ecstatic praise and singing from the little church could be heard a block away. That would have been doubly true during the homecomings of late 1865.

The sudden re-entry into civilian life must have been dizzying for the black vets. All the prayers and embraces certainly were a balm, and seeing their families two years grown would have been pure delight. White allies stepped forward to offer the vets work and continuing support. The village Methodists celebrated their bond that year by presenting a large pulpit Bible inscribed to "the Colored Congregation of the M.E. Church, Waverly, Pa." Most of the veterans came home with discharge bonuses, tangible proof of their manhood and worth as breadwinners. The Army had let them buy their muskets, and those who did could display the weapons with pride and skill. (In coming years, they could bring out the guns for the big communal hunts that happened the day before Thanksgiving.) When asked, the men might gamely tell about their victories at Petersburg and Morris Island, about seeing famous men, vanquishing the Johnnies, and setting slaves free.

Yet beneath the brave faces, the men bore indelible scars. Among them, only Wesley Baptiste, George Keys Jr., and John Sampson had returned from service physically unscathed. The reunions on Colored Hill would have brought them the grim news about Asbury Johnson. They'd reconnect with John Mason, who had been back for a year, disabled with that mangled right hand. They'd learn that George Keys Sr. had been carried home in April and remained in bad shape, bedridden in the care of his family. The vets could commiserate together about their own various wounds and ailments, which would turn out to impair most of them for the

THE COST OF COMBAT

It did not take long for the Northern public to learn the full extent of the USCT's service and sacrifices. In early 1866, the Federal Colored Bureau issued a report that one hundred eighty-six thousand sixty-seven people of color had fought for the Union cause. They comprised nearly a tenth of the federal military and saw action in nearly forty significant battles. Most of the men hailed from Southern or border states, as free-blacks or escaped slaves, while thirty-three thousand others enlisted in Northern states, including eighty-six hundred in Pennsylvania. Despite the white public's skepticism, the men acquitted themselves honorably. Fewer than five percent deserted, one-third the rate of whites. Twenty-three won the Medal of Honor.

Of the three hundred sixty thousand Union servicemen dead, thirty-eight thousand were black men. An untold number of others returned home with war wounds or injuries from accidents on duty. Disease ravaged the USCT ranks. Pneumonia, typhoid, and other ailments were the main killers, claiming black soldiers at a significantly higher rate than whites. "By the time the government had mustered them out of service, many of these men were physical wrecks, and it took months of care before they were able to work regularly," writes historian Joseph T. Glatthaar. "Still, many resumed employment immediately, but over the years they lost days and weeks battling recurrent bouts of malaria and chronic diarrhea."[12]

The racial slights did not let up. Even after the war, Glatthaar notes, "there were no black artillery batteries because the War Department thought artillery was too complicated for the black race, even though there had been numerous light and heavy artillery batteries composed of black men that performed well in the war."[13] In coming years, black veterans would frequently find their pension applications treated more harshly and white vets keeping their distance from them.

Abraham Lincoln had written presciently that when peace finally came, "there will be some black men who can remember that, with silent tongue, and clenched teeth, and steady eye, and well-poised bayonet, they have helped mankind on to this great consummation; while, I fear, there will be some white ones, unable to forget that, with malignant heart, and deceitful speech, they have strove to hinder it."

rest of their lives. Their pension paperwork reveals how, on many days, they would labor to keep their bodies working. Like combat veterans everywhere who struggle to make peace with their memories, they would sometimes drift into a distant silence. The lovely surrounding pastureland could now conjure fields of battle and evoke the carnage the men had seen, the violence they'd committed, and the comrades they'd left behind.

WHILE THE COLORED HILL VETERANS must have mulled the price they had paid, none of them joined the chorus of emboldened voices, including from within the USCT, calling for full citizenship rights. Though the war may have radicalized some of the dozen, perhaps they lacked the gift of oratory, or simply craved a return to peace and normalcy. They certainly wouldn't want to bring undue trouble on Colored Hill, knowing that the vicinity still had its share of angry, unrepentant copperheads, as well as War Democrats who looked askance at the black cause.

Some local sympathizers—white sympathizers— were speaking up on their behalf. That summer the thirty-three-church Abington Baptist Association met in Waverly and declared that God "hath triumphed gloriously" against slavery, and urged "that henceforth all Christians and all people, including the Magistracy, shall in all their political, commercial, moral and social relations, act on the principles of exact justice and equality to all people in all things, and that no distinction of color shall operate under this adjustment to restrict the right to vote for laws to which we are all amenable." In an October editorial titled "Fair Play for the Negro," the weekly *Pittston Gazette* noted how "the 'despised race' bravely mingled their blood with that of the Anglo Saxon defenders of the constitution on many well fought fields. . . . The very least that can be done for the negro is to give him a fair and equal chance with the white man in the great race of life—and if he succeeds against the odds of color and the debasing effects of generations of servitude, he will show superior capacity to those who would make color and not character the criterion of merit."[14]

Rev. William Grow, a white Baptist minister who had been a fervent abolitionist, confronted the retrograde forces on a spiritual level. In the aftermath of the war, he was asked by Rev. William Miller (son of Waverly's Elder Miller) to leave his post in Scranton and assume the pulpit in Fleetville. In his 1902 memoir, Reverend Grow recalled how he hesitated because of Fleetville's "threefold manifestations of evil, anti-Unionism, spiritualism, and universalism. The place had contributed its full portion of men to an organized resistance to Uncle Sam's draft, the organization embracing Buttermilk Falls, Factoryville, and Benton."[15] He accepted the challenge, and after three weeks of hard sermonizing "the hosts of darkness were driven back."

Then there was Lyman B. Green's Fourth of July speech at Factoryville. The 30th Pennsylvania Infantry veteran (who'd served with Waverly mulatto Wesley Baptiste) had lost a brother at the Second Battle of Bull Run, and he had a bone to pick. "I have been for the last four years slandered, maligned, traduced and abused, stabbed in the front and rear, by the Copperheads of Benton," Green declared. He accused the Lincoln-haters of a litany of seditious acts and asked his listeners to pray for them as "the most miserable God-forsaken class of sinners to be found in the country."[16]

Were many minds changed by such exhortations? It's not clear. In the October 1865 county elections, Abington and Greenfield Townships went Republican, but Benton, Newton, and Waverly stayed in the Democratic fold. In old-line Waverly, the tally was 36-26 for the Democratic slate. Waverly would eventually flip to Republican as its white war vets prodded a new generation of voters. But for the time being, the black residents of Waverly decided to keep a prudent silence in the civic realm. It would be a decade before one of their own, George Keys' son Ed, would speak out publicly for equal rights.

Elsewhere, black leaders were challenging discrimination. Early in 1865, the Pennsylvania State Equal Rights League had been organized to push for progress. James Davenger, of Pittston, and Jonathan Jasper Wright, of Wilkes-Barre, were elected to leadership roles at the league's founding convention in Harrisburg. In a strategy speech to delegates, Wright said the state must be pressured to restore "that which was unjustly wrested from us in 1838—the right of franchise. We have come to ask that our white fellow-citizens may act as though they believed in their own Declaration of Independence, and especially in its assertion, that all men are created equal."[17] It was a bold challenge to white hegemony. Republicans held a majority in the Harrisburg statehouse, but they declined to work for black suffrage. The issue lay dead in both chambers that year.

A call to abolish school segregation also went nowhere. Segregated schools retained wide support among whites, including Republicans, who "were convinced that African Americans were inferior and therefore that education could do little, if anything, to elevate them. These whites believed that the races should be separated wherever possible, particularly in the public schools, where they felt their children's welfare was most at stake."[18] The Pennsylvania legislature would not overturn the 1850s school segregation law until 1881.

THE NEXT YEAR, 1866, brought more mixed tidings. Pennsylvania Republicans once again avoided action on black suffrage. On the other hand, they also thwarted Democrats by passing a law disenfranchising war deserters and levying hefty fines on violators and election officials who tried to abet them.

In Washington, the Republican-controlled Congress enacted the Civil Rights Act of 1866 over the veto of President Andrew Johnson. Coming on the heels of

Hiester Clymer and the Democrats ran on a white supremacist platform. He lost statewide but captured Luzerne County and towns including Waverly. (Courtesy Library of Congress.)

the Thirteenth Amendment abolishing slavery, the act extended rights enjoyed by white citizens to all adult males "without distinction of race or color, or previous condition of slavery or involuntary servitude." Though it stopped short of granting the vote, the law did give blacks the considerable new rights to own property, make contracts, and testify in court.

The Democrats, true to form, were livid. "Both defeated Confederates and Democratic journalists in the North predicted that Republican policies would usher in a 'mongrel republic,'" writes historian Nancy Isenberg. "They drew paranoid comparisons to the Mexican Republic, the nineteenth century example of racial amalgamation run amok."[19] Democrats saw a political opening in Pennsylvania, where the governor's seat was up for grabs in 1866. They warned of a slippery slope toward the black vote and the power-sharing that would result. Their platform that year was explicit: "The white race alone is entitled to the control of the government of the Republic, and we are unwilling to grant to negroes the right to vote."

Pennsylvania Democrats produced a series of fear-mongering posters and rhetoric on behalf of their gubernatorial candidate, a state senator from Berks County named Hiester Clymer. One typical poster depicted buffoonish blacks crowding white men away from the polls, with the whites complaining, "Negroes rule us now. We have no chance here." That was a hallmark of the white nationalists: *It's either them or us. Yield anything and all is lost.* There could be no middle ground, no compromising, and no sharing of power. To use a modern term, it was a zero-sum game.

Democratic newspapers repeatedly accused the Republican candidate for governor, Union Maj. Gen. John W. Geary, of favoring black suffrage and its consequences. The *Lackawanna Register*, of Scranton, warned that anyone "who votes for the bombast Geary votes also in favor of negro suffrage, negro equality, high taxation, amalgamation, disunion, another war, and all the evils that abolition fanaticism can inflict upon our country and race."[20]

The Republicans equivocated. While saying the "natural rights" of black people should be protected, they wouldn't take a stand on suffrage, perhaps seeing little gain in it with the white electorate. Geary himself tried to avoid the issue.

The Republicans found a potent campaign weapon of their own, meanwhile. By pointing out that Clymer was a copperhead who had appeased the South and opposed the soldier vote, they were able to mobilize many Union war veterans. Returned servicemen began rallying for Geary much the way the "Wide-Awake" clubs strutted for Abraham Lincoln in 1860. The *Pittston*

Gazette noted that the loyalist vets wanted "'to labor patriotically to perpetuate results which every soldier had periled his life to achieve.' Let each soldier remember that while Geary marched and fought with them, Clymer opposes the cause in which the soldiers fought and opposed giving them the right to vote in the field. What soldier can hesitate in his choice between the two candidates?"[21]

"Boys in Blue" clubs formed around the state that summer to support Geary. A large rally was held September 21 in Waverly. Groups came by special train from Scranton and held their gathering on the village's main street, "there being no hall able to hold one-half of the people who were out," reported the *Scranton Weekly Republican*.[22] Sixty people enlisted on the spot for "the short and glorious campaign which will wind up, Oct. 9, with the disastrous rout of the copperheads and rebel sympathizers of these parts," the paper said. ". . . At Waverly and the Green [Clarks Green] it is thought at least 150 veterans will be enrolled."

Election Day brought a hard-fought victory for the Republicans. Geary won the governorship by seventeen thousand votes out of nearly six hundred thousand cast statewide. In Luzerne County, however, most voters were Democrats to the end. Clymer and the county's Lincoln-loathing Congressman, Charles Denison, easily won Luzerne, and Democrats swept the county row offices by a series of thirty-seven hundred vote margins. The results showed Northern Luzerne to be an electoral crazy-quilt: Geary took the two Abington districts, Greenfield, and Scott, while Clymer and the Democratic slate captured Benton, Newton, Ransom, and Waverly. The Republicans did fare reasonably well in Waverly, losing by only forty-two to twenty-four, and they might have done even better had not a village resident, William Smith, been a draw on the Democratic ticket as the

'THE DEMOCRATIC BOUNTY LIE'

In the heat of the 1866 gubernatorial race, the Democrats were manufacturing falsehoods to whip up their base. Dr. Jonathan C. Miles, Waverly's town doctor, was sick and tired of it. On October 5, four days before the election, he responded in the *Scranton Republican.*

Miles had the newspaper repeat an item of disinformation that had appeared in the Democratic weekly, the *Lackawanna Register.* According to the bogus item, "Congress passed an act giving $300 bounty to the negro soldiers. A few weeks afterwards they passed an act giving a bounty of $50 and $100 to the white soldiers who had served two years respectively. The negroes being the first provided for must be paid; and it found when they are done, there will be no money left for the payment of bounties to white soldiers. Thus the negro is not only given from three to six times as much as the white soldiers but he is paid and the white man must wait for his bounty until he can get it."

The doctor unloaded. "Every word of this about negro soldiers is FALSE — made from whole cloth, and without a shadow of foundation or excuse," he wrote. "No act giving any bounty at all to negro soldiers was passed at the last session. Dr. Miles, of Waverly, will give ONE HUNDRED dollars to any man who will prove the truth of the democratic BOUNTY LIE."

What drove the doctor to act? There were several likely reasons. He was already a Republican activist and a member of its county vigilance committee. He was a neighbor and protégé of abolitionists Rodman Sisson, John Raymond, and Leonard Batchelor (the latter having boarded in his home for a time). The doctor's rounds would have taken him to Colored Hill. In fact, throughout 1866 he'd been attending to the gravely injured George Keys Sr. Becoming intimately aware of the sacrifices of the black vets and the tribulations of their families must have made him disgusted with the *Register*'s racial calumny. It's not known if anyone took Dr. Miles up on his hundred-dollar challenge — nearly $1,500 today — but his rebuke would have reverberated in Waverly.

(winning) county commissioner candidate. Among the defeated was Benton-born Republican reformer Lyman B. Green, the "traduced and abused" war vet, who lost his freshman bid for county commissioner.

The 1866 election made it clear that Pennsylvania's inner civil war had not ended. Geary won the day, but his Democratic adversaries would recover in coming years. Waverly reflected that muddled picture: Democrats would keep a slight majority in the village for two more decades—and yet its many "Boys in Blue" had infused fresh Republican blood. That must have pleased the still-disenfranchised residents of Colored Hill.

1. *Christian Recorder* (Philadelphia), March 18, 1865 (Accessible Archives, online).
2. *Christian Recorder*, March 4, 1865 (Accessible Archives, online).
3. Trudeau, Noah Andre. *Like Men of War: Black Troops in the Civil War 18662-1865* (Toronto, Canada: Little Brown & Co.), p. 434.
4. Brooks, Noah *Washington in Lincoln's Time* (Washington, DC: Century Co., 1895), p. 235.
5. Power, J. C. *Abraham Lincoln: His Great Funeral Cortege, from Washington City to Springfield, Illinois With a History and Description of the National Lincoln Monument* (Springfield, IL: publisher not identified, 1872), p. 34.
6. Maryland land records show a 1834 deed of sale from John L. Hawkins to Hugh Cox, both of Charles County. Hawkins was Keys' owner. Hugh Cox was the father of Samuel Cox, who hid Booth and attempted to spirit him to Virginia.
7. Scott, Donald Sr. *Camp William Penn: 1863-1865* (Atglen, PA: Schiffer Publishing Ltd., 2012), p. 214.
8. Shaffer, Donald R. *After the Glory: The Struggles of Black Civil War Veterans* (Lawrence, Kansas: University of Kansas Press, 2004), p. 27.
9. *Christian Recorder*, July 8, 1865 (Accessible Archive, online).
10. Shaffer, op. cit., p. 29.
11. *Cleveland Daily Leader* (Cleveland), Nov. 17, 1865, p. 2.
12. Glatthaar, Joseph T. *Forged in Battle: The Civil War Alliance of Black Soldiers and White Officers* (New York: Free Press, 1990), p. 242.
13. Ibid., p. 234.
14. *Pittston Gazette* (Pittston, PA), Oct. 26, 1865, p. 2.
15. Grow, Rev. William B. *Eighty-Five Years of Life and Labor* (Carbondale, PA: self-published, 1902), p. 107.
16. *Pittston Gazette*, Aug. 3, 1865, pp. 1-2.
17. *Proceedings of the State Equal Rights Convention, of the Colored People of Pennsylvania, Held in the City of Harrisburg* (Harrisburg: printed by the convention in 1865, in file at the Historical Society of Pennsylvania), p. 4.
18. Davis, Hugh. *"We Will Be Satisfied With Nothing Less": The African American Struggle for Equal Rights in the North During Reconstruction* (Ithaca, N.Y.: Cornell University Press, 2011), p. 73.
19. Isenberg, Nancy. *White Trash: The 400-Year Untold History of Class in America* (New York: Viking Press, 2016), p. 182.
20. *Lackawanna Register* (Scranton), Sept. 27, 1866, p. 2.
21. *Pittston Gazette*, May 17, 1866, p. 2.
22. *Scranton Weekly Republican* (Scranton), Sept 21, 1866.

CHAPTER TEN

1867–1925

"We Ask for an Equal Footing"

———•·❖·•———

RACIAL PROGRESS would remain maddeningly uneven for the remainder of the black veterans' lives. No sooner had the war ended than the challenges became apparent. Slavery was outlawed with the Thirteenth Amendment to the US Constitution, and yet difficult fights emerged to enact the Fourteenth Amendment granting blacks citizenship, and the Fifteenth granting the vote. A supplemental equal-rights bill would be stalled in the US Congress for years. Across most of the North, including Pennsylvania, discriminatory laws and customs remained in place. The intransigent Democrats still controlled Luzerne County and were surging again statewide, while Republicans waffled on their support for black rights.

Fortunately, there were pockets of harmony like Waverly. Colored Hill had busily increased its footprint, the line of simple homes stretching farther down Carbondale Road by 1870 to house the Norrises, the Keyses, the Burgettes, the Washingtons, the Smiths, the Johnsons, the Williamses, and the Lesters. Other people were being taken in as boarders, either on Colored Hill or on the premises of white employers thereabouts. The black population for a mile around stabilized at about fifty, a mix of original inhabitants and newcomers from Montrose, Binghamton, and beyond. [*See Map 2, "Waverly, Pennsylvania, 1860–1880" on page xvi.*]

The valor of the USCT men had earned Colored Hill an extra measure of goodwill. As its veterans began applying for military disability pensions, they had no difficulty finding local whites who were ready to vouch for them in writing.

Best of all, the primary schools were still enrolling the black children without incident. In an era when Pennsylvania still authorized segregated schools, Waverly had managed to make interracial education its status quo. A white resident named George Stevenson would recall his own experience at a one-room schoolhouse, the Miller School, just south of the village, around 1870. "About half of the pupils were from the colored settlement at Waverly, this school being nearest to their homes,"[1] Stevenson wrote in a 1931 memoir. The black pupils' names were still clear to him: Ed Keys, George Brown "and various members of the Robinson, Lee, Washington, Hardy, Baptiste, Talbots, etc." Remarkably, he added that "the most popular playmates among the younger boys were the boys from the colored settlement."

The classroom integration would continue for decades. The Waverly Graded School's monthly reports for 1874 listed 12-year-old Mary Bradley as working on her Watson Speller and sister Lucretia, 5, progressing with her Towns Speller and Definer. Sarah Burgett joined the roster in 1875, followed by Lloyd Lee in 1876. The names in 1885 and 1886 included Gertie Johnson, Naomi Talbott, Daisy White, Willie Lee, and Elisha Johnson. If Stevenson's recollection was correct, his white pals not only tolerated black classmates but were drawn to them. The Keys brothers, George and Ed, and George Brown would go on to make names for themselves beyond Waverly. The education they'd received there as boys helped to instill the confidence and comportment they would need to succeed. Race relations among Waverly's adults were evidently untroubled as well, though not as carefree as among their children. Over the years, there was no indication of strong personal friendships or business partnerships across the racial line. Nor were there any hints of interracial romance, which would have been taboo. Social conventions of the day required a decorous reserve, which meant daily affairs proceeded in a polite, if superficial, manner. People were expected to be law-abiding and pious, so it must have been an everlasting relief to white allies that people on Colored Hill minded their ways. There was only one account of a troublemaker, an unnamed black fellow who raided his neighbors' gardens at night. It's said that whites and blacks banded together to run him out of town.[2] Even the reactionaries and old Democrats apparently had come to accept that Waverly's blacks, whatever they called them—"darkies," "mammies," or worse—played by the rules and were dependable laborers.

S. S. Kennedy's ledger recorded chores performed by Lot Norris and several other men of Colored Hill. (Courtesy Lackawanna Historical Society, Scranton.)

The older, slave-born residents did seem habituated to the modest work provided them. Postwar census records from the area continued to list most of the black adults as laborers and domestics. One of Waverly's white landowners, the Rev. Samuel S. Kennedy, kept a farm ledger that recorded the hard, humble tasks they did for him on the parcels behind his home. Entries in 1873 include: "making fence – Lee – 1.00," "paid Wm Bradley for cutting brush and ditching on 7-acre lot – 2.50," "paid

Lot Norris for laying wall on 7 acre lot – 2.00," "paid J. Burgett .25."[3] Similarly, the 1879 diary of local farm wife Susan Parker noted how her stout field hand, George Diggs, also called "Daddy Diggs," planted potatoes and dug the manure for her husband.

Former slave Ignatius Thomas worked in the fields well into his seventies. The Waverly correspondent for the *Scranton Republican*, probably the Reverend Kennedy mentioned above, described how everyone knew the sound of Thomas's flail threshing oats, and said he produced better bundles of straw than any machine. Ignatius Thomas was "an example of politeness, a gentleman of Southern dialect and manners. . . . All of the colored people, and many of the white people, call him 'Papa Thomas,' and give him a pleasant recognition, and always receive a polite response for their civility."[4] Another old runaway, Edward Smith, also had become a fond sight around Waverly, known for sporting a high hat and cane that villagers had presented to him. He'd grown too infirm to work much, but his wife, ex-slave "Aunty" Smith, was a hardworking washerwoman until the end. It seemed to be that way with Colored Hill's aging fugitives. Conditioned to do strenuous manual labor, they would keep their minds positive and toil away until their bodies nearly gave out.

A number of the slave-born Civil War veterans, back home, tried to return to the rigors of farm work despite their tenuous health. Having shown their mettle as soldiers, they were determined to be useful as family breadwinners as best they knew how. An affidavit from John Stone recalled how, on three occasions, he had seen Samuel McDonald trying to work, but "fall down helpless in the field and have to be carried to the house." Another villager said William Bradley, "a very reliable man," could only work intermittently because of his war wound. Dr. Frederick Van Sickle said John Washington

Waverly's main street bustled with commerce in the postwar era. Several black-owned enterprises would join the mix. (This Is Waverly, *by Mildred Mumford.)*

"was unable to perform his usual vocation more than ¼ the time and not able to do hard work even then."

But also during those years, other residents of Colored Hill, mostly younger fellows, were setting their sights higher. Waverly had become a commercial hub—bustling with agricultural and domestic supply stores, a large hotel, nearby tanneries, mills, smithies, a fish hatchery, and other businesses—and those men saw opportunity. The Waverly entry in the Scranton City Directory for 1867-68 already listed two enterprising black businessmen in Waverly: Richard Lee as a barber, and Paige Wells as a huckster selling vegetables. In coming years, Wells would become a butcher and Ed Keys a barber, or "tonsorial artist," with a shop over one of the village stores. Tom Crummel opened a small cider mill on Foundry Alley. Asbury Johnson's brother John became a busy dealer in meats and tobacco. An 1883 item in the *Scranton Evening Times* noted the opening of "a first-class meat market" in Waverly "by Mr. James, a colored man, formerly in the employ of Lindley and

Wilson, of Scranton." Their particular enterprises were acceptable to the social order and served to deepen the symbiosis between the village and Colored Hill.

WAVERLY'S RACIAL EASE would express itself in two other significant ways during the postwar era. One involved the area's veteran "Boys in Blue," and the other, the faith communities.

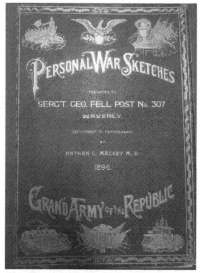

The Waverly GAR post, unlike most, was integrated from the outset. (Courtesy Lackawanna Historical Society, Scranton.)

In 1883, surviving Civil War vets gathered to establish a post of the Grand Army of the Republic in Waverly. The national GAR, much like the later American Legion and VFW, provided military veterans with fellowship and material support. The new Sgt. George Fell Post 307 was named in memory of the Waverly native who died at Gettysburg. It would number one hundred forty-five members over the years. Nearly all of them were white, and yet they integrated themselves from the start. That was not the case elsewhere in the state. The GAR organization, while officially opposing segregation, in truth acquiesced where whites refused to accept black vets as members. Pennsylvania had fifteen "colored" posts at the time (and would add a sixteenth in Wilkes-Barre in 1884). To its credit, the Waverly post enrolled black war vets William Bradley, Richard Lee, and Samuel Thomas as charter members without ado. Bradley was even appointed Officer of the Guard, an essential organizing role for reunion encampments. The Post 307 minutes referred to the three as "Comrades" and avoided the label "Colored" so often attached gratuitously to black names in newspapers and other public records of the era. The post's inclusiveness could have been due to the New England Yankee heritage of its membership. In New England, the GAR leadership was uniformly Republican and majority-white posts "were proud to accept members from black regiments, particularly if they had been wounded in action."[5]

Comrade Bradley's case showed how members of the Fell post were there for one another. By about 1880, Bradley had found farm labor too physically taxing and filed a disability claim, citing his Petersburg wound. The pension examiner denied the claim, saying Bradley was "not disabled for manual labor in any pensionable degree." Villagers, including white comrades, provided a fresh round of affidavits to attest that he was indeed "broken down in body" and at least two-thirds disabled. As a result, Bradley secured a $6 per month pension. And the GAR post did more, hiring him to be its janitor. He set up chairs for the meetings and cleaned and polished the guns, sticking to light tasks he was able to perform. Post 307 met monthly on Saturday evenings above the Cowles store, and Bradley earned a tidy seventy-five cents per meeting.

In addition to camaraderie, the GAR provided practical benefits. Its members would make sick calls to one another, pay for medicines, arrange nurse visits, offer graveside military rites, and see to the needs of widows and survivors. Unfortunately, six of Colored Hill's war veterans—Asbury Johnson, George Keys Sr., John Sampson, John Mason, Samuel McDonald, and Wesley Baptiste—could not take advantage of Post 307's services. They were all dead by the time the post formed in 1883. But in coming years, Comrades Bradley, Lee, Thomas, and their families would lean heavily on GAR beneficence. (Details of each of the thirteen veterans'

A MAN KNOWS A MAN.

"Give me your hand, Comrade! We have each lost a Leg for the good cause; but, thank God, we never lost Heart."

The ideal of comradeship across the racial line prevailed in the Waverly veterans post. (Courtesy Collection of the New York Historical Society.)

last years are presented in the chapter titled "The Final Bugle Call.")

In addition to the GAR bond was Waverly's postwar harmony through the churches. It was equally strong and even longer-lived. Every summer for at least thirty years, Waverly AME held a large outdoor revival that was open to all. Services took place over several days and nights in a clearing in the woods behind the church, evoking the "bush meetings" of slavery days. The grounds were outfitted with bleachers, a preaching platform, a refreshment stand, torches, and an old tin canal horn to call the crowd.[6] It became an interracial tradition that, at its peak, featured guest preachers and visiting choirs. White villagers, forever intrigued by the vibrancy of black worship, attended for the faith and the spectacle. In time they were joined by black church delegations and white curiosity-seekers from as far away as Wilkes-Barre. The revival became the church's primary fund-raiser so the collection plate was sure to be passed—and passed again whenever the better-off whites were present.

Waverly AME reached its zenith on the strength of those summer revivals, supplemented by the dimes and quarters its members were donating the rest of the year. By 1880, the congregation had thirty-four members and four probationers. Old-timers would later tell town historian William Lewis that the sanctuary was an impressive space in its heyday, with high-backed seats, a raised pulpit, an organ and stove at the front, a curved ceiling, and sets of lamp brackets along the walls. The Sunday school was flourishing, with two dozen youngsters enrolled, and there was a library and "a literary society, well-sustained."[7] Rev. Anthony Waldron, who lived in a snug parsonage out back, reported in 1881 that "our little church is in good condition at present."[8]

The summer revivals drew coverage in area newspapers from the 1870s into the 1900s. As the *Scranton Republican* reported in 1893, "On Sunday last the colored people of Waverly held their annual grove meeting in Fell's woods and a large number of white people attended, the attraction seeming not to diminish from year to year."[9] In 1899, the Lake Winola correspondent wrote this: "Knowing of the colored people's camp meeting at Waverly, a large number of our people wended their way in that direction. In consequence, the Lake Sunday School was nearly deserted by officers and teachers. Most of the classes were left to teach themselves or to be cared for by strangers. It has been suggested that next year someone go out to Waverly and bring the colored people here, thus saving our people a long drive and a tiresome day."

The featured sermon at the 1899 revival was "Is the World Growing Better?" The eulogist, Rev. H. A. Grant of Scranton's Bethel AME, looked to the new century in a positive light: "'There may be rotten spots on the earth, as there are sometimes on the fairest fruit,' he said of human endeavors, but in general, 'one cannot doubt for a moment that the process has been a lifting and not a depressing one.'"[10]

Reverend Grant was pointing his interracial audience toward the progress and social acceptance his community yearned to bring about. Black leaders of the era urged their people to model good citizenship and respectability. Their churches worked hard at collective uplift through literary societies, youth groups, social outings, and educational events. Newspaper items indicate that was certainly the case on Colored Hill. In 1894, Waverly AME hosted a well-attended public lecture on temperance led by a white man, George Olzer, from nearby Glenburn.[11] In 1898, a Waverly AME church item mentioned a birthday party and social that "promises to be a fine affair. The solos and duets rendered by Mesdames R.A. Robinson and A. Nelson will be a rare treat to all who attend." That same year, Waverly's white Methodist church held a winter revival whose guest preachers included an AME evangelist from Scranton. First Baptist Church of Abington got in the spirit, too, inviting Rev. J. B. Boddie, the charismatic pastor of Scranton's black Shiloh Baptist, to come to Waverly to be its guest preacher a few years later.

WITH NEW GENERATIONS COMING OF AGE, Colored Hill was housing a wide mix of personalities. Its founders were Southern transplants who stuck to their rural ways and spoke in the down-home vernacular of their upbringing. They and their unschooled, unpolished manner dominated the recollections that white old-timers would pass down. Mildred Mumford, in her folk history from 1954, *This Is Waverly*, highlighted only those people and seemed to revel in caricaturing them. She wrote, for instance, of how Hardy Lester would "break loose and howl" in church, saying "it takes a heap o' prayin', and a big wrassel wid de Lawd to get rid o' yore sins."[12] Those voices were no doubt present, but so were the dignified voices of Reverend Grant and Mesdames Robinson and Nelson. The ladies represented a worldlier new breed that was becoming an important part of Colored Hill. Some of them were the children of the village, growing into adulthood able to read and write and aspire, while some came to Waverly as adults from elsewhere. Two are of particular note: Ed Keys, the proud, enterprising younger son of fallen war hero George Keys Sr., and Grant Tillman, a formidable Scranton native who moved to Waverly after marrying Lot Norris' granddaughter, Elizabeth. Consider Ed Keys' case first:

Ed was a teenager of 16 when his father returned from the war gravely wounded. He would have been at George Keys' sickbed to help change his dressing, read to him from the newspapers, and witness his agonizing decline. Ed probably also helped his illiterate parents navigate the military's confusing pension system. By the time George Sr. died in 1867, he was receiving a mere $4 a month, one-fifth the income of an average black family. It's likely that Ed also was able to help his mother, Hannah, through the process of securing a war widow's pension. She was granted $8 a month, but it didn't come through until October 1868, more than a year and a half after his father's death, and required her to go to Wilkes-Barre to meet with an examiner.

Being interested in current events—in fact, being a budding activist—Ed would have been alert to the ways the pension system was stacked against poor and unlettered blacks. Historian Donald R. Shaffer has documented that black Civil War vets and their families "did not receive an equal share of the benefits and trod a harder path than white applicants to obtain them."[13] Pension bureaucrats "had difficulty dealing with people who had changed their names and could offer neither vital dates nor other specific information," Shaffer states in *After the Glory: The Struggles of Black Civil War Veterans*. "The inability of many black applicants to follow the conventional path of proving their worthiness led to frustration and suspicion on the part of pension bureaucrats. . . . Although [they] often overlooked defects in white pension cases, they were less likely to do so for African Americans or to give them any benefit of the doubt."[14]

Pension inequity was not the only civil rights issue that would aggrieve Ed Keys and others like him. Events built up to the point that Keys was moved to speak out publicly, in 1874. In 1868, the Pennsylvania legislature had killed an effort to drop the word *white* from the state constitution's suffrage clause. The vote was a resounding sixty-eight to fourteen, with hard-line Democrats joined by Republicans who fretted that the proposed reform was "premature."[15] Men of color did obtain the vote two years later, but only because the Fifteenth Amendment made it law on a national level. The black communities in Scranton and Wilkes-Barre celebrated the amendment with parades and prayer services, knowing how bitterly area Democrats had resisted ratification. Blacks took up the Republican banner and played crucial roles in local election victories in Philadelphia and Harrisburg, and in winning the next two governorships. However, as Ed

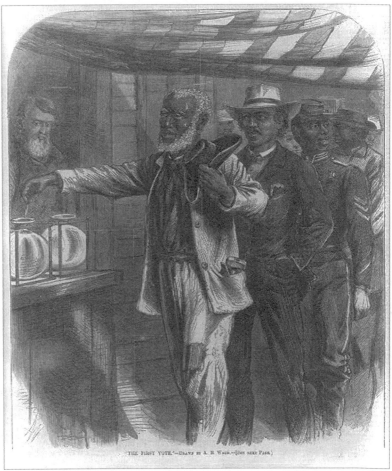

The Fifteenth Amendment gave black men the vote in 1870, but many civil rights challenges remained. (Courtesy Library of Congress.)

Keys would experience, his people soon felt Republican leaders in both Harrisburg and Washington "took them for granted, exploited their vote, and disrespected them with menial patronage jobs."[16]

Through the state Equal Rights Leagues, black activists began pressuring Republican lawmakers in Congress to make amends by passing a Civil Rights Bill put forward in 1870 by Sen. Charles Sumner, a Radical Republican from Massachusetts. Sumner's legislation sought to make the Fourteenth Amendment's guarantee

The Equal Rights League met nationally and in state conventions. Ed Keys of Waverly addressed the Pennsylvania convention as a state leader in 1874. (Courtesy Library of Congress.)

of legal equality concrete by banning racial discrimination in "public accommodations and transportation, churches, public amusements, restaurants, juries, cemeteries, and especially public schools."[17] Even though fellow Republicans controlled both houses of Congress, they kept Sumner's bill off the floor for years, arguing that the Fourteenth Amendment was sufficient—and no doubt fearing a backlash from white voters. Here's how the *Scranton Daily Times*, a Democratic organ, put it in 1874: "The extreme reluctance which the Republican members of Congress evince towards pushing the Civil Rights Bill would seem to indicate that they are doubtful of the policy of pushing the darky any farther to the front just now, or else a lingering sense of justice revolts at the idea of further pursuing oppressed and despairing white people of the South."[18] Black activists kept pressing as best as they could. In 1874, the Pennsylvania State Equal Rights League declared Sumner's bill "of paramount importance" and urged local chapters and supporters to speak out.

That is when Ed Keys, by then 25 and the Waverly barber, made himself heard. In August 1874,
he traveled to Reading to attend the state league's
annual convention. Keys felt unjustly treated on the
train ride down, which added bite to the remarks he
made on the convention floor. The *Reading Times*
quoted Keys as exclaiming, "We have been deserted
by our friends or pretended friends. The freedom of the
colored people is only a nominal thing. We insist upon
the Republican Party, upon our friends in both parties,
giving us free and impartial rights. We need these rights
for hotel, school and railroad purposes."[19]

In odd shifts of voice, the newspaper went on: "The
Republicans, at least the Republican organ of his county, Luzerne, say that we have these rights; that by the
passage of the Civil Rights Bill we will gain *more* privileges than the whites. The speaker contended that the
colored people had not the rights spoken of, and cited
an instance in his own case, where but yesterday he
was shown a smoking car to sit in, although he did not
desire to smoke, by a railroad brakeman. He said his
constituency would stand by the action of the League.
He said it was hard to denounce the whole party for the
delinquencies of a few. We ask for an equal footing, that
is all, and we ask that our Republican friends give us
this. The speaker concluded by saying that he and his
people asked for this as a right."

It's not clear when Ed Keys had joined the Equal
Rights League or what constituency he represented as
there is no evidence that Waverly had a chapter. A few
supporters may have simply pooled money to send him
to Reading on their behalf. In any case, by 1874, Ed had
been named to the league's state credentials committee,
giving him enough stature that his words bore weight.
The delegates adopted a resolution that day demanding that the Civil Rights Bill be passed, denouncing

Congressional delay as "evidence of the low standard of civilization which characterizes a large portion of the American people, and is a concomitant of slavery."

Sumner's Civil Rights Bill was finally enacted in 1875, but only after its call for integrated education had been deleted. White sentiment was steadily turning away from racial-justice measures in the North as well as in the Reconstruction South. Even many Republicans felt their constituents were tired of "the negro question." Ed would have been well aware of that. When he returned to Waverly, to barbering white heads in his shop over Cowles store, he could be satisfied knowing that *his* village, at least, had not gone cold.

Ed Keys was a restless sort who never raised a family of his own. In coming years, he would live and work as a barber in Pittston, Wilkes-Barre, and Scranton. He also tried his hand as a bootblack, shining shoes in Scranton, where he boarded for a time with his brother George. He became a Republican ward regular along with George, and is recorded as giving a speech at a black GOP campaign rally in Scranton in 1891.[20] By 1897, Ed was back in Waverly as a baker, advertising his goods as "first class in every respect." In 1898, a citizens' caucus selected him to be one of Waverly's two High Constables, serving warrants and collecting fines on behalf of the borough.[21]

TWO YEARS EARLIER, in January 1896, Grant Tillman had made town history when he was named to that same High Constable position. Since the 1870 amendment granting the vote, Waverly's black men had gained sway and probably helped to tip the hamlet into the Republican camp. Tillman's selection as constable was a crowning achievement—the first time the full citizens' caucus had reached across the color line to fill a borough post. It also picked John Johnson, son of a slave, meat dealer, and part-time gravedigger, for a seat on the Waverly borough council that year. Colored Hill, so long accustomed to subservience, now had two men with a measure of formal authority over inhabitants black and white.

Grant Tillman had been born in Scranton during the Civil War, named in honor of the famous Union general, just as his older brother was given the illustrious name Lincoln in 1860. (Lincoln "Link" Tillman followed in his father's footsteps and became a firefighter, Scranton's only firefighter of color at the time.) By 1880, Grant Tillman was a young clerk for a white butcher in Scranton. He might have met Elizabeth Norris at one of the grand summer revivals in Waverly. Their courtship led to marriage in 1888, the same year Lot Norris died. The newlyweds and their baby daughter moved into the Norris family's crowded abode on Colored Hill, even joined for a time by brother Link.

Link Tillman in his firefighter regalia. (Courtesy Collection of Anthracite Museum Complex, PHMC, Scranton.)

Grant Tillman, being of the new breed, was not afraid to challenge a wrong. Once in Waverly, he brought suit against a white man and won. This was not just any white man, either, but the future mayor of Scranton, Edmund B. Jermyn, the son of a wealthy coal operator. According to Tillman's 1895 lawsuit, which the *Scranton Republican* covered, Jermyn was a playboy who indulged in horse-racing and kept a stable of horses on a farm outside Waverly. Tillman claimed that Jermyn had hired him to tend his horses and owed him for two months' pay, plus board, for a total of $23.50. Jermyn's lawyer said only $20.00 was due. The jury sided with Tillman and added interest to his claim, awarding $27.50. It must have been a sweet night on Colored Hill.

Another article in the *Republican*, a sports story from 1894, provides a further glimpse into Tillman's strong character. "The Mud Pond Peepers of Benton were defeated in a game of base ball on the Fleetville ball grounds on Saturday, September 22, by the Wyoming Nine of Factoryville by a score of 21 to 13," the item announced. "The game was fair throughout as the umpire, Mr. Grant Tillman of Waverly, declined to be bought by the Peepers. If the Wyomings and the Peepers ever cross bats again it is said that the manager of the Peepers will not be so flush with his money."[22] On that day, racial progress played out on a ball field as two white teams agreed to be overseen—judged—by a black man. And it happened in Fleetville, of all places. Tillman showed his moxie by snubbing the home team in front of its fans in that old copperhead haven. To top it off, one of the visiting players he refereed might have been future Hall of Famer Christy Mathewson, the Factoryville teen who was already a phenom at age 14.

Grant Tillman died of unspecified causes in March 1904. He was only 40 and had returned to Scranton with his wife and their teenage daughter Ellnora. The funeral at Bethel AME was said to have been heavily attended because he was "a very popular young man . . . beloved by all who knew him."[23]

THE WIDOWED MRS. TILLMAN WOULD REMAIN a resident of Scranton, joining other Colored Hill natives who had gone to the anthracite boomtown to live or do business. George Keys Jr. was there working as a coachman, and his brother would move back and forth. John Walker came. The Burgettes would migrate en masse. John Johnson and Tom Crummel expanded their huckstering trade from Waverly into Scranton. Harry Samson came and opened a house-painting business. Mary Jane Merritt may have been the first to relocate, sometime around 1870. Within a few years, Merritt was a young mother and a widow. She took on her late husband's grocery trade and established a successful dry goods store on the flats of Wyoming Avenue. That was a rare feat for a woman of the time, especially a former slave. She also became a pillar of Scranton's Bethel AME, hosting its first services in her home before she moved to Wilkes-Barre and raised her family there.

The example of George W. Brown also shone bright. The Waverly product (one of the schoolboys who'd delighted his white classmates there years earlier) moved to Scranton in the mid-1870s, determined to test his fortunes. He worked first as a streetcar conductor—remarkable for a person of color—and then became a drayman. The white establishment considered draying, the hauling and storing of heavy goods, to be an acceptable business for black people to own and operate. Brown opened a draying firm and developed it into what the Pennsylvania Negro Business Directory would call "the largest and most complete in eastern Pennsylvania." At its peak, the G.W. Brown Co. boasted eleven double teams of horses and twelve singles, employed thirty teamsters, and had a storage warehouse on Lackawanna Avenue across from the central rail yard. His teams put in place the granite slabs for the massive soldiers and sailors monument on Scranton's courthouse square in 1900, and later moved goods under contract with the Great Atlantic & Pacific Tea Co.

Brown, self-made and prosperous, became a prominent figure around town. Some people called him "the

Waverly native George Brown built a successful hauling and storage business in Scranton. (Courtesy Mrs. Granville Smith, Collection of Anthracite Museum Complex, PHMC, Scranton.)

George Keys Jr., shown in his GAR portrait, became a coachman for a wealthy man about town in Scranton. (Courtesy GAR Library & Museum, Scranton.)

Mary Jane Merritt moved from Waverly to Scranton, where she ran a thriving store and helped to found a church. (Courtesy Constance E. Wynn Photo Collection.)

Big Mogul." The society pages took note of the birthday parties, missionary teas, and other soirees that he and his wife hosted at their home. Bethel AME made him a trustee. He was a force in black Republican circles and presided over the party's two hundred fifty-member Keystone Colored Club.

He also became an investor in new businesses. Chief among them was the Defender Publishing Co., established in 1897 in his office. It produced a weekly broadsheet that would give voice—fearless voice—to the region's black community. The *Scranton Defender* was published for about a decade. Brown was installed as vice president and treasurer, and his son, David T. Brown, as business manager. Their pastor, Bethel's Rev. H. C. C. Astwood, ran the operation as president and publisher.

The *Defender* was an extraordinary newspaper. Every Saturday its pages were laden with news filed by correspondents from Wilkes-Barre, to Waverly, to Altoona, to Bellefonte. Its "Town Notes" dispatches covered twenty-six black communities, keeping readers abreast of who was buying, selling, visiting, graduating, marrying, ailing, and deceasing. It carried news of the latest Jim Crow laws and lynchings down South, and demanded action ("To the law abiding and patriotic and Christian people of the land, you had better cry out against this wrong"). Its columns prodded readers toward propriety and collective uplift by decrying "easy divorce," for example, and admonishing black parents to do a better job keeping their youngsters in school and on track for better futures.

But the *Defender*'s primary critiques, its largest salvos, were aimed outward at the forces of bigotry right in Scranton. The Electric City had grown fast, its population hitting one hundred and two thousand in 1900, and was alive with jobs and opportunity, yet its five hundred people of color struggled to break in. Although able to vote and serve on juries, they found their civil rights gains weren't extending to other spheres of life. They were boxed out of higher-skilled, higher-wage jobs, and shunted into poor housing. Outside of their own community, employment was uniformly limited to day labor, domestic work, and service jobs like cooks, maids, janitors, and waiters. The coal industry was booming, but the white ethnic unions were ostracizing blacks, the result being that few ever found employment in the anthracite mines.[24] The segregation was so widespread that John Mitchell, president of the United Mine Workers of America, openly rebuked members about it.[25] Blacks were routinely denied service in downtown restaurants, though one fellow challenged that in court in 1900 and won.[26] Politically, their Republican party was in the thrall of the spreading "Lily White" movement (the *Defender* branded it "White Lily Republicanism") that curried conservative white voters by rejecting equal rights and excluding blacks from office. There were decent white people in town—church folks, schoolteachers, some of the neighbors—but even those relationships tended to be colored by paternalism.

Marginalized in commerce and civic life, Scranton's blacks were freely disdained in popular culture. The blackface minstrel shows that came through town mocked "Ethiopian comicalities" and played a repertoire of so-called "coon songs." Who could forget how the city's Mozart band had played one of the most popular of those ditties, "N** in the Barnyard," to wild applause in 1898? Meanwhile, the "scientific racism" of the day claimed to rank the races according to cranial measurements and other pseudo-scientific techniques. The US Sanitary Commission had fed into that ideology with its postwar finding that black soldiers tended to be smaller than whites, with smaller brains, and

DR. HOLLISTER'S SECOND THOUGHTS

During the postwar decades, some Northern whites questioned their own prejudices and racial indoctrination, even if only later in life. Horace Hollister was one. In addition to being a physician in Providence, now northern Scranton, Hollister was the author of the official *Contributions to the History of the Lackawanna Valley*. Here is his initial entry about Waverly, from 1857: "The only colored feature in the picture of Abington is a colony of negroes living there, who, with all the boasted advantage of farming and freedom, possess all the abandoned, lazy habits of the race, and who hardly draw from the frosty hills around them as plenty a sustenance as that enjoyed by their brethren at the South."[27]

That disdain sat in print through the Civil War and the postwar struggle for black rights, until Hollister revised his entry in 1885. It became kindlier, though still condescending: "The only colored feature in the picture of Abington is a colony of negroes which in spite of the double disadvantage of prejudice and hereditary indolence, has drawn from the frosty hills thereabouts, the wherewithal to sustain animation in a very creditable manner."[28]

But the doctor wasn't done. By the time he died, his condescension had given way to full remorse over his words. He had wielded a poison pen, he realized. In a powerful account published after his 1883 death, Hollister wrote that by the 1830s, "the North, not only in Congress, but out of it, was controlled wholly by the South. Southerners taught us to believe that without slavery the country would go to the devil at once. Nearly everybody believed it. . . . every Northern man was told and taught that to catch a runaway 'n***' was a duty he owed his God and his country. The poor, sore-footed, hungry slave who sought liberty in flight, found only here and there a friend to give him aid, shelter and food. Those who did were called Abolitionists, in disdain. They were hooted and howled at almost as bad as the escaping slave and everywhere and time were treated with contempt."[29]

Horace Hollister's progressive revisionism was hardly winning the culture war, however. By the end of the century, the memory of slavery's atrocities was giving way to Northern indifference, and even to sympathy for the South and its mythology of the Confederacy's "Lost Cause." As the *Pittston Gazette* opined in 1902, "We can hardly blame the Southerners for objecting to the production of 'Uncle Tom's Cabin' on the stage in their country . . . It will do no good to be everlastingly rubbing it in upon them that they were once slaveholders. We have forgiven, now let us forget."[30] George B. Kulp, in his 1890 compendium of illustrious men of Luzerne County, praised George W. Woodward for demanding black disenfranchisement in 1837, saying black people's "political and social inferiority must be recognized. . . . It is gravely to be regretted that principles so sound and salutary have come to be abandoned."[31]

were more likely to succumb to disease. To many white people, the meaning was obvious: freedom itself was bad for black people's health.[32] This built on an 1869 study by the War College, which claimed blacks' physical characteristics place them "very low in the seals of human evolution" and which found black soldiers "too animal to have moral courage or endurance."[33]

In that benighted atmosphere, George Brown's *Scranton Defender* strove to be "The Brightest and Bravest Exponent of the People." Its issues from 1904-05, the only ones still extant, seethe with the frustrations of its journalists and readers.

The Laurel Line streetcar tunnel was one of the paper's causes. In 1904, a subcontractor provoked "considerable agitation" when he imported non-union black laborers to dig the tunnel in South Scranton, at half the pay of union wages. The white "rockman" union and the *Scrantonian*, the city's large Democratic newspaper, pressed to have only union men hired or "trouble may occur."[34] The *Defender* took direct aim at the sense of white entitlement that the impasse had exposed. "Labor organizations formed by these men [European immigrants] who quickly become educated by the Democratic Southern prejudices, shut out the colored men from the labor organizations of the country for which they suffered, bled and died, depriving them of the right to gain a common livelihood in the affairs of the common country. These foreigners, whose cause the Scrantonian undertakes to champion, attempt to build a Chinese wall around every known industry in the county, claiming it is their own individual heritage, and when they, for any cause, refuse labor or work, the colored laborer at the peril of his life must attempt to earn his daily bread."[35]

During Scranton's election season that autumn, the *Defender* accused Democratic tax assessors of a blatant effort to disenfranchise blacks. Under a law in place in Pennsylvania until 1933, every voter had to pay a poll tax and then present the receipt on Election Day in order to vote. The *Defender* complained that assessors were systematically rejecting black applicants as a way "to nullify and disenfranchise every colored voter they can, in Democratic districts." The goal was "to win the election by counting out sufficient colored votes to effect the election in case of a close contest. Let every colored voter presenting to pay his poll tax file a protest."[36] In addition, the *Defender* accused the "white autocracy in local Republican politics" of colluding with an unnamed "colored trickster" to double-cross black loyalists by neither refunding their campaign contributions nor awarding a patronage position as promised. The paper warned of a reckoning because "we will no longer be trifled with."

On the eve of the election, a *Defender* editorial gave this weary summation of conditions in Scranton: "The prejudice against the colored man is just as pronounced as it is in any portion of the South, and but [for] the stringent state laws the position of the colored man would be intolerable. As it is with the free State of Pennsylvania, the colored man or woman, no matter how decent, cannot rent a house to live in in any public street, and only in certain courts, and but for the stringent state laws, he would not be accommodated in a single public restaurant, and even now it is with difficulty that there are accommodations. Politically they are ostracized in every way although they are at times the balance of power in local elections, yet not a single place is obtainable by them in this great Republican center; the only place held by a colored man is that of a dogcatcher."

Like the *Chicago Defender* and other "race papers" of the day, the *Scranton Defender* provided a forum for everyday readers to speak their minds. Jennie Dorsey, a cook in Wilkes-Barre, was one such subscriber. A lynching report in 1904 moved her to write this disgusted letter to the editor:

> *Show me a race that has made the progress the Negro has in thirty-seven years! We cope with the Caucasian in every sphere—judges, lawyers, doctors, authors, statesmen, poets, artists, etc. Our girls and boys graduate with the same honor, carry off the honors from your highest and best colleges. Now show me where they are an inferior race and we can never be assimilated. As a law-abiding race we have yet to find our equal. What race stands by the Stars and Stripes with more honor than the Negro soldier? During our civil war, when you tried to fight without them, before they knew their right foot from their left, when to drill them properly it was necessary to tie straw to one foot and hay to the other, thus enabling them to mark time correctly—then you placed them in battle. Who was it that caused your victory at Richmond, Va.? The Negro. Is this an instance of inferiority?*[37]

THAT WAS HOW IT WAS with black people down in the fray of the anthracite belt. They felt held back and belittled, and the *Defender* did its best to launch their grievances out to the wider world. At the same time, behind the rhetorical ramparts, its pages continued to chronicle everyday happenings in calmer communities like Waverly.

"Mr. John R. Johnson has returned from Scranton where he has been to visit his daughter, Mrs. Frank Johnson, who has had the relapse, but is reported today to be doing very nicely," reported the "Waverly Notes" of March 1904. "Mr. Henry Hundley is kept quite busy slaughtering calves for the Scranton market. Mrs. Henrietta Walker is much better this week of neuralgia."

The Waverly correspondent also included news of white allies. The same March roundup noted that "Dr.

N. C. Mackey is sick with the grip and is scarcely able to attend to his patients, who are very numerous." In April, it brought news that Samuel Whaling had died "at the ripe old age of 83. He was formerly a great friend and did much for our race." In May, it noted that Waverly's white Baptists hosted the pastor of Scranton's black Shiloh Baptist, Rev. J. B. Boddie, as guest preacher: "His sermon was very interesting and also well attended."

While Colored Hill escaped the animosity so prevalent in Scranton and elsewhere, it was undergoing its own struggle: against time. "Scranton seems to be the attraction of our people in this village nowadays," the (anonymous) Waverly correspondent lamented in September. A month later: "We regret to hear that Mrs. Fanny Johnson intends to spend the winter in Brooklyn, N.Y., with her aunt Madame Robinson. It will make one less in our small community." Deaths, too, had steadily reduced the numbers. By 1893, the last of Colored Hill's resident USCT veterans, William Bradley, was dead. Other founding fugitives were passing on with him: Edward Smith in 1877, Aunty Smith in 1886, Rev. William Johnson in 1886, Lot Norris in 1888, and Ignatius Thomas in 1897. They were buried at Hickory Grove Cemetery, where Aunty Smith's epitaph reads "Forty years in slavery, now safe in the arms of Jesus."

By the turn of the century, Rev. Charles Garner was living in Waverly and pastoring the AME churches there and in Pittston and Montrose. As he reported to his superiors in 1898, "it will not be long before all of our people will have passed over the river into the land of rest. The few people in our church are old and feeble, hence we are not able to keep up the expenses of the churches. Yet the minister must go and preach to them as long as they live."[38]

The last report of a summer revival was in 1905. Waverly's black population dwindled steadily, to ten households in 1910, and three in 1920. By 1920, Waverly AME was down to six congregants and holding services only twice a month with visiting preachers and evangelists. In 1923, the church lost its final member and was shuttered. (Fittingly, it was the same year Waverly's last USCT veteran,

The façade of the 'extinct' Colored Hill church. (Courtesy Peter and Sally Bohlin.)

Joshua Norris, died, far away in western Pennsylvania.) The church building sat vacant for three years until the AME denomination entrusted Elizabeth Tillman, Grant's widow, and Scranton pastor William Dawkins to dispose of it. The legal notice described the church as "inactive and extinct by reason of the death or removal of its members from Waverly" and "liable to be wasted or destroyed."[39] The two trustees sold the property for $975 to its white neighbor, lawyer Charles Wells.

Dick Norris, brother of Joshua and Peter, was the last of the founding descendants left on Colored Hill. As of 1910 he was taking in Italian-born boarders—the new face of Waverly's incoming labor. By 1924, Dick Norris was dead, and Charles Wells bought up the Norris property. A newer black family, the Hundleys, would remain in Waverly until about 1940, at which time they moved a few miles away.

By then, Colored Hill was only a memory. The village itself had a new look, its central block of old stores replaced by the innovative Waverly Community House, its outskirts boasting grand estates of the wealthy. The humble homes along Carbondale Road were either knocked down or modernized by new owners. Waverly's remarkable era of interracial harmony had quietly passed away.

1. Stevenson, George E. *Reflections of an Anthracite Engineer* (Scranton: Hudson Coal Co., 1931), p. 2.
2. Mumford, Mildred. *This Is Waverly* (Waverly, PA: Waverly Women's Club, 1954), p. 114.
3. Rev. S.S. Kennedy farm expense ledger for 1873-74, at Lackawanna Historical Society, Scranton.
4. "Waverly Notes," *Scranton Republican* (Scranton), Dec. 31 1892, p. 7.
5. Egerton, Douglas R. *Thunder at the Gates: The Black Civil War Regiments That Redeemed America* (New York: Basic Books, 2016), p. 336.
6. Lewis, William. "Colored Settlement at Waverly" (unpublished manuscript, undated), p. 3.
7. *History of Luzerne, Lackawanna and Wyoming Counties* (New York: W.W. Munsell & Co., 1880), p. 459.
8. "Church News" item, *Christian Recorder* (Philadelphia) Jan. 20, 1881 (Accessible Archives, online).
9. "Waverly Report," *Scranton Republican*, Aug. 9, 1893.
10. "Sermon of Rev. H.A. Grant," *Scranton Tribune* (Scranton), Aug. 7, 1899, p. 3.
11. *Scranton Tribune*, Oct. 24, 1894, p. 8.
12. Mumford, op. cit., pp. 71-72.
13. Shaffer, Donald R. *After the Glory: The Struggles of Black Civil War Veterans* (Lawrence, Kansas: University of Kansas Press, 2004), p. 118.
14. Ibid., pp. 129, 131.
15. Davis, Hugh. "The Pennsylvania State Equal Rights League and the Northern Black Struggle for Legal Equality," article in *Pennsylvania Magazine of History and Biography*, October 2002, p. 627.
16. Davis, Hugh. *We Will Be Satisfied With Nothing Less": The African American Struggle for Equal Rights in the North During Reconstruction* (Ithaca, N.Y.: Cornell University Press, 2011), p. 73.
17. Ibid., p. 103.
18. *Scranton Daily Times* (Scranton, PA), June 4, 1874, p. 2.
19. *Reading Times* (Reading, PA), Aug. 19, 1874, p.4.
20. "The Keystone Boys Parade," *Scranton Republican*, Oct. 20, 1891, p. 6.
21. *Scranton Tribune*, Jan. 26, 1898, p. 6 .
22. "Wyoming Notes," *Scranton Republican*, Sept. 26, 1894, p. 7.
23. *ScrantonDefender* (Scranton), March 26, 1904.
24. Smith, Eric Ledell. "The African American Community of Wilkes-Barre, 1870 to 1900." (Nanticoke, PA: Proceedings of the 12th Annual Conference on the History of Northeastern Pennsylvania, 2000), p. 17, p. 58.
25. *Scranton Republican*, July 11, 1903, p. 5.
26. "Drawing the Color Line," *Scranton Republican*, Dec. 11, 1900, p. 5.
27. Hollister, Horace. *Contributions to the History of the Lackawanna Valley* (New York: W.H. Tinson, 1857), p. 212.
28. Lewis, William. "Underground Railroad in Abington, Pa.," (unpublished manuscript, 1944), p. 2.
29. Hollister, Horace. *Historical Record, Vol. 8* (Wilkes-Barre, PA:Press of the Wilkes-Barre Record, 1899), p. 337.
30. *Pittston Gazette* (Pittston, PA), Jan. 17, 1902, p.2.
31. Kulp, George Brubaker. *Sketches of the Bench and Bar of Luzerne County, Pennsylvania, Vol. 3* (Wilkes-Barre: E. B. Yordy, 1890), pp. 1152-3.
32. Glathaar, Joseph T. *Forged in Battle: The Civil War Alliance of Black Soldiers and White Officers* (New York: Free Press, 1990), p. 255.
33. Hunt, Dr. Sanford B. "The Negro as Soldier," *Anthropological Review 7*, no. 24 (London, England: January 1869), p. 43.
34. *Scranton Republican*, Aug. 15, 1904, p. 5.

35. *Scranton Defender* (Scranton), Aug. 6, 1904.
36. *Scranton Defender*, Oct. 15, 1904.
37. "The Race Problem," *Scranton Defender*, Sept. 17, 1904.
38. Minutes of the Thirty-Second Session of the Pittsburgh Annual Conference of the African Methodist Episcopal Church. Oct. 12-17, 1899. p. 16.
39. *Scranton Republican*, May 29, 1924, p. 25.

CHAPTER ELEVEN

Epilogue

⊷•◈•⊶

A S TIME PASSED, the legacy of Colored Hill and Waverly's progressivism fell to the margins of memory. The consequences were predictable. Interracial high-mindedness would give way to the same low stereotyping of black people that was common elsewhere. No sooner had the Waverly AME church closed than the Ku Klux Klan gained force for a time in the area. Hundreds of local nativists donned the white robes and set enormous crosses ablaze in a showing of WASP (white Anglo-Saxon Protestant) power.[1] Dalton, Factoryville, and Nicholson were among the gathering points. Local newspapers reported on nighttime Klan rallies in Clarks Summit[2] and Benton[3] as well. The Klan eventually petered out in the Abingtons in the 1930s—but the low regard toward non-whites, Roman Catholics, and other "outsiders" did not. Unfortunately, black people became reduced to the foolish caricatures of *Amos 'n' Andy* and Stepin Fetchit. Waverly High School formed a Minstrel Club,[4] with students sporting blackface makeup. The Waverly Men's Club put on annual minstrel-show spoofs for the town well into the 1950s. If *This Is Waverly*, an anecdotal folk history published in 1954, is any guide, bygone Colored Hill had become seen as a quirk rather than a point of pride. The author, Mildred Mumford, depicted people on Colored Hill as amusing simpletons. She collected reminiscences that had one elderly fugitive slave somehow mistaking a carnival organ grinder's monkey for a black child, and that mocked another fugitive as a "laaa-zy, s-h-i-f-t-less d-o-n-u-t-h-i-n kind." The fugitives' heartfelt praise and worship, to her way of thinking, illustrated "the simple child-like faith of the Negro." Without a strong black presence or white reformers left to counter such derogatory attitudes, Waverly became an ordinary, insular white town like so many others where minority concerns, even during the modern civil rights movement, were distant abstractions with no special hold on the conscience.

Attitudes have improved since then. Today, the village is a welcoming place to live. It is upscale, politically moderate, still overwhelmingly white, but accommodating of a mix of lifestyles and of its current racial minorities: a smattering of Asian professionals. In recent years, as broader perspectives about our nation's development have taken hold, Colored Hill has worked its way back into the heart of Waverly's self-understanding. An Underground Railroad marker was erected at the entrance to Hickory Grove Cemetery in 2003. Efforts to salvage the historic Fell School where the fugitive slaves were first taught and worshipped helped to raise public awareness. Walking and driving maps of the town highlight abolition-related sites and tell of the fugitive settlement.

Colored Hill certainly deserves an honored place in the area's history. It is an important human chronicle— one of good and ill, of charity, bravery, bigotry, and never-ending vigilance. Its story needs to be told in full, the old voices heard again, their lessons grasped.

Consider the powerful lesson left to us by Rev. J. B. Boddie, a Scranton pastor and the son of ex-slaves, who visited and preached in Waverly. One Sunday in 1904, Reverend Boddie delivered a sermon at his black Shiloh Baptist Church in Scranton that must have had the amen corner alive with praise. His subversive topic: "The Place in the Bible Where the White Man Obeyed the Negro."

Like other black people of his day, the pastor had seen the good and the bad in white people. His new church had been accepted into the otherwise all-white Abington Baptist Association. The association's member congregations even extended funds that enabled Shiloh to purchase property to erect a new church building in Scranton. That was to the good. Mad-

Rev. J. B. Boddie. (A Giant in the Earth, by Charles E. Boddie [Berne, Ind.: Berne Witness Co., 1944].)

deningly, however, neighbors of the property objected, and "discriminatory tactics" forced Shiloh out. It had to build its new sanctuary elsewhere in the city[5].

That day Reverend Boddie rose in the pulpit, all six-feet-seven and two hundred sixty pounds of him, and gave a spiritual response. At a time when much of the country deemed the difficulties of black progress "the Negro Problem," he dared to turn that notion on its head. The problem is essentially a white one, a problem of white prejudice, he preached—and it goes directly against God's will. The *Scranton Defender*'s item about the sermon didn't identify his biblical proof text, but it could well have been Jeremiah 38. In that chapter of scripture, a black Ethiopian eunuch persuades the king and his minions to spare the imprisoned prophet Jeremiah. The royal court follows the lowly eunuch's counsel—which finds divine favor.[6] Reverend Boddie drew an obvious contemporary lesson. The crux of his sermon, the *Defender* reported, was: "The White Man

Must Recognize the Negro as his Brother, or They Will Never See God's Face in Peace."

With that profound message, Reverend Boddie could have been speaking for Gildersleeve and Batchelor, for Brown and Douglass, and for others of expanded spirituality. He was speaking for the Keyses and the Norrises and their comrades in arms who fought for a more perfect union. Do not be deluded, he was warning the likes of Woodward, Gritman, Bedford, and the klansmen. Your "white republic" hubris jeopardizes not only the bonds of society but your own individual salvation. *The White Man Must Recognize the Negro as his Brother, or They Will Never See God's Face in Peace.*

For the God-fearing, it's a message with resonance today. For everyone, believer or not, it is a reminder that the high ideal of human brotherhood has a way of putting us all to the test in every generation.

1. Brauer, Norm. *Revisiting Bailey Hollow: A History of Dalton* (copyright Norm Brauer, 1988), pp. 88, 93.
2. "Wedding Features Meeting of Thousand Klansmen in Field at Clark's Summit," *Scranton Republican* (Scranton, PA), Aug. 14, 1924, p.1.
3. "Klansmen in Kloreo Held Near Fleetville," *Scranton Republican*, Sept. 8, 1924, p. 3.
4. "Waverly Notes," *Scranton Republican* (Scranton), Dec. 13, 1932, p. 9.
5. Williams, James T. *Northern Fried Chicken: A Historical Adventure Into the Black Community of Scranton, Pa.* (Scranton, unpublished manuscript, 1993), p. 14.
6. Based on a conversation with the Rev. James Pollard, Bible scholar and pastor of Zion Baptist Church in Ardmore, PA.

CARRIED THE COLORS.

W. R. ACKERSON,
Age 72.

J. B. HOBDAY,
Age 82.

GEORGE KEYS,
Colored.

A photograph from the Scranton Tribune, *August 21, 1902, shows Waverly native George Keys Jr. standing proud as a GAR standard-bearer, his race duly noted. His age at the time was 56. Keys would die six years later. (Courtesy Newspapers.com, the* Scranton Times-Tribune.)

CHAPTER TWELVE

The Final Bugle Call

WAVERLY'S THIRTEEN Civil War soldiers went to war willingly and died unsung. They not only witnessed history, they made history. Remarkably, only three returned from the war with bodies undamaged. For the rest, bullet and shell wounds and the ravages of camp diseases brought chronic suffering. And what could they do but persevere? In many ways, they fit the profile described by historian Joseph T. Glatthaar. Overall, the nation's black war vets remained mentally stable, rarely divorced, and did not descend into alcoholism and other "vicious habits." At the same time, many were physical wrecks beset by rheumatism, arthritis, and "recurrent bouts of malaria and chronic diarrhea."[1]

Regrettably, none of the Colored Hill veterans left behind diaries or other direct accounts of their thoughts and experiences. The only insights into their challenging final years come from service and pension paperwork bound in old manila folders at the National Archives in Washington. The following accounts of the men's last chapter, and the crucial support they and their families received from neighbors black and white, is drawn primarily from those archival records.

The thirteen veterans are listed here in the order of their deaths.

FRANCIS ASBURY JOHNSON

Freeborn son of a slave
Enlisted as a private in 22nd USCT
Mortally wounded in action; died 1865

Asbury Johnson, a five-feet-five teenager, was shot on July 4, 1864, somewhere along the Petersburg siege lines. He was hospitalized for months until, infection worsening, he was shipped to the care of his family. Johnson died on February 3, 1865, in upstate New York where his family was then living. He was only 16 at the time. His father, Rev. William Johnson, eulogized him as described in Chapter 9. Asbury left behind his slave-born parents, William and Eliza; brothers Ezra and John R. (who would later serve on the Waverly borough council); and sisters Masilla, Rebecca, Rachel, and Sarah.

Asbury's place of repose is unknown; the photo shows his father's headstone at Waverly's Hickory Grove Cemetery, along Row Five.

GEORGE KEYS SR.

Born into slavery in Maryland
Enlisted as a private in 22nd USCT
Mortally wounded in action; died 1867

George Keys, Colored Hill's founding father, was 42 when he signed up in early 1864. Five months later he was shot in the left thigh near the hip, probably while on patrol alongside Asbury Johnson. Keys received a disability discharge in spring of 1865, and returned to Waverly. Though fully bedridden, he received only a "one-half disability" pension of $4 a month. He applied for an increase to $25 a month (signing with an X), and received supporting statements from his doctor, Waverly's J. C. Miles, and Norman Phelps; no decision was recorded by the time he died in February 1867. Dr. Miles would later describe Keys' agonizing injury: "This wound extended to the hip joint, ulcerated from time to time and continued to discharge pus and occasionally  a piece of bone until he became entirely exhausted. For months before his death, the discharge was constant. The wound was the only cause of his death."

Keys, five-feet-five and gray-eyed, died never knowing how to read or write. He left behind his freeborn wife, Hannah, sons George Jr. and Edward, and a slave family that had been sold away from him decades earlier in Maryland. He was interred in the Waverly Methodist Episcopal churchyard, a testament to the respect he'd earned from that white congregation.

Hannah Keys applied for a widow's pension in November 1867, with a supporting affidavit from Waverly native George Bedford. She was granted $8 a month, retroactive to her husband's death, but it took her a year to get it. Her burial place is unknown.

JOHN T. SAMPSON

Freeborn in New York
Enlisted as a private in 3rd USCT
Returned from war unscathed; died 1869

John Sampson first appeared on the Waverly census in 1860, as an eighteen-year-old farm laborer. His army muster papers list him as five-feet-nine and born in

Binghamton, New York. Sampson returned from duty without injury or even ailment, remarkable considering the time he'd spent in close quarters attending to sick and infected soldiers in the military hospital wards at Morris Island and Hilton Head, South Carolina. Back in Waverly, he went to work for the Sherman family and boarded on their premises on the eastern slope of Colored Hill.

Sampson died of unknown causes in September 1869. He left behind a young wife, Susan, and their two youngsters. His gravestone is an obelisk at Hickory Grove Cemetery, along Row Five. His 3rd Regiment comrade, Peter Norris, and Norris's wife took in Susan and the children at first, until Susan became a live-in servant for the Shermans for many years. There is no record of her or John Sampson's applying for or receiving pensions.

JOHN MASON
Born into slavery in Maryland
Enlisted as a private in 22nd USCT
Shot in hand and maimed; died 1870

Farm laborer John Mason was among the heroes of the vaunted June 15 assault at Petersburg. During that ferocious penetration of the Rebel lines, Mason was shot in the right hand. The wound was so shattering that he spent five months in military hospitals in Virginia, New Jersey, and New York. He returned to Waverly with a disability discharge, the army doctor classifying him as "totally incapacitated for obtaining his subsistence by manual labor." With one hand still functioning, he was given only a one-half disability status and granted a pension of $8 a month. In 1866, having a wife and newborn daughter, Mason applied for an increase, signing the form with his X mark. It's not clear whether the extra ever came through.

Mason was one of Colored Hill's older war recruits. His muster papers list him as age 40, a mulatto standing five-feet-six. He died of unspecified causes in August 1870, and was laid to rest in Hickory Grove Cemetery, Row 5. His widow, Catherine, went on to remarry twice, first to John Walker and, when Walker died, to William Bradley.

It seems Mason's daughter, Ella, had a physical disability of her own. A letter in Mason's file, written to the pension bureau in 1911 by an Ida Rowe, said Ella had been nearly blind since birth and was left "an orphan" without government support and unable to support herself. Rowe asked if Ella might qualify retroactively under an 1890 law that allowed relief for soldiers' children up to age 16. The bureau turned her down.

WESLEY W. BAPTISTE
Freeborn in Pennsylvania
Enlisted as a private in 30th Penna. Infantry Militia
Returned from service unscathed; died 1878

Wesley Baptiste was working as a laborer for the Shermans when a freak accident took his life in August 1878. The story goes that he was climbing over a wall and tumbled onto the prongs of a cradle scythe, puncturing an artery. According to Waverly historian William Lewis, people attempted to stop Baptiste's copious bleeding with cobwebs from the Madison Academy tower but could not save him.[2] Baptiste, whom old-timers described as a "refined colored man," was 28 and single when he died.

Baptiste (often listed as *Baptist*) was a mulatto. He is recorded as white in the 1870 census, and Lewis was told that Baptiste was a half-brother of Waverly blacksmith George Perry, a Maryland native. That may explain how Baptiste was able to join the ranks of the white 30th Pennsylvania. The regiment was formed on an emergency basis to defend the state against the Confederate invasion of 1863. Three months later, when the emergency ended, the unit was dissolved. Baptiste never sought a pension and may not have seen combat.

He is interred at Hickory Grove Cemetery, among the white veterans near the flagpole rather than along Row Five with the black soldiers.

SAMUEL McDONALD
Born into slavery in Virginia
Enlisted as a private in 11th USC Heavy Artillery
Discharged for "miasmatic disease" (malaria); died 1882

McDonald's case is particularly sad. He saw duty as a teamster, out of the line of fire, but nevertheless returned from the war a broken young man. His unit had been sent to the swamps of southern Louisiana to defend Union-held New Orleans, remaining in place there until well after the war ended. Though the 11th saw a bit of combat, what felled McDonald was disease. After eighteen months of incessant "fever and ague," he received a medical discharge for "disability from miasmatic disease complicated with enlargement of the hepatic gland [liver]." The examining doctor said McDonald "has continually complained of internal fever, loss of appetite and spitting up blood."

It's not clear when McDonald settled in Waverly and why. As with many others on Colored Hill, the particulars are sketchy. He had enlisted in Providence, Rhode Island, as a farmer, recorded variously as *McDonnell, McDonell,* and *McDonald.* He does not appear in the Waverly census until 1870, when he is listed as a mulatto laborer with a wife, Susan, and 12-year-old son, Robert. By 1880, Susan and Robert are gone, and McDonald is living with Eliza Johnson, Asbury Johnson's mother, and perhaps Susan's mother, too. One thing was clear: McDonald was not a well man.

Pension filings describe him as trying to perform manual labor though barely able to move. He applied for an invalid pension in 1874, saying his "constitution was shattered by the disease." Villagers John Stone and G. W. Bailey filed affidavits attesting to McDonald's disability. Said Stone, "I'd seen him trying to do work during the last year, at three different times, and fall down helpless in the field and have to be carried to the house." McDonald never received a pension, evidently because his paperwork was incomplete. He fell under the care of the Waverly Poor Board, and died a pauper in 1882 at age 42. McDonald is buried at Hickory Grove, Row Five.

JOHN W. WASHINGTON
Born into slavery in Virginia
Enlisted as a private in 22nd USCT
Disabled by a shell wound to the head; died 1886

Washington ("5-10½, complexion yellow, eyes blue, hair brown") enlisted at age 38 and returned south to fight. He was the highest-ranking of the Waverly contingent, being promoted to sergeant by the end of 1864. Washington survived Petersburg and took part in Lincoln's funeral march and the hunt for John Wilkes Booth before limping back to Colored Hill, wounded.

Two decades of health and money problems would follow. Having a wife and daughter, Washington aimed to resume work as a farm laborer but "was unable to perform his usual vocation more than ¼ the time and not able to do hard work even then," stated his Waverly physician, Dr. Frederick Van Sickle. The doctor made that assessment in 1889, in a widow claim filed after Washington died. The doctor attributed death to diabetes, but said Washington had also suffered from a shell wound sustained at Petersburg: "At the location named by him was a depression in the outer table of the skull. Much pain was also experienced in the side."

Though Washington never applied for an invalid pension, his wife Sarah tried to claim his due posthumously along with her own widow's pension. Dr. Nathan Mackey, William Rice, and Ed Keys joined Dr. Van Sickle in support of the claim. Sarah formally declared that she had married Washington in Virginia in 1849, lived with him until his death, and bore him nine children:

"They all died but one [adult daughter Georgianna]. I was married when I was a slave and have no certificate of my marriage." She signed the form with an X.

The government rejected the invalid claim, saying her husband's military records yielded "no evidence of disability." It did grant her a widow's pension of $8 per month in 1890, but more trouble soon came. In addition to being "absolutely penniless," Dr. Mackey noticed that Sarah Washington was developing "imbecility," and required continual watching by Georgianna, who he said was also impoverished. The county court convened a special panel under a law to aid "deranged" people. The panel confirmed that Sarah Washington was "a lunatic without lucid intervals." John Johnson, by then Georgianna's husband, was appointed caregiver and entrusted with $1,000. The support helped Sarah Washington linger until 1892, when she passed away and was buried next to her husband at Hickory Grove, Row Five.

RICHARD LEE
Born into slavery in Maryland
Enlisted as a private in 25nd USCT
Discharged for disability; died 1891

Richard Lee was an Underground Railroad fugitive who entered the Army at age 32, leaving behind a wife and young son. A year later, he was hospitalized with a spinal injury suffered while carrying timber in July 1864. His regiment was on garrison duty at Fort Barrancas, Florida, at the time. He was sent north to a military hospital in New York and finally discharged for "disability, one third."

As of 1867, Lee was drawing $4 a month disability pay, working in Waverly as a barber, and living in a small house atop Academy Street.

The 1870 and 1880 censuses show Lee working as a laborer, which must have wracked his body further. The Waverly GAR post minutes would record Comrade Lee as being in "deplorable condition." By mid-1890, he was getting regular visits from the post's sick committee, along with financial aid and a waiver of dues. Members even moved to petition the pension bureau about his "pressing need for immediate relief." Lee died the following March. The post voted that a joint "resolution of respect" for him and a white comrade be published in a local newspaper as a final tribute. He lies buried at Hickory Grove, Row Five.

By the time of his death, Lee had been widowered and remarried. His will, signed in a scratchy hand, granted son Lloyd a priceless object: a green trunk that belonged to Lloyd's late, slave-born mother. Lee's second wife, Sarah, received the little family home, which Lee had been able to hold onto throughout his ordeals. Sarah Lee died in 1913, bequeathing the property to Dr. N. C. Mackey with instructions to hold a public sale "for the payment of all my just debts."

SAMUEL THOMAS
Born into slavery in Virginia
Enlisted as a private in 54th Massachusetts
Suffered effects of malaria; died 1892

Samuel Thomas, a blacksmith by trade, was part of the pioneering black regiment immortalized for its heroics at Fort Wagner and elsewhere. He'd enlisted early, in April 1863, in Massachusetts and served until August 1865. Regimental papers list Thomas as five-feet-four and a

company cook. While it's not clear he ever saw battle action, postwar pension files show he fought a war of his own against a host of ailments. A comrade at Folly and Morris Islands, South Carolina, testified that Thomas contracted chronic diarrhea there and became "thin in flesh and in a debilitated state." The cause was "drinking bad water and extreme fatigue," said another comrade, Benjamin Naylor of Montrose. Throughout his service, Thomas was also treated for "pain around his heart and shortness of breath." He was made a cook only because he was "not able to do duty in the ranks."

After the war, Thomas moved to Binghamton with his wife, Mahala, and their young son. Over the years, he made regular trips to Colored Hill, where Ignatius and Elizabeth Thomas were evidently kinfolk. While living in Waverly in 1890, he filed a disability claim for "rheumatism resulting from malaria." Affidavits from Colored Hill residents Elizabeth Thomas and Catherine Bradley and from villagers Benjamin Green and Dr. Mackey vouched that Thomas was lame and "wholly unable to earn a support." He was awarded $12 per month, which he drew until his death in Binghamton from stomach ulceration. Thomas had been admitted to the Waverly GAR post in 1891, and the post covered his funeral expenses: $7.

Mahala Thomas sought a widow pension in 1895, but was rejected on grounds that her husband's cause of death "was not due to service." She tried again in 1904, gathering more affidavits, and won $12 per month, which supplemented her income as a laundress. She died in Binghamton in 1913 and was buried beside her husband at Hickory Grove, Row 5.

WILLIAM BRADLEY
Born into slavery in Maryland
Enlisted as a private in 22nd USCT
Disabled by shell shrapnel; died 1893

William Bradley was a familiar figure in Waverly after the war. Though hobbled by a back wound sustained during the unforget-table charge at Petersburg, he set to work on the farms again to support his growing family. He made do until 1883, when he sought an invalid pension claiming he'd become "unable to labor more than one half his time and is unable to gain a support for his family by his occupation as a laborer." Character references came from villagers Norman Phelps ("a very honest man, complains of a war wound"), George Fell ("a very reliable man"), Benjamin Green ("broken down in body"), and Dr. Miles ("a sound man when he enlisted but since his discharge has always seemed to be in poor health"). Dr. Mackey classified him as two-thirds disabled. Bradley was granted a monthly pension of $6, raised to $12 in 1890.

Bradley benefited from the mercies of the Waverly GAR post. First, the post hired him for light duty caring for its meeting room. Then, as he grew "sick and short of money," the comrades sent several $5 relief payments during his final months. Bradley, 66, died in August 1893, from what Dr. Mackey termed Bright's Disease, now known as nephritis. "He was a temperate and moral man," the doctor noted, "and his disease was not due to any vicious or immoral practice." The post's help did not end there. According to its minutes, it handled Bradley's funeral and covered food and coal costs for "widow Bradley" intermittently for several years. When Catherine Bradley, by then thrice-widowed, applied for a widow pension, her character references included this testimonial from post adjutant George Warner: "She is a highly respectable old woman and is known and recognized in this community. She has no property of any kind, or any income from any source except from what she earns by the work of her hands, together with the help given her by our Post, and the charity of her neighbors. She is 80 years of age, and cannot and does not earn more than 25 or 30 dollars a year. She has no vicious habits, and her inability to earn a living is due solely to her advanced age. No person or persons are legally bound to support her."

The pension bureau granted Catherine Bradley $8 per month, which she received until her death in 1903. Her burial place is unknown. William Bradley lies buried at Hickory Grove, Row Five.

GEORGE KEYS JR.

Freeborn son of a slave
Enlisted as a private in 22nd USCT
Returned from the war unscathed; died 1908

Still barely 20, bugler George Keys Jr. returned dutifully to the family home to help care for his wounded father, and then for his widowed mother. The 1870 Waverly census shows him working as a laborer. By 1880, Keys had broken away and was boarding in Scranton. He worked as a newspaper pressman until fortune struck and he  was hired as a coachman and "body servant" for one of

"SMOKING BY PROXY"

Accounts of the day report that Ira Tripp loved to be out and about with "his loyal Negro," George Keys Jr. It seems Tripp was an inveterate cigar smoker, so much so that his doctor told him it would kill him if he kept at it. Tripp agreed to quit, but dumped the task on his trusty body servant. Keys' bizarre assignment became to smoke as many as 15 cigars a day, and to direct the fumes into his employer's waiting mouth. The pair would stroll around town in a cloud of smoke, with passersby sometimes doing double-takes that drew guffaws from Tripp. This went on for years until Tripp died in 1891.

A 1970s newspaper column treated Tripp's so-called "smoking by proxy" as amusing, but Keys' death certificate listed his cause of death in 1908 as *"phthisis pulmonalis,"* an archaic term for tuberculosis—a wasting condition greatly exacerbated by smoking. In his last days Keys had gone to a country retreat "in search of health," but in vain.

He died on July 4, 1908—forty-four years to the day after his father was shot on the Petersburg battlefield. Father died a painful death in loyal service to liberty; son died a painful death in loyal service to a boss's guilty pleasure.

Ira Tripp, Keys' employer. (Courtesy The City of Scranton and Vicinity and Their Resources.)

George Keys Jr., Tripp's valet. (Courtesy GAR Library & Museum, Scranton.)

the city's most prominent men, the wealthy Ira Tripp. Keys would keep that plum job for years, living in an apartment behind his boss's mansion even after Tripp's death in 1891. Tripp was a Civil War vet like him—in fact, had been a prisoner of war—shared a Republican viewpoint, and operated two farms up in the Abington area. The two men bonded in some unusual ways. (See box, "Smoking by Proxy," above.)

Accompanying his gregarious boss gave Keys visibility and stature around town. Even after Tripp's death, he managed to keep up his perambulations as a coachman for the wealthy railroad executive Garrett Bogart. Keys became politically influential, serving during the 1890s as Republican ward committeeman and a judge of elections. He was a founder of a political clubhouse called the Oriental Social Club, and of a fire-hose company on the West Side. In addition, he became active in Scranton's large, integrated Ezra Griffin GAR post, serving as its color-bearer at parades and events. He socialized with black movers like George Brown, and was a familiar figure in white circles. Keys' wedding in 1894 merited this article in the *Scranton Tribune*: "Probably the most notable marriage of colored people which has occurred in recent years in this part of the state was that of Miss Ella F. Miller to George W. Keyes, at [Bethel] A.M.E. at 8 o'clock last night. Additional interest was added to the event by the large number of white people, well known in Scranton social circles, who witnessed the ceremony."[3]

Upon Keys's death in 1908, the *Scranton Truth* remembered him as "one of the most prominent colored men in this section . . . a man of character, integrity and common sense."[4] His comrades in the Griffin post attended the funeral en masse. Keys was interred in the GAR section of Dunmore Cemetery. He was divorced at the time and left no heirs.

PETER NORRIS

Freeborn son of a slave
Enlisted as a private in 3rd USCT
Sustained hernia in action; died 1909

Peter Norris was never the same after rupturing his abdomen on the beach at Fort Wagner. Added to that was the rheumatism resulting from fevers he'd contracted in Florida. A laborer before the war, he struggled to find steady work afterwards and was particularly unsettled. "Immediately after my discharge I came to Waverly, Luz. Co., Pa. (now Lackawanna Co.) where I lived for two years," he stated in an 1890 pension form. "I then moved to Scranton. I lived

on Franklin Ave. I lived there about 18 months. I then moved back to Waverly, where I lived for about 4 years. I then moved to Scranton again where I lived about two years, on Franklin Ave. I then moved to Clarks Green, same county, where I lived about 7 years. I then moved to Waverly again, where I resided about one year. I then moved to Bridgewater Township [bordering Montrose], where I have lived up to the present time."

He and his wife, the former Jane Williams of Waverly, remained at Bridgewater until his death. Like his father, Lot, Peter Norris served as "a loyal, regular exhorter," or lay preacher, at his AME church, in this case in Montrose[5], as he coped with ill health. Lift too much or move too suddenly and "my abdomen seems to almost break in two and causes fearful pain and suffering, and entirely lays me up for some days," Norris testified in 1890. With neighbors and his doctor repeatedly vouching for him, he won a disability pension that began at $12 per month in 1888, and reached $30 in 1907.

Peter Norris died at age 66 in January 1909—"an esteemed colored gentleman," remarked the *Montrose Democrat*—and was buried in Montrose Cemetery. Jane Norris received a $12 widow pension until her death in 1911. They had no known children.

JOSHUA NORRIS

Freeborn son of a slave
Enlisted as a private in 3rd USCT
Injured by shell explosion; died 1923

After the war, Joshua Norris, a farmer "5-foot-6, complexion yellow," returned to the fold as a 21-year-old impaired by the back injury sustained when an explosion buried him in the sand on Morris Island. He also lost hearing and would suffer bouts of vertigo, which he blamed on the malaria and scurvy that hit him in Florida. Back home he persevered, marry-

(Courtesy Michael D. Kilgore.)

ing Paige Wells's daughter Malvina in 1867 and fathering four children. When Wells died, Joshua took in his mother-in-law, a German-born woman who was listed in the 1870 census as "deaf and dumb."

Life for the Norris family took a dramatic turn in the 1880s. Joshua became "an itinerant minister of the Gospel," traversing western Pennsylvania and West Virginia, according to his 1912 pension declaration. His travels for the AME church easily matched his brother Peter's footloose ways: "Pittsburgh 2 yrs, Monongahela 2 yrs, Bellefonte 3 yrs, New Haven 4 yrs, Altoona 3 yrs, West Bridgewater 4 yrs, West Newton 3 yrs, Morgantown 2 yrs, New Kensington 2 yrs, Bradford 2 yrs, Kane 3 yrs, Titusville 1½ yrs."

He began drawing an invalid pension, $6 per month, in 1899. An appeal for more in 1901 included an affidavit describing the clergyman as "lame in the back and quite deaf." The increases came through. By the time of his death in January 1923 from kidney disease, he was receiving $72 a month. His second wife Isabella, whom he'd wed in 1914 following Malvina's death in 1901, was left with "no property, income or family help." The pension bureau recommended a $30 monthly widow pension. Bella Norris lived until 1939, when she was laid to rest with him in Green Lane Cemetery in Fayette County, Pennsylvania.

1.   Glatthaar, Joseph T. *Forged in Battle: The Civil War Alliance of Black Soldiers and White Officers* (New York: Free Press, 1990), p. 242.
2.   Lewis, William. "Colored Settlement at Waverly,' unpublished manuscript, p. 2.
3.   *Scranton Tribune*, March 22, 1894, p. 5.
4.   *Scranton Truth*, July 7, 1908, p. 6.
5.   Adleman, Debra. *Waiting for The Lord: 19th Century Black Communities in Susquehanna County, Pa.* (Rockland, Me.: Picton Press, 1997), p. 71.

Bury Me in a Free Land

(By Frances Ellen Watkins Harper, 1825-1911,
freeborn African American poet-activist)

Make me a grave where'er you will,
In a lowly plain, or a lofty hill;
Make it among earth's humblest graves,
But not in a land where men are slaves.

I could not rest if around my grave
I heard the steps of a trembling slave;
His shadow above my silent tomb
Would make it a place of fearful gloom.

I could not rest if I heard the tread
Of a coffle gang to the shambles led,
And the mother's shriek of wild despair
Rise like a curse on the trembling air.

I could not sleep if I saw the lash
Drinking her blood at each fearful gash,
And I saw her babes torn from her breast,
Like trembling doves from their parent nest.

I'd shudder and start if I heard the bay
Of bloodhounds seizing their human prey,
And I heard the captive plead in vain
As they bound afresh his galling chain.

If I saw young girls from their mother's arms
Bartered and sold for their youthful charms,
My eye would flash with a mournful flame,
My death-paled cheek grow red with shame.

I would sleep, dear friends, where bloated might
Can rob no man of his dearest right;
My rest shall be calm in any grave
Where none can call his brother a slave.

I ask no monument, proud and high,
To arrest the gaze of the passers-by;
All that my yearning spirit craves,
Is bury me not in a land of slaves.

References

Books

Adleman, Debra. *Waiting for The Lord: Nineteenth Century Black Communities in Susquehanna County, Pa.* (Rockport, Me.: Picton Press, 1997).

Bates, Samuel P. *History of Pennsylvania Volunteers, 1861-5* (Harrisburg: B. Singerly, State Printers, 1871).

Billingsley, Rev. Amos S. *From the Flag to the Cross: Or, Scenes and Incidents of Christianity in the War; the Conversions . . . Sufferings and Deaths of Our Soldiers, on the Battle-field, in Hospital, Camp and Prison; and a Description of Distinguished Christian Men and Their Labors* (Philadelphia: New-World Publishing Co., 1872).

Blackett, R.J.M. *Freedom, or the Martyr's Grave: Black Pittsburgh's Aid to the Fugitive Slave* (Pittsburgh: University of Pittsburgh, 1997).

Blackman, Emily C. *The History of Susquehanna County* (Baltimore: Regional Publishing Co., 1873, reprinted 1970).

Blight, David W., editor. *Passages to Freedom: The Underground Railroad in History and Memory* (Washington, DC: Smithsonian Books, 2004).

Blockson, Charles L. *The Underground Railroad in Pennsylvania* (New York: Berkley Books, 1987).

Bradsby, Henry C. *History of Luzerne, Lackawanna, and Wyoming Counties, Pa: With Illustrations and Biographical Sketches of Some of Their Prominent Men and Pioneers* (New York: W.W. Munsell & Co., 1880).

Brauer, Norm. *Revisiting Bailey Hollow: A History of Dalton* (copyright Norm Brauer, 1988).

Brooks, Leonard L. *Who Freed the Slaves? The Fight Over the Thirteenth Amendment* (Chicago: University of Chicago Press, 2015).

Brooks, Noah. *Washington in Lincoln's Time* (Washington, DC: Century Co., 1895).

Brower, Edith. *Little Old Wilkes-Barre As I Knew It* (Wilkes-Barre, PA: Fowler, Dick & Walker, 1923).

Brown, Barbara W., and Rose, James M. *Black Roots in Southeastern Connecticut, 1650-1900* (New London, Conn.: New London County Historical Society, 2001).

Brown, William Wells. *Narrative of William W. Brown, an American Slave, Written by Himself* (London: Charles Gilpin, 1850).

Coco, Gregory A. *Killed In Action* (Gettysburg, PA: Thomas Publications, 1996).

Cooper, H.C. Jr. *The Twentieth Century Bench and Bar of Pennsylvania, Vol. 2* (Chicago: Brown & Cooper, 1903).

Davis, Hugh. *"We Will Be Satisfied With Nothing Less": The African American Struggle for Equal Rights in the North During Reconstruction* (Ithaca, N.Y.: Cornell University Press, 2011).

Djupe, Paul A., and Olson, Laura R., editors. *Encyclopedia of American Religion and Politics* (Infobase Publishing, 2014).

Dobak, William A., *Freedom by the Sword: The U.S. Colored Troops, 1862-1867* (Washington DC: Center of Military History, US Army, 2011).

Egerton, Douglas R. *Thunder at the Gates: The Black Civil War Regiments That Redeemed America* (New York: Basic Books, 2016).

Foner, Eric. *Gateway to Freedom: The Hidden History of the Underground Railroad* (New York, W.W. Norton & Co., 2015).

Freeman, Aileen Sallom. *Lincoln: The Northeastern Pennsylvania Connection* (Paupack, PA: Fosi Ltd., 2000).

Furnas, J. C. *Goodbye to Uncle Tom* (New York: Sloane, 1956).

Gara, Larry. *The Liberty Line: The Legend of the Underground Railroad* (Lexington, Ky.: University of Kentucky Press, 1961).

Glatthaar, Joseph T. *Forged in Battle: The Civil War Alliance of Black Soldiers and White Officers* (New York: Free Press, 1990).

Graber, Mark A. *Dred Scott and the Problem of Constitutional Evil* (Cambridge, England: Cambridge University Press, 2008).

Grow, Rev. William B. *Eighty-Five Years of Life and Labor* (Carbondale, PA: self-published, 1902).

Hitchcock, Frederick L., and Down, John P. *History of Scranton and Its People, Vol. 1* (Scranton: Lewis Historical Publishing Co., 1914).

Hollister, Horace. *Contributions to the History of the Lackawanna Valley* (New York: W.H. Tinson, 1857).

Howe, Thomas J. *The Petersburg Campaign: Wasted Valor, June 15-18, 1864* (Lynchburg, Va.: H.E. Howard Inc., 1988).

Hunter, Carol M. *To Set the Captives Free: Reverend Jermain Wesley Loguen and the Struggle for Freedom in Central New York, 1835-1872* (New York: Garland Publishing, 1993).

Johnson, Frederick C. *The Historical Record of Wyoming Valley: A Compilation of Matters of Local History from the Columns of the Wilkes-Barre Record* (Wilkes-Barre: Press of the Wilkes-Barre Record, 1902).

Kulp, George Brubaker. *Sketches of the Bench and Bar of Luzerne County, Pennsylvania, Vol. 3* (Wilkes-Barre: E. B. Yordy, 1890).

Lapsansky, Emma. *Black Presence in Pennsylvania: Making It Home* (University Park, PA: Historical Association, Pennsylvania History Studies, No. 21, 2001).

Lilley, Stephen R. *Fighters Against American Slavery* (San Diego, Calif.: Lucent Books, 1999).

Longacre, Edward G. *Army of Amateurs: General Benjamin F. Butler and the Army of the James, 1863-65* (Mechanicsburg, PA: Stackpole Books, 1997).

Moss, Emerson I. *African-Americans in the Wyoming Valley, 1778-1990* (Wilkes-Barre: Wyoming County Historical and Geological Society, 1992).

Mumford, Mildred. *This Is Waverly* (Waverly, PA: Waverly Women's Club, 1954).

Neely, Mark E. *The Fate of Liberty: Abraham Lincoln and Civil Liberties* (Oxford Paperbacks, 1991).

Pierce, Frederick Clifton. *Batchelder, Batcheller Genealogy* (Chicago: W.B. Conkey Co, 1898).

Power, J. C. *Abraham Lincoln: His Great Funeral Cortege, from Washington City to Springfield, Illinois With a History and Description of the National Lincoln Monument* (Springfield, Ill: publisher not identified, 1872).

Redkey, Edwin S. *A Grand Army of Black Men: Letters from African-American Soldiers in the Union Army 1861-1865* (Cambridge, England: Cambridge University Press, 1992).

Sacks, Howard L. and Judith R. *Way Up North in Dixie: A Black Family's Claim to the Confederate Anthem* (Champaign, Ill.: University of Illinois Press, 2003).

Sandow, Robert M. *Deserter Country: Civil War Opposition in the Pennsylvania Appalachians* (New York: Fordham University Press, 2009).

Scott, Donald Sr. *Camp William Penn: 1863-1865* (Atglen, PA: Schiffer Publishing Ltd., 2012).

Shaffer, Donald R. *After the Glory: The Struggles of Black Civil War Veterans* (Lawrence, Kansas: University of Kansas Press, 2004).

Siebert, William H. *The Underground Railroad From Slavery to Freedom* (New York: Macmillan, 1898).

Spear, Sheldon. *Wyoming Valley History Revisited* (Jemags & Co.,: Shavertown, Pa, 1994).

Stampp, Kenneth M. *The Peculiar Institution: Slavery in the Ante-Bellum South* (New York: Vintage, 1956).

Stevenson, George E. *Reflections of an Anthracite Engineer* (Scranton: Hudson Coal Co., 1931).

Sweet, Frank W. *Legal History of the Color Line: The Rise and Triumph of the One-Drop Rule* (Palm Coast, Fla.: Backintyme, 2005).

Taylor, Frank H. *Philadelphia in the Civil War, 1861 1865* (Philadelphia: City of Philadelphia, 1913).

Tomasek, Peter, editor. *Avery Harris Civil War Journal* (Wilkes-Barre: Luzerne National Bank, 2000).

Trudeau, Noah Andre. *Like Men of War: Black Troops in the Civil War 18662-1865* (Toronto, Canada: Little Brown & Co.).

Wise, Stephen R. *Gate of Hell: Campaign for Charleston Harbor, 1863* (Columbia, S.C.: University of South Carolina Press, 1994).

Wooden, Sherman. *The Place I Call Home: How Abolition and the Underground Railroad Shaped the Communities of Northeastern Pennsylvania* (Montrose, PA: Center for Anti-Slavery Studies, 2009).

Undesignated Author. *Historical Record: The Early History of Wyoming Valley and Contiguous Territory* (Wilkes-Barre, PA: Press of the Wilkes-Barre Record, 1893).

Articles and Manuscripts

Davis, Hugh. "The Pennsylvania State Equal Rights League and the Northern Black Struggle for Legal Equality," article in *Pennsylvania Magazine of History and Biography*, October 2002.

Derr, Allean F. "Factoryville: The Hollow in the Beech Woods" (unpublished manuscript, in the holdings of Keystone College Library, Factoryville, PA).

Diemer, Andrew. "Pennsylvania, Black Citizenship Rights, and Slavery in the 19th Century," article in *Historical Society of Pennsylvania Legacies* magazine, Fall 2016.

Holzer, Harold. "America's Second Declaration of Independence," article in *America's Civil War*, January 2013.

Hudson, Leonne. "Valor at Wilson's Wharf," article in *Civil War Times Illustrated*, March 1998.

Kashatus, William C. "In Immortal Splendor: Wilkes-Barre's Fugitive Slave Case of 1853," article in *Pennsylvania Heritage*, Spring 2008.

Jackson, Kellie Carter. "At the Risk of Our Own Lives: Violence and the Fugitive Slave Law in Pennsylvania," article in *Civil War in Pennsylvania: The African American Experience*, edited by Samuel W. Black (Pittsburgh: John Heinz History Center, 2013).

Lewis, William. "Colored Settlement at Waverly" (unpublished manuscript, undated).

Lewis, William. "Underground Railroad in Abington, Pa." (unpublished manuscript, 1944).

Lewis, William. "Waverly and the Underground Railroad (unpublished manuscript, 1952).

Malone, Christopher. "Rethinking the End of Black Voting Rights in Antebellum Pennsylvania: Racial Ascriptivism, Partisanship and Political Development in the Keystone State," article in *Pennsylvania History*, November 2005.

Price, Edward. "The Black Voting Rights Issue in Pennsylvania, 1780-1900," article in *Pennsylvania Magazine of History and Biography*, July 1976.

Schuelke, Frieda. "Activities of the Underground Railroad in Oswego County," *Journal of the Oswego Historical Society* (Oswego, N.Y.: Palladium-Times Inc., 1940).

Shankman, Arnold. "Draft Resistance in Civil War Pennsylvania," article in *Pennsylvania Magazine of History and Biography*, April 1977.

Smith, Eric Ledell. "The African American Community of Wilkes-Barre, 1870 to 1900." (Nanticoke, PA: Proceedings of the 12th Annual Conference on the History of Northeastern Pennsylvania, 2000).

White, Jonathan W. "A Pennsylvania Judge Views the Rebellion: The Civil War Letters of George Washington Woodward," article in *Pennsylvania Magazine of History and Biography*, April 2005.

Williams, James T. "Northern Fried Chicken: A Historical Adventure Into the Black Community of Scranton, Pa." (unpublished manuscript, 1993).

Wood, Nicholas. "A Sacrifice on the Altar of Slavery: Doughface Politics and Black Disenfranchisement in Pennsylvania, 1837-1838," article in *Journal of the Early Republic* (Philadelphia: University of Pennsylvania Press, Spring 2011).

Zbick, Jim. "Pennsylvania's 'Perfect Hell,'" article in *America's Civil War Magazine*, January 2013.

Newspapers

Charleston Mercury (Charleston, SC)—accessible-archives.com, online.

Christian Recorder (Philadelphia, PA)—accessible-archives.com, online.

Cleveland Daily Leader (Cleveland, Ohio)—newspapers.com, online.

Port Tobacco Times & Charles County Advertiser (Port Tobacco, MD)—microfilm collection, Southern Maryland Studies Center, La Plata, MD.

Frank Leslie's Illustrated Weekly (New York, NY)—accessible Archives, online.

Gettysburg Compiler (Gettysburg, PA)—newspapers.com, online.

Jeffersonian (Stroudsburg, PA)—newspapers.com, online.

Lackawanna Register (Scranton, PA)—microfilm collection, Albright Library, Scranton.

Liberator (Boston, MA)—newspapers.com, online.

Montrose Democrat (Montrose, PA)—microfilm collection, Susquehanna County Historical Society, Montrose.

National Anti-Slavery Standard (Philadelphia.)—accessible-archives.com, online.

North Branch Democrat (Tunkhannock, PA)—microfilm collection, Wyoming County Historical Society, Tunkhannock.

Northern Pennsylvanian (Carbondale, PA)—microfilm collection, Carbondale Public Library, Carbondale.

Pennsylvania Freeman (Philadelphia, PA)—microfilm collection, Haverford College Library, Haverford, PA.

Pittsburgh Daily Commercial (Pittsburgh, PA)—newspapers.com, online.

Pittsburgh Gazette (Pittsburgh, PA)—newspapers.com, online.

Pittston Gazette (Pittston, PA)—newspapers.com, online.

Reading Times (Reading, PA)—newspapers.com, online.

Republican Farmer & Democratic Journal (Wilkes-Barre, PA)—newspapers.com, online.

Scranton Defender (Scranton, PA)—microfilm collection, Pennsylvania State Library, Harrisburg.

Scranton Daily Times (Scranton, PA)—microfilm collection, Albright Library, Scranton

Scranton Republican (Scranton, PA)—microfilm collection, Albright Library, Scranton.

Scranton Times (Scranton, PA)—microfilm collection, Albright Library, Scranton.

Scranton Tribune (Scranton, PA)—newspapers.com, online.

Scranton Weekly Republican (Scranton, PA)—microfilm collection, Albright Library, Scranton.

Spectator and Freeman's Journal (Montrose, PA)—microfilm collection, Susquehanna County Historical Society, Montrose.

Star of the North (Bloomsburg, PA)—newspapers.com, online.

Volunteer (Montrose, PA)— microfilm collection, Susquehanna County Historical Society, Montrose.

Wayne County Herald (Honesdale, PA)—microfilm collection, Wayne County Historical Society, Honesdale.

Weekly Standard (Raleigh, NC)—newspapers.com.

Wilkes-Barre Advocate (Wilkes-Barre, PA)—newspapers.com, online.

Wyoming Republican (Tunkhannock, PA)—microfilm collection, Wyoming County Historical Society, Tunkhannock.

Wyoming Republican (Wilkes-Barre, PA)—newspapers.com, online.

Wyoming Republican & Farmer's Herald (Kingston, PA)—newspapers.com, online.

Index

About the Author

JIM REMSEN is a journalist and author of two prior books, *The Intermarriage Handbook* (HarperCollins, 1988) and *Visions of Teaoga* (Sunbury, 2014). Since retiring as Religion Editor at the *Philadelphia Inquirer*, Jim has pursued his keen interest in history, with a focus on underappreciated aspects of our nation's local histories. Being a native of Waverly, PA, he is pleased to be bringing his old hometown's remarkable black and abolitionist histories to light.

—

Readers are invited to visit **embattledfreedom.org**, a related, free educational website. There you will find:

Learning segments based on themes in the book
Author's blog
Classroom materials
Gallery of illustrations
Recommended reading

74534159R00149

Made in the USA
Columbia, SC
01 August 2017